DEFENDING THE JURY

Crime, Community, and the Constitution

This book sets forth a new approach to twenty-first-century criminal justice and punishment, an approach that fully involves the community and provides a better way to make our criminal process more transparent and inclusive. The American criminal justice system faces numerous challenges because of its ongoing failure to integrate the community's voice. Using the lens of the Sixth Amendment jury trial right, this book offers fresh and much-needed ways for incorporating the citizenry into the procedures of criminal justice, resulting in greater investment and satisfaction in the system. Ultimately, the people's right to participate in the criminal justice system through the criminal jury – a right that is all too often overlooked – is essential to truly legitimizing the criminal process and ensuring its democratic nature.

Laura I Appleman is a professor of law at the Willamette University College of Law. She received the Meisner Award for Faculty Scholarship in 2011 and frequently speaks to local and national news media on topics of crime, incarceration, and sentencing. For five years, Appleman was a criminal appellate public defender at the Center for Appellate Litigation, where she briefed and argued approximately fifty appeals in front of the New York appellate courts, including the New York Court of Appeals. Appleman currently blogs at the Faculty Lounge (www.thefacultylounge.org).

Defending the Jury

CRIME, COMMUNITY, AND THE CONSTITUTION

Laura I Appleman
Willamette University College of Law

CAMBRIDGE
UNIVERSITY PRESS

CAMBRIDGE
UNIVERSITY PRESS

32 Avenue of the Americas, New York NY 10013-2473, USA

Cambridge University Press is part of the University of Cambridge.

It furthers the University's mission by disseminating knowledge in the pursuit of education, learning and research at the highest international levels of excellence.

www.cambridge.org
Information on this title: www.cambridge.org/9781107043541

First published 2015

A catalogue record for this publication is available from the British Library

ISBN 978-1-107-04354-1 Hardback
ISBN 978-1-107-65093-0 Paperback

CONTENTS

ACKNOWLEDGMENTS

I am deeply indebted to numerous individuals who helped me conceive, contemplate, and write this book. Particular thanks are owed to John Langbein, Judith Resnik, and Hans Linde, three scholars who have served as mentors for many years. I would also like to thank Douglas Berman, Stephanos Bibas, Bennett Capers, Jennifer Collins, Caroline Davidson, Carissa Hessick, Elizabeth Kaplan, Peter Letsou, Dan Markel, Risa Mealus, Alice Ristroph, Darren Rosenblum, Nick Rosenkranz, Rose Villazor, Bob Weisberg, Norman Williams, and Ron Wright for their patience and their willingness to endlessly read, review, and debate my work. Thanks are also owed to Dean Curtis Bridgeman and Willamette University College of Law for helping fund this project. Finally, this book is dedicated to David and Graham, without whose constant support and encouragement this project would never have happened.

1 INTRODUCTION

The grand jury's failure to indict Darren Wilson – a Ferguson, Missouri police officer – for fatally shooting Michael Brown in 2014 provoked a nationwide outcry, sparking days of protests, riots, and arrests all over the country. Foremost among the denunciations was an expressed dismay that the community would not have an opportunity to determine Wilson's fate in an open, public trial. Even the embattled officer expressed hope that his resignation from the police force would help the community heal.

Less than one week later, this anger flared up in New York City – and all over the country – when the public learned that a Staten Island grand jury had failed to indict NYPD officer David Pantaleo in the choking death of Eric Garner during an arrest. Protests, rallies, "die-ins," and traffic tie-ups broke out in Manhattan, all over the United States, and in major cities worldwide. Once again, the public was outraged that the community had not received a chance to weigh Pantaleo's actions in a court of law and determine guilt or innocence through jury trial. This desire for community-determined justice was so widespread that soon after the Staten Island grand jury's decision, the New York attorney general asked the governor for the power to investigate and prosecute killings of unarmed civilians by law enforcement officials. Additionally, the U.S. Justice Department announced that it would open a civil rights inquiry into Garner's death.

Following these two grand jury declinations to indict, there was a call to bypass the grand jury's role entirely in the case of Tamir Rice, a twelve-year-old Cleveland boy fatally shot by Officer Timothy Loehmann. Outrage at the boy's death prompted requests to have the prosecutor charge the officer for homicide without the use of the grand jury, despite the fact that Ohio law mandates grand jury issuance of indictments. Concerns about the secrecy and the lack of public accountability inherent in the grand jury proceeding, as well as a need for more transparency and a more expedient route to an open, public trial, helped motivate this desire to eliminate the institution entirely.

In a similar vein, once the news of Trayvon Martin's death (2012) began to spread, both local community members in Florida and the greater public nationwide were infuriated that George Zimmerman was not initially charged with any crime. The public was equally perturbed that Zimmerman was released on bail after his eventual indictment for second-degree murder. The simmering anger was such that the public citizenry, both local and national, directed the prosecutors to evidence of Zimmerman's falsehoods regarding his access to funds, eventually uncovering a secret internet fundraising scheme that netted Zimmerman and his wife close to $200,000. This discovery resulted in the revocation of Zimmerman's bail, to the satisfaction of much of the populace, both local and far flung, satisfaction that later dissolved into more anger when Zimmerman was re-released at a much higher bail.

Likewise, New Yorkers expressed intense wrath about Bernard Madoff's pretrial release. Confined to supervised house arrest at his luxurious Park Avenue apartment, Madoff could barely shuttle to and from his court appearances without being hounded by angry investors and fellow New Yorkers. News of his limited-bail release sparked outrage worldwide as victims of his Ponzi scheme expressed resentment about Madoff's freedom after his commission of fraud on a vast scale. Equal rage and dismay was aired when Madoff's guilty plea was announced, as victims and bystanders alike desired a full jury trial, both to formally broadcast the details of Madoff's financial misdeeds and to provide for a more public expiation and punishment.

Similar dismay was voiced by both the local and national communities when the news broke that Dominique Strauss-Kahn, then-Managing director of the International Monetary Fund was granted bail after his indictment for sexually assaulting a hotel chambermaid, despite his high risk of flight. Although Strauss-Kahn was halted at the airport, ready to flee the country, and arrested there, he was still permitted to reside in his posh Upper East Side penthouse while electronically monitored, serving an extremely upscale version of house arrest. The disquiet continued when Strauss-Kahn's case was ultimately dismissed for lack of credible evidence, with many community members arguing that the alleged victim's untruths about her background should not undermine her accusations against Strauss-Kahn, who had a long history of harassing and sexually assaulting women.

This type of community and countrywide frustration is nothing new, of course. Earlier indicators of this pattern of citizen outrage were present in the 1990s. The socially historic explosion of fury at the not-guilty verdicts handed down in the LAPD/Rodney King and O. J. Simpson trials, from very different segments of the Los Angeles populace, highlighted the local community's great frustration about its inability to truly participate in the decision-making and adjudication of these high-profile cases.

Although the high-profile cases of Garner, Brown, Zimmerman, Madoff, and Strauss-Kahn are recent and spectacular, they serve to expose a recurring problem with our criminal justice system. Indeed, much of this outrage, politicking, and commentary points to one primary question: What role *should* the community play in deciding matters of criminal justice? Today, society, media, and politicians pay close attention to the latest high-profile crime, but the general public usually finds itself at a great remove, watching the system from the sidelines. Our current model of criminal justice marginalizes the local populace to mere bystanders during criminal adjudication, thus creating fear, confusion, and anxiety over how crime is addressed. As a result, punishment for crimes continues to increase and prison populations mushroom, despite the lowest crime rates in over forty years.

Much of this unease and misunderstanding can be attributed to the modern community's exile from the justice system. In the past thirty years, the local public has been almost entirely eliminated from the criminal justice process, as approximately 95 percent of all criminal indictments are disposed of by guilty plea. This virtual elimination of the criminal jury trial has resulted in a system in which justice is dispensed by courts, bureaucrats, and prosecutors, with little room for the community's voice. These backroom criminal procedures completely upend the way our criminal justice system was originally constituted. Not only does our current system eviscerate the Sixth Amendment jury trial, but it also makes a mockery of constitutional criminal justice, which was specifically designed to incorporate the local public.

How, then, to return to the correct path without overturning the current structure of our justice system? In other words, how do we offer "we the people" a way back into the criminal justice process, granting them their *constitutional right* to decide an offender's punishment, and give them a stake in regulating their own society? One potential path is to create space within our current criminal process for the community's voice, whether this means recognizing the Sixth Amendment's role in sentencing, creating plea juries, inserting a community representative into pretrial detention procedures, or other innovative procedures that allow the greater participation of citizens.

Interjecting the community's voice into criminal justice, of course, can raise the difficulty of distinguishing the jury from the maddened public during a highly publicized trial, such as those of Casey Anthony and O. J. Simpson. In these circumstances, often the public – local and nationwide – desires a different outcome than what the jury decides. Here, however, it's a simple answer: we need juries to defy the larger, often more emotional community when justice requires it, playing a mediating role between the raw sentiments of the populace and the need for community input. The community – whether in the form of petit juries, plea juries, or bail juries – must play a similar, buffering role in nontrial situations.

This responsibility of mediating the outrage of the public is precisely the role that the drafters of the Sixth Amendment envisioned for jury members, particularly after the public outcry following events such as the Boston Massacre trial. Instead of mob justice, the jury, or other, similar bodies of selected community representatives, builds a bridge between the sometimes-raw emotions of the general public and a more careful, considered selection of local citizens who take their job as delegates very seriously.

Circling around, over, and through this, the Sixth Amendment right to a jury trial plays a critical part in helping incorporate the community back into the criminal justice system. Although the Supreme Court has repeatedly reaffirmed the Sixth Amendment jury trial right in a variety of contexts, this most critical of rights is still being pushed to the wayside by our system of hidden criminal adjudication, where decisions concerning life and liberty are made far from the public sphere and the public eye.

With the help of the Sixth Amendment, we can reverse this trend by focusing on the community, assisted by the integration of practical ways to return the people's voice to the criminal justice process. Conveniently, such an undertaking – fostering citizen participation and investment in the criminal justice process – will also assist in returning us to the type of criminal adjudication originally envisioned by the Founders of this nation. The community-based criminal procedures I advocate were in the past believed so important that they were enshrined in our Constitution and our Bill of Rights, and have been routinely reaffirmed by the modern Supreme Court.

In response to these problems, this book sets forth a new, community-based approach to twenty-first-century punishment and criminal justice, providing a way to make our criminal process more transparent and inclusive of all. Using the lens of the Sixth Amendment jury trial right, this book will offer fresh and much-needed ways to incorporate the citizenry into the procedures of criminal justice, thereby resulting in greater investment and satisfaction in the system. I hope to demonstrate the power of the Sixth Amendment paradigm by applying it to all aspects of criminal adjudication, from bail to jail and beyond.

A primary goal of this book is to expose some of the various challenges the American criminal justice system faces from its ongoing failure to integrate the community's voice. For instance, the victim's rights movement has gained prominence and power in criminal justice over the past twenty years, often at the expense of the rights of both the defendant and the community, both of whose roles are shrinking. Equally troubling, the collapse of the jury trial into an assembly-line system of guilty pleas, relying on backroom bargaining between prosecutors and defense attorneys, not only shortcuts constitutional criminal process, but also has almost entirely shut out the local community. Finally, the resulting shift of power from jury trials to plea and sentencing hearings (and, indeed, inflexible state and federal sentencing systems) has again eliminated the community from the feedback loop, creating a criminal justice system in which the local public is denied any input or participation, causing frustration, anger, and resentment.

Careful scrutiny of the problems arising from the criminal justice system's shift to hidden adjudication and the concomitant suppression of the public voice leads to two distinct questions, each of which has been given insufficient attention until now. First, how does the criminal justice system in this country approach the issue of community rights? Second, how should community rights be recognized, if at all, in a criminal justice system situated within a liberal democracy?

This book tries to answer both of these questions, taking a careful look at how the community is involved in the criminal justice system and arguing why there is a strong need for more participation by the local public, for the benefit of all. Ultimately, I show that the people's right to participate in the criminal justice system via the petit jury – a right all too often overlooked – is critical to truly legitimize the criminal process and ensure its democratic nature.

The book proceeds in three major parts. Part I, entitled "History in the Crucible: Rediscovering the Original Community Right in Criminal Justice," delves into the historical aspects of the jury trial right, illustrating how the original jury trial right was a community right, not an individual one as we commonly envision it. I argue that although the Court's recent decisions relying on the collective right to jury trial have caused a rethinking of sentencing and punishment, the Court has failed to buttress its reasoning with proper historical and scholarly support. This is a major oversight, as the Court's current understanding of sentencing and punishment relies upon the scope, meaning, and provenance of the jury trial right. In response, Part I provides a missing historical and constitutional justification for the Court's fidelity to the community as arbiter of punishment and traces the evolution of the jury trial right through the modern day.

Chapter 2, entitled "The Collective Jury Right and the Sixth Amendment," offers a textual-historical reading of the Sixth Amendment, based on seventeenth- and eighteenth-century legal theory, linguistic usage, and colonial and Revolutionary practices, and concludes that the jury trial right was originally the community's right, not an individual right. This chapter explores the historical evolution of the right to a jury trial and the community's role in imposing punishment, tracing it from its early beginnings in England through its full fruition in the post-Revolution and Constitutional drafting periods.

Within this chapter, I also explain why this collective jury trial right should still be recognized today.

Chapter 3, "The Supreme Court and the Reaffirmation of Community," discusses the ascendance of the Sixth Amendment jury trial right and explains why the Court has been so focused on the role of the jury as the representative voice of the community. This chapter illustrates how the Supreme Court has laid groundwork for a vast criminal procedure policy shift by gradually "rediscovering" the Sixth Amendment jury trial right, a right it continues to reaffirm in its latest terms. The third chapter explores this function of the community and expands upon why these founding origins have structured the legitimacy of recent reforms in criminal law and sentencing.

Part II of the book, entitled "Old Becomes New: Sixth Amendment Jury Rights and Twenty-First Century Criminal Procedure," provides the theoretical and philosophical heart of the book. In it, I explore what motivates this community jury trial right, both historically and today, and what it means to be part of a community in the criminal justice context. This part explores the jurisprudential underpinnings of the Court's latest decisions, focusing on the jury trial right, investigating the retributive and restorative aspects of criminal justice that animate these holdings. In addition, this part also delves into the contested and complicated definitions of *community* as applied to criminal justice, and teases out the negatives and positives that linger within.

Chapter 4, "Retribution, Restorative Justice, and the Sixth Amendment Jury Right," studies the jurisprudential underpinnings of the Court's latest decisions focusing on the jury trial right. Here, I flesh out my argument that these late twentieth- and early twenty-first-century sentencing decisions suggest a punishment philosophy based on expressive, restorative retribution. This theory of punishment is grounded both in the historical jury right to decide all punishments and in community determinations of blameworthiness. As I will show, expressive, restorative retribution not only helps explain why the Supreme Court has become the champion of the Sixth Amendment jury trial right at a time when most indictments are settled through guilty pleas, but also gives us a blueprint to help navigate future challenges in the criminal justice system.

In Chapter 5, entitled "Defining Community in the Twenty-First Century: Cities, Counties, and Collective Action," I investigate the significance and fluidity of the term *community*. In our dynamic twenty-first-century digital world, community has many functional and social meanings. The criminal jury setting, however, has long defined notions of "the community" in geographical terms, limiting the term to local human peers of the defendant, often the model members of the relevant community. In a world with newly defined online crimes and online communities, the notion of "community rights" and the means to incorporate the community into criminal justice decision-making needs to be premised on more than just traditional conceptions of the community. This chapter explores the various forms that community can take in today's criminal justice system, and discusses as well the problems that can arise from relying on an amorphous "community" to dispense justice.

The final and most substantive part of the book, Part III, "Theory into Practice: Origins and Community in Modern Criminal Procedure," takes this newly expanded understanding of the history and theory of the jury trial right and applies it to several forms of modern criminal procedure and punishment, including pretrial detention, guilty pleas, bench trials, post-prison sentences, victim's rights procedures, and jury nullification. Since so much of criminal practice and punishment now revolves around nontrial process, I explain why the Court's focus on juries and communities should apply to any type of criminal process that imposes punishment, whether it happens before, during, or after adjudication.

Chapter 6, "Bail, Jail, and the Community Voice," analyzes how the reality of pretrial detention in today's criminal justice system means that punishment is often imposed by nonjury, nonjudicial actors, such as bail bondsmen, probation officers, and correction officials. This is far from the aggressive public oversight imagined by the Framers of the Constitution and fails to comply with the spirit of the Sixth Amendment jury trial right, which requires collective decisions on the imposition of punishment. The terrible conditions in local and county jails frequently turn pretrial detention into a form of punishment, despite the fact that the offender has not yet been adjudicated. Accordingly, I conclude that some subsection of the local public should take some part in deciding whether an offender should be granted or denied bail, particularly in issues involving community safety.

In Chapter 7, "Infusing Community through Criminal Procedure: The Plea Jury," I address a critical question: How important is the jury trial right in a world of guilty pleas? This chapter explores the ways in which the Court's new jury-centered philosophy of punishment affects the procedures of the guilty plea. I contend that although the Court focused its analysis on community participation in juries, there is nothing in *Apprendi-Blakely* or its progeny to suggest that this type of participation should be limited only to the criminal trial. Accordingly, I argue that the logical next step is the incorporation of the community into the guilty plea procedure, through the use of a plea jury, and I describe one potential way this integration could be achieved.

Chapter 8, "Eradicating the Bench Trial," addresses the constitutional and theoretical problems with bench trials. This chapter contends that one important way we should exercise the community jury trial right is by eliminating bench trials. Bench trials occupy a peculiar middle ground in the realm of the jury trial right. Neither a full waiver of the jury trial such as by guilty plea, nor a carefully regulated criminal procedure such as a full jury trial, the bench trial is a strange beast. As such, it requires a full reevaluation under our new understanding of the community jury right.

In Chapters 9 and 10, I discuss how the use of expressive restorative retribution as a philosophy of punishment provides a concrete policy of community involvement and participation, similar to what was practiced during the Constitutional era. Taking a page from the past, these two chapters argue that community involvement can help structure ancillary sentencing, giving guidance not only to the players in the criminal justice system, but also to the legislative and executive branches as well.

Chapter 9, "Restoring the Offender to Society," explains how the community jury trial right should apply to all pre-sentence proceedings, including pre-sentence reports, persistent felony offender statutes, prior convictions, and probation (or suspended sentences).

Similarly, Chapter 10, "Back-End Sentencing: The Sixth Amendment and Post-Prison Procedures," investigates the often-lengthy aftereffects of a modern sentence and includes all aspects of supervision to which the offender is subject, such as parole, post-release supervision, fines, and restitution. I conclude that these back-end sentencing proceedings, which can increase the length and the burden of an offender's sentence, must also be considered in the wake of *Apprendi-Blakely*.

In Chapter 11, "Jury Nullification and Victim Rights: Going Past Procedure," I discuss two extraordinary procedures seen in the criminal adjudication process: jury nullification and victim's rights. Although profoundly dissimilar in most ways, both jury nullification and victim's rights have one important commonality they both go beyond the normal envisioning of the criminal adjudication process, tipping the scales in balance of their unique and sometimes quite-powerful voices. Both can also be seen as the extreme culmination of the community voice expanded to its greatest power, having extensive power over either the actual offense found or the punishment imposed.

The book winds up in Chapter 12 with a look toward the future of criminal procedure if the community jury trial right is fully understood and applied to all aspects of the criminal justice system. I conclude that although the implementation of community participation within criminal adjudication might be challenging, over all, it will have positive consequences for both our understanding of and our comfort level with the processes of criminal justice.

PART I

History in the Crucible: Rediscovering the Original Community Right in Criminal Justice

2 THE COLLECTIVE JURY RIGHT AND THE SIXTH AMENDMENT

When we discuss the role of juries and the rights of the community in modern criminal justice, we must understand the precise contours of our modern jury trial right. Our historical Sixth Amendment right to a jury trial has been misapplied and misunderstood, and, as a result, too easily dismissed. Contrary to popular understanding, the original jury trial right was not an individual right, but a community one. We need a proper understanding of the Sixth Amendment jury trial right to provide both historical and constitutional justification for the community's involvement in criminal justice. Thus, fully comprehending the collective nature of the jury trial right is critical to our project of incorporating the community right into current criminal process.

Much of our current understanding of the community jury trial right relies on a recent spate of Supreme Court decisions revitalizing the Sixth Amendment right to a jury trial and making the jury trial right central to criminal justice. Although these recent decisions reinvigorating the collective right to jury trial have prompted a large-scale rethinking of sentencing and punishment, we are still lacking proper historical and scholarly support for these changes. In response, Part I of the book provides a missing historical and constitutional justification for the Court's fidelity to the community as arbiter of punishment and traces the evolution of the jury trial right through the modern day. First, Chapter 2 offers a textual-historical reading of the Sixth Amendment based on seventeenth- and eighteenth-century legal theory, linguistic usage, and colonial and Revolutionary practices, and concludes that the jury trial right was originally the community's right, not an individual right. Bringing the discussion to the modern day, Chapter 3 provides an overview of why the Sixth Amendment jury trial right has recently reassumed great importance in criminal procedure and explains how and why the Court's primary focus has been on the role of the jury as a critical voice of the community.

THE COLLECTIVE JURY RIGHT AND THE SIXTH AMENDMENT

Understanding the historical evolution of the right to a jury trial and the community's original role in imposing punishment during the founding of this country is paramount to repairing the criminal justice system. Not only is this history a key factor in the Supreme Court's recent reinvigoration of the Sixth Amendment jury trial right in criminal process, but it is also an excellent template for modeling twenty-first-century community involvement in the criminal justice system. The scope, meaning, and provenance of the historical jury trial right all provide proof that it was a collective right, not an individual right as we now understand it. This has important ramifications for modern criminal process. With this as background, the current chapter focuses on the collective right to a jury trial, tracing it from its early beginnings in England through its full fruition in the post-Revolution and Constitutional drafting periods. In doing so, I also argue why this collective jury trial right should still be recognized today.

Community, Crime, and the Colonials

The original historical right to a jury trial, particularly in the criminal context, was viewed almost exclusively as the *people's right*, not as a right of the accused. This understanding of the jury trial right can come as a shock to our modern sensibilities, given as we are to thinking about jury trials as solely the prerogative of the defendant. But for the British colonies and later the confederation of states, a trial by jury was primarily about the fledgling American community's ability to judge its own people and pronounce its punishment.

Accounts from contemporary newspapers, legal treatises, and popular writing show that the jury trial right, as handed down from England, was understood as the right to have an offender's crimes tried before the local community. Thus, returning to historical origins teaches us that the right to a jury trial was and still is grounded in the community's central role of deciding punishment for criminal offenders and in its ability to determine moral blameworthiness. The ideas underlying this community-based jury trial right were widespread and influential at the time the Constitution was drafted and ratified, and provided a valuable context for understanding the right to a jury trial.

English Roots

The origins of the jury – and its intertwinement with the community – stretch far back into the Anglo-American past. Although jury-based trials existed in the twelfth and thirteenth centuries, they were vastly different than our model of a jury trial today.[1] Jurors were drawn from the immediate neighborhood where the crime occurred and chosen for their knowledge of the crime or their ability to find out about the crime.[2] In other words, the jurors were to make inquiries, collect testimony, weigh the evidence, and state the verdict[3] – a far cry from the role played by juries today. These community-based aspects of the jury trial remained even as the English jury stopped personally investigating the facts of each crime, thus becoming more passive.[4]

Trial by jury also played a significant part in the seventeenth-century English Bill of Rights.[5] Enumerated ninth on the list of complaints was the Crown's habit of allowing "partial, corrupt, and unqualified persons [to be] returned and served on juries in trial. . . ."[6] In response, Parliament demanded that "jurors ought to be duly impaneled and returned, and jurors which pass upon men in trials for high treason

[1] *See* John H. Langbein, The Origins of Adversary Criminal Trial 64 (2003).
[2] *See id.*
[3] *See id.*
[4] *See id.*
[5] The English Bill of Rights was promulgated in 1689 by the House of Lords and Commons against the reign of James the Second. *See* The English Bill of Rights (Dec.16, 1689), *available at* http://www.constitution.org/bor/eng_bor.htm.
[6] The English Bill of Rights (Dec.16, 1689), *available at* http://www.constitution.org/bor/eng_bor.htm.

ought to be freeholders."[7] Notably, however, the individual rights mentioned in the document were separately listed in another clause.[8] Thus, in one of its earliest documented forms, the Anglo-American jury trial right was envisioned as an exclusively local one – concerned with providing fair and qualified jurors to represent the community, not the individual.

Most important to our tour through the early history of the jury trial right, however, is the eighteenth century. This era saw some of the "most fundamental attributes of modern Anglo-American criminal procedure"[9] arise, including the relationship between the judge and the jury. Of course, eighteenth-century criminal trials, both in England's Old Bailey and in the colonies, were also significantly different than today's.[10] Jury trials were conducted extremely rapidly, with judges often hearing between twelve and twenty felony cases a day, and it was not uncommon for juries to render verdicts "at the bar."[11]

Despite these differences from modern conditions, there were some critical aspects that survive in today's juries. "Twelveman juries" were commonplace by 1750, and the men drawn for them resided in the same small venue in which the offense occurred.[12] In addition, the eighteenth-century jury's most important task was to decide the punishment. Only a few eighteenth-century trials actually were concerned with separating guilt from innocence; instead, "[t]o the extent that trial had a function in such cases beyond formalizing the inevitable conclusion of guilt, it was to decide the sanction."[13] The jury's ability to "down-charge" an offense[14] gave it great power over the social and psychological ramifications of crime.

[7] *Id.*

[8] "That excessive bail ought not to be required, nor excessive fines imposed; nor cruel and unusual punishments inflicted." *Id.*

[9] John H. Langbein, *Shaping the Eighteenth-Century Criminal Trial: A View from the Ryder Sources*, 50 U. CHI. L. REV. 1, 2 (1983). Langbein notes, however, that the sources for any history of the eighteenth-century criminal trial are "suspect," "scarce," and "unsystematic," as "the contemporary press contains relatively little in the way of trial reporting." *Id.* at 4.

[10] John H. Langbein, *Understanding the Short History of Plea Bargaining*, 13 LAW & SOC'Y REV. 261, 262 (1979).

[11] *Id.* at 262–63.

[12] Langbein, *Shaping the Eighteenth-Century Criminal Trial*, *supra* note 9, at 15.

[13] *Id.* at 41.

[14] *Id.*

In the same vein, the English Murder Act of 1752 also added a very public aspect to the Anglo-American jury's role in punishment, as the Act stipulated that the sentence must be pronounced in open court immediately after the conviction, to "impress a just Horror in the Mind of the Offender, and on the minds of such as shall be present, of the heinous Crime of Murder."[15] Although the judge pronounced sentence it was the jury's role as the public moral arbiter that gained prominence and importance.

Put another way, the primary role of the jury in English criminal trials was fourfold: (1) to determine the defendant's level of *moral culpability*; (2) to sanction the offender; (3) to restore the victim to his or her original state; and (4) to try to repair the community by publicly denouncing the crime and the criminal. It is these particular aspects of criminal jury trials – the size, the vicinage, the aspects of compassion or restorative justice, and the role of moral arbiter – that made their way across the ocean to the British colonies. All of these would become imperative to the ideals of American community justice.

Colonial America

Colonial America did not import its legal system part and parcel from the mother country.[16] Instead, the colonists created "a layman's version of English legal institutions,"[17] drawing on English local and customary law in creating a legal order. The legal stronghold of the American colonies was the institution of the local jury, used both to resolve conflict and to adjudicate criminal offenses. Most importantly for our purposes, the jury trial was the conduit for the community's expression of restorative, retributive justice.

Colonial justice and jury trials varied widely. The several colonies had substantial differences in their "social arrangements, populations, ideologies, institutional developments, and economic organization."[18]

[15] *Id.* at 46.
[16] *See* Kermit L. Hall, Paul Finkelman & James W. Ely, American Legal History 23 (1996).
[17] Daniel J. Boorstin, The Americans: The Colonial Experience 27 (1958).
[18] Douglas Greenberg, *Crime, Law Enforcement, and Social Control in Colonial America*, 26 Am. J. Legal Hist. 293, 296 (1982).

This was often true within colonies as well.[19] Nonetheless, there were enough similarities among the types of criminal justice meted out in the British colonies that enables fair generalization.

Colonial juries guided the public trial and punishments of offenders, leaving courts with such minor tasks as delivering jury instructions or deciding pleas in abatement.[20] The jury provided an important way for the community to control the discretion of judges and curtail their authority.[21] As a symbol and a tool of popular power, the petit jury represented the vox populi and was thus intimately tied to the local community.[22] In many villages, the community and the jury were one and the same. Both grand and petit juries played a central role in mediating conflicts of interest between local interests and the governing authorities.[23] Most significantly, the right to trial by jury was understood as the people's right.

In all of the British colonies, jury trials and the law reinscribed the mores of the community. This was necessary, of course, in a system that allowed juries to decide both the law and the facts; in the early days of the colonies, law was determined from generally accepted moral principles and community norms.[24] The jury's authority over the law meant that the local community was able to both create and control the content of the colony's substantive law. In other words, the custom of the town meant more than any social policies created by political authorities.[25]

In fact, the main function of the colonial judicial system was to "punish and restrain crime and to maintain a cooperative harmony in the community"[26] – something that the local citizens were

[19] *See id.*

[20] *See id.* at 20.

[21] *See id.*

[22] *See id.* at 21.

[23] *See* J. R. Pole, *Reflections on American Law and the American Revolution*, 50 Wm. & Mary Q., 123, 126 (1993); *see also* Roger A. Fairfax Jr., *The Grand Jury's Jurisdictional Heritage*, 91 Minn. L. Rev. 398 (2006); Kevin Washburn, *Restoring the Grand Jury*, 76 Fordham L. Rev., 2333, 2387 (2008) (discussing grand jury's role in reflecting community's voice).

[24] William E. Nelson & Robert C. Palmer, Liberty and Community: Constitution and Rights in the Early American Republic 20 (1987).

[25] *See* William E. Nelson, Americanization of the Common Law: The Impact of Legal Change on Massachusetts Society, 1760–1830, at 29 (1994).

[26] J. R. Pole, *Reflections on American Law and the American Revolution*, 50 Wm. & Mary Q., 123, 132 (1993).

eager to undertake. Criminal justice functioned as social drama,[27] and the community often made the law. As such, the jury right was often simply an arm of the community's decision-making power. How these communities used this power varied from colony to colony and from town to town.

The colonies of both New England and New York provide examples of how local communities used the power of the jury to help mediate and communicate the community norms within the confines of criminal justice. In Puritan New England, for example, which had strong religious values, the legal system largely served to reinforce common ideals.[28] Very early on, the New England colonies generally recognized the right of the accused to be tried by a jury.[29] The institution of the grand jury was established as early as 1635.[30] The right to a civil jury trial was guaranteed in New Plymouth in 1623.[31] And Massachusetts Bay Colony provided for jury trial in virtually all felonies; serious crimes were required to go through a jury trial unless the defendant expressly waived the right.[32]

More specifically, Massachusetts Bay nicely illustrates how community values were transmitted through the use of the jury trial. The consensus-building and common ethical values present in the Bay colony communities made the role of the jury relatively simple. The jury's job was to promulgate moral standards reinforced by the church through the law. All parts of the legal system were continually under the tight scrutiny of the community as a whole, responding to community needs and interests.[33]

Public sanction was another critical way in which the New England colonies punished offenders. This was particularly true in the seventeenth

[27] *See* LAWRENCE M. FRIEDMAN, CRIME AND PUNISHMENT IN AMERICAN HISTORY 25 (1993).

[28] *See* Warren M. Billings, *Law in Colonial America: The Reassessment of Early American Legal History*, 81 MICH. L. REV. 953, 956 (1983).

[29] *See* EDGAR J. MCMANUS, LAW AND LIBERTY IN EARLY NEW ENGLAND: CRIMINAL JUSTICE AND DUE PROCESS, 1620–1692, at 99 (1993).

[30] Pole, *supra* note 26, at 126.

[31] *See* Julius Goebel, *King's Law and Local Custom in 17th Century New England*, 31 COLUM. L. REV. 416, 436 (1931).

[32] *See* MCMANUS, *supra* note 29, at 99. Granted, in the very early days of the colony (i.e., before 1660), the difficulty of impaneling juries meant that there were fewer jury trials. *Id.* at 103.

[33] *See id.* at 15.

century, when punishment tended to be extremely public and often shame-based.[34] As time went on, however, the public humiliation factor became just one of many expressive options for the community to express its displeasure.

Seventeenth-century juries determined both the facts and the law through a network of community norms, mediating between law and colonial society.[35] Because all colonial juries determined both the law and the facts, they were the ultimate arbiters of justice. Courts could not grant a new trial if a civil jury ignored the law, and juries could not be forced to adhere to the court's legal instructions.[36] In the New England colonies, then, the community's determinations of restorative and retributive justice, as mediated through the local justice system, continued to resonate even after the rigid hold of religion began to dissipate.

In contrast, the colony of New York lacked strong religious underpinnings yet still held its jury rights dear as a way to inculcate community norms. In 1683, the New York General Assembly passed a Charter of Liberties and Privileges specifying three separate instances when any criminal offender had the right to be tried by a jury.[37] Likewise, the New York Judiciary Act of 1691 reaffirmed the right to a jury trial and enshrined the jury's responsibility to determine questions of fact.[38]

Colonial New York's dedication to the role of a jury trial as a tool to reinscribe community values was exemplified through two prominent cases: the 1733 John Peter Zenger trial[39] and the case of *Forsey v. Cunningham*.[40] Both cases publicized the rights of the jury and

[34] *See* FRIEDMAN, *supra* note 27, at 37.

[35] Bruce H. Mann, *Law, Legalism, and Community Before the American Revolution*, 84 MICH. L. REV. 1415, 1425 (1986).

[36] *See* William E. Nelson, *The Eighteenth-Century Background of John Marshall's Constitutional Jurisprudence*, 76 MICH. L. REV. 893, 913–15 (1978).

[37] New York Charter of Liberties (1663), *available at* http://www.montauk.com/history/seeds/charter.htm.

[38] Matthew T. Tulchin, *An Analysis of the Development of the Jury's Role in a New York Criminal Trial*, 13 J.L. & POL'Y 425, 443 (2005).

[39] Tried for criminal seditious libel, Zenger carried the jury against the instructions of the court and garnered an acquittal, becoming famous as an example of the jury's power to overrule the court. *See* LEONARD W. LEVY, LEGACY OF SUPPRESSION: FREEDOM OF SPEECH AND PRESS IN EARLY AMERICAN HISTORY 133 (1960).

[40] In *Forsey*, an assault and battery case, the jury refused to follow the law and awarded the complainant £1500. *See* Pole, *supra* note 26, at 130.

made them resonate for American colonists – in New York and throughout the rest of the colonies.

The Zenger trial involved a New York publisher who printed assertions of incompetence and corruption against the colonial governor, William S. Cosby. Charged with libel, Zenger refused to name the authors involved, and the trial court directed a verdict. At trial, however, the jury ignored the court's instructions and acquitted Zenger of all charges.[41] For our purposes, the most significant aspect of the Zenger trial was the argument that colonial juries should *on principle* have broader prerogatives than English ones because of the differences in forms of government.[42] If we interpret this argument to mean that the community element was more powerful in the colonies than in England, as has been suggested by other scholars,[43] then the ringing endorsement of the Zenger trial's outcome by the colonists reinforces the power of the community's voice in the law.

Forsey was a 1763 assault and battery case in which the jury refused to follow the law and awarded the complainant £1,500.[44] In this case, the colonial governor's subsequent interference with a jury verdict caused an uproar because it was correctly interpreted as an executive usurpation of traditional jury rights.[45] During this era, the jury's primary role was seen as transmitting and preserving the norms of the people, not simply adjudicating the law.[46] The potential diminution of jury rights was seen as quashing the community's ability to participate in local disputes. This theoretical diminution was unacceptable to colonial New Yorkers. The *Forsey* case fits more broadly into the way pre-Revolutionary colonial juries generally "functioned as resistance bodies," refusing to convict or indict political and religious dissenters.[47]

[41] *See generally* JILL LEPORE, NEW YORK BURNING: LIBERTY, SLAVERY AND CONSPIRACY IN EIGHTEENTH-CENTURY MANHATTAN 72–7 (Knopf 2005).

[42] *See* Pole, *supra* note 26, at 127.

[43] *See id.*

[44] *See* Pole, *supra* note 26, at 130.

[45] *See* Historical Society of the New York Courts, *available at* http://www.nycourts.gov/history/legal-history-new-york/legal-history-eras-01/history-new-york-legal-eras-forsey-cunningham.html.

[46] *Id.* at 130.

[47] JEFFREY ABRAMSON, WE, THE JURY: THE JURY SYSTEM AND THE IDEAL DEMOCRACY 22–24, 68–75 (1994).

This fidelity to the jury's power remained true well past the War of Independence; even after 1800, New York judges did not always agree that they could set aside verdicts against law or evidence.[48] In seventeenth- and eighteenth-century New York (and in most other jurisdictions of that time), the power of the jury reigned supreme.[49]

In both New York and the other colonies, then, colonials relied on juries to maintain and reify their social values through the criminal law. Such shared social values were one reason that most socioeconomic decisions – including the application of substantive criminal law – were made at the local level. These collective values allowed local juries to decide both law and fact with little problem, as well as to continuously reinforce community norms.

In light of these shared legal ideals, it made sense to leave most of the determinations of criminal justice to the jury, since jury duty was most likely distributed among a random and representative cross section of the white, male, landowning, and taxpaying population.[50] In colonial America, decisions on criminal justice – and community governance – trickled up. Juries took an active and critical role in self-government, both by translating the law down to the community and by translating values up to the governing bodies.[51]

To these citizen-juries, the law was created both through the formal governmental channels and in the community's interpretation and acceptance of the law. With the additional, though infrequently used, threat of jury nullification (which I discuss in more detail in Chapter 11), the community had a way to respond to laws it decided were overly oppressive or unfair. Although the community was not responsible for writing the law, the people transmogrified it through their own lived experience, thus invigorating it from the cold text to a living, responsive body.[52]

This pattern of local governance in decisions about crime and punishment would continue through the War of Independence and

[48] Nelson, *The Eighteenth-Century Background of John Marshall's Constitutional Jurisprudence*, *supra* note 36, at 915.

[49] *See id.* at 916.

[50] *Id.* at 919.

[51] *See* SHANNON C. STIMSON, THE AMERICAN REVOLUTION IN THE LAW: ANGLO-AMERICAN JURISPRUDENCE BEFORE JOHN MARSHALL 59–61 (1990).

[52] *See* Jenny E. Carroll, *Nullification as Law*, 102 GEO. L.J. 579, 588, 590, 595 (2014).

beyond, despite the vast changes in almost all other areas. The people's right to the jury trial would not only remain unchanged, but gain even more power in the Revolutionary and Constitutional eras.

Revolutionary Juries

The American Revolution created great change in the patterns of justice[53] as more and more conflicts were resolved through the courts, as opposed to informally.[54] The jury trial, however, would retain its centrality to both the fledgling American government and the criminal justice system.

At the beginning of the War of Independence, the majority of colonists wished to maintain the general political structure.[55] Most wanted to keep an order that "generally required officials to govern according to *common values or principles* which nearly all citizens accepted as right or otherwise legitimate."[56] Although the colonial political structure would be thoroughly upended,[57] the colonists' desired to maintain the role of common principles. It was this desire – combined with the theory that all law springs from popular will[58] – that placed the role of the community and the jury in the center of American ideals of government and justice.

These ideals of government and justice were envisioned as specifically American and independent.[59] During the Revolutionary era, as in the colonial era that preceded it, law was "mediated to society" through the courts and the representative roles of the grand and petit juries.[60] Juries and the judicial process provided a critical contribution in both the social psychology and substance of the representative nature of new government.[61] Stated differently, some of the heft of America's

53 *See* Billings, *supra* note 28, at *id.*
54 *See id.*
55 *See* Nelson, *supra* note 45, at 924.
56 *Id.* (emphasis added).
57 *See id.* at 924–25.
58 *Id.* at 925.
59 *See* Pole, *supra* note 26, at 123.
60 *Id.* at 125.
61 *See id.*

new representative government came not only from the jury's key role of dispensing the law to the community, but also from its role of maintaining the community's centrality to politics and the polity. The jury trial right was absolutely critical to both.

Getting to the Sixth Amendment: Legal and Political Theory

The role of the community in interpreting and mediating legal disputes was given crucial support by legal writers and theorists read by colonists before, during, and after the Revolution. The role of the local populace in adjudicating the law can be found in the influential theoretical works and law treatises of Edward Coke, Matthew Hale, Cesare Beccaria, William Blackstone, and other seventeenth- and eighteenth-century authors who discussed the right to a jury trial.

Edward Coke was a highly influential, widely read theorist at the time of the formation of the American Constitution.[62] His *Institutes of the Laws of England*, originally published in the Elizabethan age, shaped the understanding of English law for generations and was familiar to the colonies' educated class.[63] Coke's discursions on the workings of the jury trial clarified that the right belonged to the county, or community, where the accused had committed the crime.[64] Coke never raises the notion that the twelve-man jury trial was a right of the accused. Instead, the focus was consistently on the area from which the jurors were chosen. For Coke, the importance of the local, as translated through the literal site of the jury trial and its composition, was part and parcel of the jury trial right.

[62] *See generally* ALLEN D. BOYER, SIR EDWARD COKE AND THE ELIZABETHAN AGE (2003).

[63] *See id.*

[64] For example, in Coke's discussion of where an Englishman should be tried for treason, his gloss on Edward Littleton, the fifteenth-century English jurist, explains that "it shall be tried by twelve men of the countie [sic], where the kings [sic] bench shall sit ..." SIR EDWARD COKE, *Of Continuall Claime*, *in* 2 THE FIRST PART OF THE INSTITUTES OF THE LAWS OF ENGLAND, OR, A COMMENTARY UPON LITTLETON 261 (19th ed., Garland Publishing 1979) (1832). Likewise, in a more detailed exposition on petit treason, Coke notes that the decision in such cases rests on "trialls [sic] by the verdict of twelve men *de vicineto*, of the place where the offence is alleadged [sic]. ..." SIR EDWARD COKE, *Petit Treason*, *in* THE THIRD AND FOURTH PARTS OF THE INSTITUTES OF THE LAWS OF ENGLAND 19, 26 (19th ed., Garland Publishing 1979) (1644) (emphasis added).

Matthew Hale's *History of the Common Law*, penned in 1713, also helped shape eighteenth-century American lawmaking and demonstrated concern about the scope and meaning of the jury trial right.[65] Like Coke's work, Hale's discussion of the jury trial concentrated largely on the selection and nature of the jurors comprising the jury, which he lauded as "an institution most admirably calculated for the preservation of liberty, life, and property."[66]

Hale's jury was an institution that drew power from the community, not an individual defendant. A key aspect of this "institution" was that its members – the jurors – were to be chosen from those who lived, preferably, in the neighborhood, or at least the county or bailiwick.[67] The author's use of four separate terms to delineate the locality of the jury trial right – *de vicineto*, *neighbourhood*, *county*, and *hundred* – denoted the inseparable nature of the community and the jury trial right. The judgment of the local community was part and parcel of the jury trial right and legal adjudication, as understood by Hale and his contemporaries.

Another of these contemporaries, Cesare Beccaria,[68] also had great influence on Founding-era thinkers and writers. Beccaria's writing

[65] Indeed, Hale's very first remark about England's criminal courts focused, unsurprisingly, on the role of the jury trial: "no Man shall be put out of his Lands or Tenements, or be imprisoned by any Suggestion, unless it be by Indictment or Presentment of lawful Men, or by Process at Common Law." MATTHEW HALE, *III. Concerning the Common Law of England, its Use and Excellence, and the Reason of its Denomination, in* THE HISTORY OF THE COMMON LAW OF ENGLAND 24, 27 (1713). Similarly, in discussing the parallels between Norman and English law, Hale noted that in England, "in Cases of Trials by Twelve Men, all ought to agree, and any one dissenting, no Verdict can be given." MATTHEW HALE, *VI. Concerning the Parity or Similitude of the Laws of England and Normandy, and the Reasons Thereof, in* THE HISTORY OF THE COMMON LAW OF ENGLAND, at 60, 65.

[66] SIR MATTHEW HALE, *XII. Touching Trial by Jury in* THE HISTORY OF THE COMMON LAW OF ENGLAND AND AN ANALYSIS OF THE CIVIL PART OF THE LAW 336, 336 (Charles Runnington, ed., 6th ed. 1820) (1713).

[67] As Hale explains in a footnote:

> [T]he jury was to come *de vicineto*, from the neighbourhood of the place where the action was laid; and therefore, they were summoned from the very hundred in which the cause of action arose; ... [l]iving in the neighbourhood, they were most unquestionably of the very county, or *pais*, to which both parties had thought proper to appeal. ...

Id. at n.B. The significance of this passage lies in Hale's focus on the local derivation of the jurors. Of the four aspects of the jury Hale mentioned, it is only this neighborhood requirement that Hale deemed imperative enough to devote a page-long explanation. *See id.* at 338.

[68] Beccaria, an Italian political theorist, was well known in his native country, in England, and in the colonies.

covered many topics, but significant for our purposes are his discussions of public trial and punishment. In his seminal work, *An Essay on Crimes and Punishments*, Beccaria penned a paean to the jury trial as a public right, which he saw as critical in establishing and strengthening the people's rights.[69] Beccaria's belief that any trial and resulting judgment should be performed openly became part of the common belief for the newly created United States that the jury needed to be a popular bulwark against government and sovereign oppression. And by emphasizing the importance of the public's *opinion* as well as the openness of any trial, Beccaria also underlined the importance of the people's involvement in the criminal justice process – "the only cement of society."

Likewise, in the course of discussing secret accusations, Beccaria asked, rather dramatically, "can there be any crime, committed against the public, which ought not to be publicly punished?"[70] Even writing from a tradition that did not use the jury as a way to involve the community in an offender's trial and punishment, Beccaria still viewed crime as a wrong "committed against the public," something that ought to be "publicly punished." This philosophy of punishment fit well with the colonial understanding of the community's right to judge an offender and penalize him, openly and in full view of the populace. In other words, Beccaria's understanding of punishment supported an expressive, retributive punishment philosophy – one that fit well into the existing American framework.

William Blackstone was perhaps the most influential legal writer for the fledgling Americans. His *Commentaries on the Law of England*,[71] published in the mid-1760s, quickly became a cornerstone for developing American jurisprudence.[72] It is useful, then, to look at Blackstone's

[69] Specifically, Beccaria argued that "All trials should be public; that opinion which is the best or, perhaps, the only cement of society, may curb the authority of the powerful, and the passions of the judge; and that the people may say, 'We are protected by the laws; we are not slaves.'" CESARE B. BECCARIA, AN ESSAY ON CRIMES AND PUNISHMENTS 30 (Philadelphia, R. Bell 1778).

[70] *Id.* at 32.

[71] 3 SIR WILLIAM BLACKSTONE, COMMENTARIES ON THE LAW OF ENGLAND (Philadelphia, Robert Bell 1772) (1765).

[72] *See* Pole, *supra* note 26, at 143.

chapter concerning the jury trial to comprehend further the late eighteenth-century meaning of the institution.

In his *Commentaries*, Blackstone focused on the roots of jury trial to show the close relationship between the composition of the jury from the local community and the ability to judge the defendant properly.[73] In this way, Blackstone rooted the entire theory underlying jury trial in the village or country in which the cause was tried. Although Blackstone later noted that the practice of impaneling jurors from the actual neighborhood had been abolished in favor of the larger county, due to concerns over excessive prejudice,[74] his focus still remained on the importance of having the surrounding community's direct participation in criminal adjudication and punishment.

In lauding the practice of using juries to decide criminal cases, Blackstone literally defines it as that great right of the *people*, describing it thus: "the trial by jury, or *the country, per patriam*, is also that trial by the peers, of every Englishman, which, as the grand bulwark of his liberties, is secured to him by the great charter. . . ."[75] In other words, the criminal jury trial right is explained as *per patriam*, or by the country, or by the peers. This "grand bulwark" of liberties was provided to everyone by giving the right of judgment to the *community*.

Blackstone ended his written discussion of the criminal trial by referencing Beccaria to explain how guilty pleas and even voluntary forgiveness were "contrary to the good of the public"[76] since they put a stop to the essential function of the criminal jury trial. Blackstone's message was that the primary purpose of the criminal jury trial was not to give rights either to the accused or the victim. Rather, the jury trial's overarching role – that of determining truth and dispensing

[73] As Blackstone argued, "[b]y policy of the ancient law, the jury was to come *de vicineto*, from the neighborhood of the vill or place where the cause of action was laid in the declaration. . . . For, living in the neighborhood, they were properly the very country, or *pais*, to which both parties had appealed; and were supposed to know before-hand the characters of the parties and witnesses, and therefore the better knew what credit to give to the facts alleged in evidence." Blackstone, Commentaries, *supra* note 71, at 359–60.

[74] *Id.* at 360.

[75] 4 Sir William Blackstone, Commentaries on the Law of England 342 (Philadelphia, Robert Bell 1772) (1765) (emphasis added), *available at* http://avalon.law.yale.edu/18th_century/blackstone_bk4ch27.asp.

[76] *Id.* at 343 (emphasis added).

punishment – belonged to the public, or "society in general."[77] The "necessity of public example" was a key part of the criminal jury trial right, or the right of the local community to publicly adjudicate any alleged crimes committed against it.

Jury Rights in the New Union of States

The first Continental Congress saw the right to a jury trial as collective, or belonging to the offender's community.[78] A key aspect of the jury trial right, as understood at the time and incorporated into the Continental Congress's proceedings, was the local community's right to participate in the trial. This was accomplished by holding the proceedings in open court.[79] By doing away with secret trials, the jury trial right existed to preserve the open, public aspect of justice. A jury trial was an expressive right possessed and practiced by the entire local community, not just those who were chosen for the jury.

Although aware of the dangers of local prejudice, Americans of the Constitutional era fervently believed that only local juries that could fully adjudicate and represent the community.[80] Revolutionary colonists understood that the jury trial right was inextricably linked to the moral judgment of the community and ultimately constructed the constitutional right to a jury trial based on that understanding.

[77] 4 Blackstone, *supra* note 74, at 343 (emphasis added).

[78] As the notes reflect:

> The next great right is that of trial by jury. This provides, that neither life, liberty nor property can be taken from the possessor, until twelve of his unexceptional countrymen and peers, of his vicinage, who from that neighbourhood may reasonably be supposed to be acquainted with his character, and the characters of the witnesses, upon a fair trial, and full enquiry face to face, in open Court, before as many of the people as chuse [sic] to attend, shall pass their sentence upon oath against him. . . .

U.S. Cont'l Cong., Journal of the Proceedings of the Congress, Held at Philadelphia, September 5, 1774 121 (Philadelphia, William and Thomas Bradford 1774).

[79] The public aspect of the jury trial was unlimited, "before as many of the people as chuse to attend." *Id.*

[80] *See* Steven Engel, *The Public's Vicinage Right: A Constitutional Argument*, 75 N.Y.U. L. Rev. 1658, 1673 (2000).

Following the War of Independence, many states, as well as the Northwest Ordinance, secured the right to a collective jury trial.[81] Georgia,[82] Maryland,[83] Massachusetts,[84] North Carolina,[85] and New York[86] all ascribed the jury right to the community, listing it separately from the individual rights belonging to the accused, such as the right of presenting proof, the right of confrontation, and the right of defense. In contrast, Pennsylvania,[87] Vermont,[88] and Virginia[89] almost simultaneously grant the jury trial right to both the individual and the community.

81 *See* Gaspare J. Saladino, *Synthesizing the Origins of the Bill of Rights*, H-NET REVIEWS 3 (1999) (reviewing LEONARD W. LEVY, THE ORIGINS OF THE BILL OF RIGHTS (1999)), *available at* http://www.h-net.org/reviews/showrev.php?id=3505.

82 GA. CONST. of 1777, art. XXXIX, *reprinted in* 2 THE FEDERAL AND STATE CONSTITUTIONS COLONIAL CHARTERS, AND OTHER ORGANIC LAWS OF THE STATES, TERRITORIES, AND COLONIES NOW OR HERETOFORE FORMING THE UNITED STATES OF AMERICA 777, 783 (Francis Newton Thorpe, ed.) (1909) [hereinafter FEDERAL AND STATE CONSTITUTIONS], *available at* http://avalon.law.yale.edu/18th_century/ga02.asp.

83 MD. CONST. of 1776, art. III, *reprinted in* 3 FEDERAL AND STATE CONSTITUTIONS, *supra* note 82, at 1687, 1686–87, *available at* http://avalon.law.yale.edu/17th_century/ma02.asp.

84 MASS. CONST. art. XII.

85 N.C. CONST. of 1776 art. IX, at 2787, *reprinted in* 5 FEDERAL AND STATE CONSTITUTIONS, *supra* note 82, at 1287,1287–88, *available at* http://avalon.law.yale.ed u/18th_century/nc07.asp.

86 N.Y. CONST. of 1777 art. XLI, *reprinted in* 5 FEDERAL AND STATE CONSTITUTIONS, *supra* note 82, at 2623, 2637, *available at* http://avalon.law.yale.ed u/18th_century/ny01.asp.

87 *See* PA. CONST. of 1776 art. IX, *reprinted in* 5 FEDERAL AND STATE CONSTITUTIONS, *supra* note 82, at 3081, 3083, *available at* http://avalon.law.yale.edu/18th_century/pa08.asp ("That in all prosecutions for criminal offences, a man hath a right to be heard by himself and his council, to demand the cause and nature of his accusation, to be confronted with the witnesses, to call for evidence in his favour, and a speedy public trial, by an impartial jury of the country, without the unanimous consent of which jury he cannot be found guilty; nor can he be compelled to give evidence against himself: Nor can any man be justly deprived of his liberty except by the laws of the land, or the judgment of his peers.")

88 *See* VT. CONST. of 1777, chap. 1, art. X, *reprinted in* 6 FEDERAL AND STATE CONSTITUTIONS, *supra* note 82, at 3737, 3741, *available at* http://avalon.law.yale.edu/18th_century/vt01.asp (declaring a right to "a speedy public trial, by an impartial jury of the country; without the unanimous consent of which jury, he cannot be found guilty," and declaring that no man can "be justly deprived of his liberty, except by the laws of the land or the judgment of his peers").

89 *See* VA. CONST. of 1776, § 8, *reprinted in* 7 FEDERAL AND STATE CONSTITUTIONS, *supra* note 82, at 3812, 3813, *available at* http://avalon.law.yale.edu/18th_century/jeffcons .asp (declaring that a "speedy trial by an impartial jury of twelve men of his vicinage" was critical to the people's rights as citizens).

The understanding of the jury trial right as the local community's right was in full evidence during the drafting and ratification of the Constitution. Early versions of the right to a jury trial in the document required criminal cases to follow the "accustomed requisites" – the historical jury trial customs practiced both in England and colonial America.[90] It is not surprising, then, that in every discussion recorded of the debates concerning the drafting of the Constitution, jury trial as a right of the accused was rarely, if ever, mentioned. It was simply assumed.

In the constitutional debates during the 1787 Federal Convention, all versions of the nascent Constitution possessed only a collective version of the jury trial right.[91] Article XI addressed the judiciary and its various jurisdictions but made sure to establish, in Section 4, that "The trial of all criminal offences (except in case of impeachments) shall be in the State where they shall be committed; and shall be by Jury."[92] This original criminal jury trial right focused on the community's ability to adjudicate crimes, not on any individual rights of the defendant.[93] Indeed, there were no individual rights at all in this first draft of the Constitution.

So focal was the collective jury trial right that several public voices, including some prominent anti-Federalists, strongly criticized the Constitution's first iteration for inadequately protecting it. To repair this oversight, the anti-Federalists insisted on the addition of a jury trial right – one that was specifically communitarian.

The importance of the collective jury trial right was thrown into sharp relief by the debate over the definition of *vicinage*, defined as the boundaries of the area from which the jurors would be drawn. Vicinage – inseparable from the community's right to judge its wrongdoers – was presumed in the Anglo-American legal system[94]

90 Kory A. Langhofer, *Comment, Unaccountable at the Founding: The Originalist Case for Anonymous Juries*, 115 YALE L.J. 1823, 1826 (2006).

91 James Madison, *Debates in the Federal Convention of 1787 as Reported by James Madison*, *reprinted in* DOCUMENTS ILLUSTRATIVE OF THE FORMATION OF THE UNION OF THE AMERICAN STATES, *supra* note 82 at 109, 479.

92 *Id.* at 479.

93 Stephanos Bibas, *Originalism and Formalism in Criminal Procedure: The Triumph of Justice Scalia, the Unlikely Friend of Criminal Defendants?* 94 GEO. L.J. 183, 196–97 (2005).

94 *See* Henry G. Connor, *The Constitutional Right to a Trial by a Jury of the Vicinage*, 57 U. PA. L. REV. 197, 197–98 (1909).

and was envisioned as the community's or public's right.[95] The local character of the jury was more than just functional, however, since it was critical for the jury's representation of the community.[96] Indeed, common law assumed that vicinage was part of the jury trial right.[97]

The right of vicinage was of concern to the anti-Federalists in the Constitutional drafting period, because the draft Constitution guaranteed a state trial, but failed to secure the participation of the local community members on the jury.[98] In fact, the anti-Federalist understanding of the jury trial right was inextricable from the vicinage right.

This concern over the draft Constitution's failure to properly safeguard the rights of the community was articulated in many ways, including various requests from the states ratifying the Constitution – including Pennsylvania,[99] New York,[100] and Maryland – to amend or add the criminal jury trial right. This battle over the jury trial right spilled out into the various states as they considered ratification.

Prominent anti-Federalists such as Elbridge Gerry objected to the draft Constitution due to its insufficient restraints of governmental power and limited guarantees of personal liberties. The jury trial right, civil and criminal, was at once a part of that general concern, and an issue all to itself. As such, the debates over its articulation in the Constitution raged fiercely.

For example, in the ratifying debates of the Massachusetts Convention, anti-Federalist Abraham Holmes argued against ratifying

[95] *See* Engel, *supra* note 77, at 1674–75.

[96] *Id.* at 1674.

[97] *Id.*

[98] *Id.* at 1687.

[99] These dissenters included the minority committee from the Pennsylvania and New Jersey delegation. *See The Address and Reasons of the Dissent of the Minority of the Convention of Pennsylvania to Their Constituents*, PA. PACKET & DAILY ADVERTISER, Dec. 18, 1787, *reprinted in* THE ANTI-FEDERALIST, at 201, 206–07, *available at* http://www.constitution.org/afp/pennmi00.htm; *see also* SAUL CORNELL, THE OTHER FOUNDERS: ANTI-FEDERALISM AND THE DISSENTING TRADITION IN AMERICA, 1788–1828, at 32 (1999).

[100] New York's Ratification Convention, which took place on July 26, 1788, demanded that a number of amendments be added to the draft Constitution in order to secure that state's vote. *See* NEW YORK RATIFICATION CONVENTION (July 26, 1788), *reprinted in* FOUNDING AMERICA: DOCUMENTS FROM THE REVOLUTION TO THE BILL OF RIGHTS 600–604 (Jack N. Rakove, ed., 2006) [hereinafter FOUNDING AMERICA].

the draft Constitution because of its failure to define the word *jury*.[101] According to Holmes, the understanding of what comprised a jury comprised needed to be specifically articulated to properly preserve the right in criminal trials – something that the Constitution failed to do.

In all of these ratification debates about the jury trial right, the primary question was, in the words of Melancton Smith, "How was the will of the community to be expressed?"[102] Community rights were the mainstay of the complaints about the draft Constitution, specifically, regarding the jury trial right, and more generally, regarding the people's representation in the new republic.

By the time the Constitution had been ratified by the necessary nine states, several bodies had drafted amendments to be inserted in the text of the Constitution, but no proposal had been made for a declaration of rights.[103] After a number of states provided their drafts of potential amendments, James Madison proposed a bill of rights to the House on June 8, 1789.[104] Madison's amendments contained a variety of protections for the criminal jury trial right. Madison proposed striking the existing Constitutional provision for the jury trial right and inserting instead the following: "The trial of all crimes . . . shall be by an impartial jury of freeholders of the vicinage, with the requisite of unanimity for conviction, of the right of challenge, and other accustomed requisites. . . ."[105] This alteration reflected the deep concern that many had regarding the lack of specific vicinage provision. Madison's revision of the criminal jury trial right signaled the importance of the

[101] *Debates in the Convention of the Commonwealth of Massachusetts on the Adoption of The Federal Constitution*, *in* 2 The Debates in the Several State Conventions, on the Adoption of the Federal Constitution, as Recommended by the General Convention at Philadelphia, in 1787, at 1, 109–12 (Jonathan Elliot, ed., 1836) (statement of Abraham Holmes), *available at* http://press-pubs.uchicago.edu/founders/documents/a3_2_3s15.html.

[102] Melancton Smith, Address to the Convention (June 20, 1788), *reprinted in* The Essential Federalist and Anti-Federalist Papers 42, 46 (David Wootton, ed., 2003), *available at* http://www.constitution.org/rc/rat_ny.htm#msmith01.

[103] *See Framing the Bill of Rights*, Founding America, *supra* note 100, at 611–12.

[104] *See* James Madison, Speech Introducing Amendments in the House of Representatives (June 8, 1789), *reprinted in* Founding America, *supra* note 100, at 613, 618.

[105] *Id.*

local citizenry's participation in criminal adjudication to the creators of the new American government. It also signified a recognition that the common meaning of jury trial right centered on the community.

The Senate, however, would not accept the "local" aspect of the criminal jury right, despite Madison's best efforts.[106] Article X of the House Amendments, concerning vicinage, was acknowledged only by a reference to "the State and district wherein the crime shall have been committed," which was less robust than what the House had originally provided.[107]

After the proposed amendments shifted from the House to the Senate to the House again, the ultimate text of what became the Sixth Amendment listed the collective jury trial right alongside the traditional rights of the accused. Despite the jury trial right's placement in the Sixth Amendment, however, there is no evidence to show that its meaning suddenly switched from a collective right to an individual right.

The phrasing of the Sixth Amendment deserves our careful scrutiny and analysis. Let us look at the text in full:

> In all criminal prosecutions, the accused shall enjoy the right to a speedy and public trial, by an impartial jury of the State and district wherein the crime shall have been committed, which district shall have been previously ascertained by law, and to be informed of the nature and cause of the accusation; to be confronted with the witnesses against him; to have compulsory process for obtaining witnesses in his favor, and to have the Assistance of Counsel for his defence.[108]

In its first clause, the Amendment grants the accused the right to a speedy and public trial – a fairly simple and straightforward

[106] *See* Stanton D. Krauss, *The Original Understanding of the Seventh Amendment Right to Jury Trial*, 33 U. RICH. L. REV. 407, 426 (1999) (reviewing AKHIL REED AMAR, THE BILL OF RIGHTS: CREATION AND RECONSTRUCTION (1998)).

[107] *Amendments Proposed By the House*, *reprinted in* FOUNDING AMERICA, *supra* note 100, at 631.

[108] U.S. CONST. amend. VI.

proposition.[109] A defendant is entitled to a prompt, free, and open trial, not one hidden behind closed doors or conducted years later.

The second clause of the Sixth Amendment, however, is quite different from the first. This clause, demarcated from the first by a comma, denotes the collective nature of the jury trial right: that is, that the jury must not only be "impartial," but must be comprised from the "State and district wherein the crime shall have been committed."[110] Why phrase it like this? Because the Framers wanted to emphasize that the *jury* aspect of the trial is local and communal, belonging to those (white, landowning men) who reside in the immediate district. In other words, the accused has a right to a trial that is speedy and public, but the jury trial piece is a right reserved to the community.

If the authors of the Bill of Rights had wished to grant the accused the jury trial right as well, then the Amendment could have looked more like this: "the accused shall enjoy the right to a speedy and public JURY trial, drawn from the State and district wherein the crime shall have been committed." The fact that the second passage of the Sixth Amendment separates out the jury aspect of a defendant's trial indicates that this right was separate from the rest of the individual rights listed.

Ultimately, what looks to our eyes like a purely individual jury trial right would have been interpreted quite differently when the Bill of Rights was drafted. Contemporaneous understanding of the jury trial right would have seen it as a right of the community, no matter where or how it was inserted into the Constitution. Unlike the contested definition of vicinage, the jury trial right was solidly interpreted as belonging to the local community, so much so that its placement within the bundle of defendants' rights would not have changed its common public meaning. It was only the passage of time and habits of careless interpretation that altered the original understanding of the right to trial by jury.

Why, then, was this collective jury trial right placed in a list of individual rights? First, a study of the various draft Amendments shows that many of the rights that made it into the Bill of Rights were truncated and/or combined with other rights for brevity's sake. The

[109] *Id.* cl. 1.
[110] *Id.* cl. 2.

Sixth Amendment cataloged all the rights attached to criminal indictment and trial; it is possible that, given the popular understanding of the jury trial right, adding the right to the rest of the trial rights, whether individual or collective, was done as a measure of expediency.

Second, the jury trial right was added to the list of the individual rights in the Sixth Amendment possibly as a way to quiet the fears of those (vocal) Framers who claimed that the new system of government was designed to trample on individual rights. As Akhil Amar has documented, the anti-Federalists' distrust of the federal legislature's ability to truly represent the people resulted in their strong focus on the average person's right to serve as a juror.[111] The anti-Federalists were disturbed at the application of national laws onto the local communities, unadulterated by the particular needs of that area.[112] Thus, adding the jury trial right to the list of individual rights protected in the Sixth Amendment was likely a gesture to quiet anti-Federalist unrest.

Amar observes that the jury trial right was never "simply and always an individual right but also an institution of localism and popular sovereignty."[113] But the criminal jury trial right has always been greater than this conceptualization. As understood in the colonial and Revolutionary era, the jury trial right was envisioned primarily as a local, community-based right with little thought given to the rights of the defendant.

As Amar noted, the actions of the American jury "were expected to be informed by community values"[114] – thereby not only allowing the community the specific right of a public trial, but also ensuring that the populace could retain its role as local arbiters of punishment. Moreover, the ability to participate in a criminal jury trial provided representation and voice on a variety of different levels.

Finally, the right of the accused to a "public" trial, as articulated in the Sixth Amendment, was also a nod to the rights of the local community. This public, expressive aspect of the jury trial right was another way in which the power of the local community was formalized into the

[111] *See* Akhil Reed Amar, The Bill of Rights: Creation and Reconstruction 11 (1998).

[112] *See id.*

[113] *Id.* at 106.

[114] *Id.* at 88–89.

Constitution. The right to a jury trial, then, signified both expressively and morally, allowing the average citizen a way to contribute simultaneously to the politics of the local as well as a greater national polity.

Accordingly, the right to a jury trial, despite its location in the collection of defendants' rights articulated in the Sixth Amendment, was never anything but an integral right of the community. This new historical understanding requires us to reconsider how easily we allow the collective jury trial right to be ameliorated in our current world of bail hearings, plea bargains, guilty pleas, and ancillary sentencing proceedings.

Erosion and Decline

The fidelity to the role of the community in the right to a jury trial began to waver as the eighteenth century turned into the nineteenth. Jury trials came increasingly under judicial control.[115] Juries lost their right to decide the law, and their role in deciding the facts became increasingly restricted.

Nonetheless, juries were still performing their typical mediating functions well into the latter parts of the nineteenth century.[116] In his masterwork, *Democracy in America*,[117] Alexis de Tocqueville marveled at the primacy of the jury as an essential aspect of America's democratic experiment. Recognizing that the jury had great influence on "the destinies of society at large,"[118] Tocqueville admired the American jury trial because it placed "the real direction of society in the hands of the governed, or of a portion of the governed, and not in that of the government."[119] Loosely decoded, Tocqueville admired how the jury trial gave control to the people.

Tocqueville's appreciation of the jury trial was entirely predicated on the benefits that resounded to the community. As he noted, although he was unsure whether the jury was a useful tool to those being judged,

[115] *See* Pole, *supra* note 26, at 134.
[116] *See id.*
[117] ALEXIS DE TOCQUEVILLE, DEMOCRACY IN AMERICA (Francis Bowen, trans., Alfred A. Knopf, Inc. 4th prtg. 1948) (1835).
[118] *Id.* at 282.
[119] *Id.*

he was "certain it is highly beneficial to those who judge them."[120] Tocqueville was greatly impressed with the jury's ability to be "the voice of the community represented by that institution."[121]

The idea that jury trial rights meant community rights held sway until at least the mid-nineteenth century. Even in the latter part of the nineteenth century, state supreme courts continued to hold that trial-less procedures such as guilty pleas were unconstitutional, in part because they took away the community's right to adjudicate the offender's guilt and punishment.[122] For example, in 1865 the Tennessee Supreme Court reversed a guilty plea with the admonishment that a public trial could not "be defeated by any deceit or device whatever."[123]

As the nineteenth century hastened toward the twentieth, however, the role of the jury trial began to diminish. The climbing number of felonies in both the state and federal arenas, combined with the increasing length of trials and the complexity of evidentiary rules, has resulted in many fewer jury trials and a great many more guilty pleas. The twenty-first century has only exacerbated this trend, with approximately 95 percent of all criminal indictments adjudicated through guilty pleas.[124]

Our current extreme diminishment of the jury's role, however, does not change the original meaning and practice of the jury trial right. Ultimately, a textual-historical analysis of original sources from the colonial era through the Constitutional ratification period strongly indicates that the right to a jury trial was collective. The jury trial right, particularly the criminal jury trial right, was almost entirely predicated on validating the community's right to propound moral judgments on local citizens and little concerned with the defendant's individual rights and liberties.

120 *Id.* at 285.

121 *Id.* at 286.

122 *See* Adam H. Kurland, *Providing a Federal Criminal Defendant with a Unilateral Right to a Bench Trial: A Renewed Call to Amend Federal Rule of Criminal Procedure 23(a)*, 26 U.C. Davis L. Rev. 309, 320 (1993).

123 David J. Bodenhamer, Fair Trial: Rights of the Accused in American History 86 (1992).

124 *See* Ron Wright, *Trial Distortion and the End of Innocence in Federal Criminal Justice*, 154 U. Penn. L. Rev. 79, 90–91 (2005).

This history should have profound effects on how we view the criminal jury trial right today. Although twentieth-century courts have assigned the jury trial right almost exclusively to defendants,[125] there is no reason why the rights of the community could not be taken into consideration as well. This understanding has been repeatedly endorsed by the Supreme Court over the past fifteen years as the Court has continued to expand the community's role in determining all sorts of punishment for offenders.

[125] *See* Patton v. United States, 281 U.S. 276 (1930) (assigning jury trial right to defendant).

3 THE SUPREME COURT AND THE REAFFIRMATION OF COMMUNITY

Why has the Sixth Amendment right to a jury trial recently reassumed such great importance in modern criminal procedure? More specifically, why has the Supreme Court focused so heavily in recent years on the role of the jury as an essential voice of the community? The answer lies in both a return to the historical patterns in adjudicating crimes and a renewed appreciation for the need for community participation in the criminal justice process. The former we discussed at length in Chapter 2; the latter we will explore as we launch into Chapter 3.

For approximately the past fifteen years, the Supreme Court has renewed its focus on the role of the community jury as a constitutional requirement. Based on a return to origins, this heightened interest in the work of the jury, in its role as a representative of the community, has helped buttress the legitimacy of recent sentencing and criminal law reforms.

The Supreme Court only recently focused its sights on the history of the jury trial right as a way to bolster its Sixth Amendment jurisprudence, most notably through *Apprendi v. New Jersey* and *Blakely v. Washington*. As I discuss throughout this chapter, the Court's new understanding of proper criminal adjudication is grounded in the rediscovered historical right of the jury to decide punishment for offenders – specifically, in the community's central role of determining an offender's moral blameworthiness.

In short, this chapter will explore the broader question of what this invigoration of the Sixth Amendment jury trial right means for all aspects of criminal punishment. I accomplish this by analyzing a combination of sentencing doctrine, punishment theory, and empirical observations of sentencing schemes and applying them to hidden sentencing.

For this analysis, it is useful to first review the Court's use of the jury trial right in cases involving punishment, pointing out where its historical evidence has proved thin as well as noting where the two conflicting conceptions of the jury trial right have muddied the waters of its jurisprudence.

THE APPRENDI-BLAKELY REVOLUTION

Apprendi, *Blakely*, and their progeny, which have revolutionized sentencing and punishment, may be relatively recent decisions, but over the past decade and a half, the Supreme Court has been building the foundation for policy shift by gradually "rediscovering" a criminal offender's Sixth Amendment jury trial right. Of course, the Constitution has always protected each criminal defendant against conviction "except upon proof beyond a reasonable doubt of every fact necessary to constitute the crime with which he is charged"[1] and gives the defendant the right to insist that "a jury find him guilty of all the elements of the crime with which he is charged."[2] As the Court recently commented, these two basic ideas – that all elements of a crime must be found by a jury, beyond a reasonable doubt, for a valid conviction – "provided the basis for [its] . . . decisions interpreting modern criminal statutes and sentencing procedures."[3]

Until quite recently, however, a century's worth of decisions submerged the community's right to these Sixth Amendment guarantees, effectively concealing their applicability to criminal sentencing and punishment. To best see how this right was uncovered, we must return to the cases directly preceding the *Blakely* line that laid the groundwork for this supposed "watershed" change in Court sentencing jurisprudence.

The first real sign of the Court's Sixth Amendment rediscovery was in *Jones v. United States*,[4] a case largely ignored until *Blakely*. One of the

1 *In re* Winship, 397 U.S. 358, 364 (1970).
2 United States v. Gaudin, 515 U.S. 506, 511 (1995).
3 United States v. Booker, 543 U.S. 220, 230 (2005).
4 526 U.S. 227 (1999).

chief concerns in *Jones* was to determine the history and boundaries of the constitutional safeguards for fact-finding procedures, particularly the identity of the fact finder. By expounding the history of criminal sentencing as well as the Framers' concerns over jury rights, the *Jones* Court underlined the importance of the jury's control over the ultimate verdict. In doing so, the Court signaled that *any* future "relative diminution of the jury's significance"[5] would raise Sixth Amendment concerns.

Accordingly, the *Jones* Court's steadfast championing of the Sixth Amendment community jury right laid the groundwork for much of the change in criminal punishment that was – and is – to follow. *Jones* suggested that in a battle between the recent focus on speed and process in the criminal justice system and the safeguarding of traditional jury rights, jury rights must triumph.

A year later, in *Apprendi v. New Jersey*,[6] the Court broadened its rediscovery of the historical Sixth Amendment collective jury trial right. The Court held that a lengthened sentence resulting from the addition of a "sentence enhancement" was impermissible because "any fact that increases the penalty of a crime beyond the prescribed statutory maximum must be submitted to a jury, and proved beyond a reasonable doubt"[7] – thus reaffirming what it had suggested in *Jones*. Sentencing facts had to be proven beyond a reasonable doubt, just like those of any offense, to preserve the jury's prerogative.

In *Apprendi*, as in *Jones*, the Court returned to the communitarian role of the jury to ensure that the state did not overreach its powers. These twelve jurors, representing "the great bulwark of [our] civil and political liberties," were supposed to be "twelve of [the defendant's] equals and neighbors" or part of the offender's community.[8] Notably, *Apprendi* focused on how the traditional jury trial right required the jury to determine the truth of each accusation in *every* stage of the legal process, from start to finish.

[5] *Id.* at 247.

[6] 530 U.S. 466 (2000) (declaring unconstitutional a New Jersey hate crime statute enabling a sentencing judge to impose a sentence beyond the statutory maximum for various crimes without imprimatur of a jury).

[7] *Id.* at 490.

[8] *Id.* at 477.

The *Apprendi* Court's emphasis on the community's role in measuring levels of culpability was first discussed in *Jones*, where the Court considered how eighteenth-century English juries devised extralegal ways of avoiding a guilty verdict if the punishment for a certain offense seemed disproportionate to the offender's conduct.[9] This community focus strongly suggests that a retributive philosophy of punishment, based on the defendant's moral blameworthiness, may best explain what motivated the Court's decision, at a jurisprudential level, that the jury (and, by extension, the community) had the right to determine punishment.

The importance of the community's role as arbiter of criminal justice is best explained by the progenitor of collective jury rights, Justice Antonin Scalia. In his powerful *Apprendi* concurrence, Scalia rightly argued that the Founders of the American Republic had no intentions of leaving criminal justice to the states. Thus, the jury trial guarantee was a very important provision of the Bill of Rights. This guarantee promised the criminal offender that "all the facts which must exist in order to subject the defendant to a legally prescribed punishment *must* be found by the jury."[10]

In later opinions, Scalia explained that his strong championing of the community jury right resulted from the realization that "the right of trial by jury is in perilous decline"[11] – indeed, he stated outright, in a later opinion, that he had "discarded [his] old ignorance"[12] (i.e., jury trial rights do not matter). This was something he, and a majority of the Court, would remedy in *Blakely* and its successors.

Blakely v. Washington fully articulated the community's historical right to a jury trial. In its most narrow form, *Blakely* specifically held that "[o]ther than the fact of a prior conviction, any fact that increases the penalty for a crime beyond the prescribed statutory maximum must be submitted to a jury, and proved beyond a reasonable doubt."[13] By holding that a court can only sentence a defendant on facts found by

[9] *See* Jones v. United States, 526 U.S. 227, 245 (1999) (cited in *Apprendi*, 530 U.S. at 480 n. 5).

[10] *Id.* at 499 (Scalia, J., concurring) (quoting Breyer, J.).

[11] Ring v. United States, 536 U.S. 584, 612 (2002) (Scalia, J., concurring).

[12] *Id.* at 611 (Scalia, J., concurring).

[13] Blakely v. Washington, 542 U.S. 296, 301 (2004).

the jury beyond a reasonable doubt or admitted by the defendant himself, the *Blakely* Court eliminated all judge-made enhancement of sentences beyond their maximum.[14]

Blakely's holding, however, had far more import than simply determining which body may find facts that increase an offender's maximum sentence.[15] In responding to the slow diminution of the jury right's traditional and proper scope, the *Blakely* Court firmly reestablished the paramount territory of the jury in criminal decision-making and punishment. This broad *Blakely* mandate stems from the importance the Court has invested in the role of the jury. The *Blakely* Court drew its constitutional and historical bases from a variety of sources, including the Sixth Amendment's "reservation of jury power,"[16] the "common-law ideal of limited state power,"[17] the rediscovered "Framers' paradigm for criminal justice,"[18] and the constitutional requirement that all facts legally essential to the punishment be proved to a jury beyond a reasonable doubt.[19] All these ideas combined in *Blakely* to form a new guiding principle for imposing punishment within criminal justice.

The local jury trial, the *Blakely* Court explained, was a key reservation of the community's power in the structuring of our government: "Just as suffrage ensures the people's ultimate control in the legislative and executive branches, [a] jury trial is meant to ensure their control in the judiciary."[20] As *Blakely* illustrated with a number of historical sources, the jury trial right was a critical right during the nation's

[14] Critically, the majority found that "[w]hen a judge inflicts punishment that the jury's verdict alone does not allow, the jury has not found all the facts 'which the law makes essential to the punishment,' and the judge exceeds his proper authority." *Id.* at 304 (internal citation omitted) (quoting 1 JOHN BISHOP CRIMINAL PROCEDURE 55 (2nd ed. 1872)).

[15] It is possible, of course, to interpret *Blakely* more narrowly. A more restrained *Blakely* reading would only mean that juries must find facts increasing the "statutory maximum." If the definition of "statutory maximum" is itself limited to only the actual length of time the offender spends in prison, as opposed to all the other ancillary sentencing proceedings that can increase an offender's punishment, then *Blakely*'s scope is considerably constricted. However, this reading is extremely formalistic, with little to no underlying theory supporting it. A broader understanding of *Blakely* is indicated in both the pre-*Blakely* line of cases and, as we explore throughout the book, in its progeny.

[16] *Blakely*, 542 U.S. at 308.

[17] *Id.* at 313.

[18] *Id.*

[19] *Id.* at 313.

[20] *Id.* at 306.

founding – so much so that the Framers decided to entrench it in the Constitution because "they were unwilling to trust government to mark out the role of the jury."[21]

Moreover, *Blakely*'s wider understanding of the historical jury role also relied on the jury's function as the public's representative and as the primary provider of community-based punishment. The Court placed such importance on the jury's role in part because of its recent emphasis, in decisions such as *Apprendi*, on the community's traditional role in determining moral blameworthiness.

Blakely contended that the liberal democratic decision-making vested in the jury's determination of blameworthiness relies on the community's role in linking punishment to the crime committed, so that the offender will feel more responsibility for her actions. Put another way, there is a strong link between community-based retribution and the jury's role in finding all facts relevant to punishment.

As we explored previously in Chapter 2, colonial Americans believed that the best way to ensure that the offender felt the moral weight and indignation of the community (as part of the punishment) was having a fair cross-section of said community determine that punishment via the jury. Indeed, this was so important to early Americans that they interpreted the jury trial right as a right of the community, not the offender. This is an important distinction, because when the determination of culpability is handed down by an offender's fellow citizens, rather than the state, the punishment is fully legitimized and the normative judgment of the community is fully imposed.

This collective punishment ideal was reinforced by the *Blakely* Court. In *Blakely*, the Court articulated how from the earliest days of our nation the jury trial was considered an essential part of criminal justice. This was because the jury ensured that the interests of the local public were incorporated into the institution of the judiciary. In other words, one of the key roles of the jury at the time of the founding was to make sure that the community's concerns and beliefs remained central in the punishment of an offender. This punishment was not something left to the judge, but rather a responsibility and right of a defendant's immediate society. As Amar observed, "[t]he

[21] *Blakely*, 542 U.S. at 308.

jury was not simply a popular body, but a local one as well . . . composed of Citizens from the same community and . . . informed by community values."[22]

As noted in Chapter 2, the criminal jury trial right was protected in both Article III of the Constitution and the Sixth Amendment because Article III had no specific promise of the jury trial, and "many Anti-Federalists wanted an explicit guarantee that juries would be organized around local rather than statewide communities."[23] From the beginning, then, a key aspect of the criminal jury trial was the *community's* role in conveying punishment to criminal offenders.

In addition, considering how many Revolutionary-era Americans deeply distrusted the judicial branch,[24] one of the primary reasons for enshrining the jury as arbiter of criminal punishment was to ensure that adjudication of crime was never severed from popular authority. Thus the desire to protect the community jury trial right cannot be seen merely as a way to incorporate popular checks and accountability into the justice system, because the jury trial right guaranteed that the citizenry would have a direct hand in determining moral blameworthiness of punishment.

Ultimately, *Blakely* underlined the jury's function as the lay public's representative and as the primary provider of community-based punishment. And the Court has been faithful to this renewed appreciation of the jury and the community's role in arbitrating punishment in its post-*Blakely* decisions involving the need for the collective imposition of punishment. This is immediately evident in recent cases such as *Shepard*,[25] *Cunningham*,[26] *Southern Union*,[27] and *Alleyne*,[28] all of which contain examples the Court's ever-broadening understanding of the community jury right's scope.

[22] Akhil Amar, *The Bill of Rights as a Constitution*, 100 YALE L.J. 1131, 1186 (1991). As Amar explains, the jury was central to both the Bill of Rights and the Constitution: "Not only was it featured in three separate amendments (the Fifth, Sixth, and Seventh), but its absence strongly influenced the judge-restricting doctrines underlying three other amendments (the First, Fourth, and Eighth)." *Id.* at 1190.

[23] *See id.* at 1197.

[24] Revolutionary-era Americans' distrust stemmed from their experience with the British court system and the Stamp Act, among other outrages.

[25] Shepard v. United States, 544 U.S. 13 (2005).

[26] Cunningham v. California, 549 U.S. 270 (2007).

[27] Southern Union Co. v. United States, 567 U.S. __, 132 S. Ct. 2344 (2012).

[28] Alleyne v. United States, 570 U.S. __, 133 S. Ct. 2151 (June 17, 2013).

For example, *Shepard* seemed to deal with a very narrow issue: a judge's ability to determine certain facts in weighing an offender's prior conviction. Specifically, the *Shepard* Court held that judges must confine their review of evidence concerning prior convictions to the charging document, the terms of the plea agreement, or the offender's admissions in an exchange with the trial judge.[29] In other words, the decision cabins the judge's discretion regarding already-determined facts when deciding on proper punishment. For our purposes, however, *Shepard* is most interesting in its broader implications for the future of the prior conviction exception, which permits a nonjury, noncommunity actor to increase an offender's punishment when he or she has previously been convicted of a separate offense, since it hinted that the Court might eliminate the last remaining exception to the ban on judicial fact-finding. Justice Clarence Thomas, writing separately, argued in his *Shepard* concurrence that the exception carved out in *Almendarez-Torres v. United States*[30] had been continually eroded by the *Apprendi-Blakely* principles, and, thus, the exception should be eliminated.[31]

Shepard is significant for a number of reasons, then. First, so much of today's punishment is made much more severe due to prior convictions, which relies on the continuing constitutional validity of *Almendarez-Torres*. And because most states have some sort of compulsory recidivism statute on the books, eliminating the prior conviction exception could have tremendous effect on state punishment, essentially requiring the states to fully recognize the community jury trial right in all aspects of punishment. Second, *Shepard* illustrates how the Supreme Court's interpretation of the Sixth Amendment is shifting toward more jury involvement. If an exception even as sacred as that of prior conviction can be questioned and challenged, this can be seen as a signal that the Court's understanding of the jury's role points in the direction of expansiveness.

Another exception that prior to *Blakely* seemed sacrosanct was state-required mandatory minimums. These compulsory minimum

[29] *See* Shepard, 544 U.S. at 26.

[30] Almendarez-Torres v. United States, 523 U.S. 224 (1998).

[31] Shepard, 544 U.S. at 28 (Thomas, J., concurring). Thomas had joined the *Almendarez-Torres* majority but has since said that he "succumbed" to error in joining that ruling. Apprendi v. New Jersey, 530 U.S. 466, 520 (2000) (Thomas, J., concurring).

sentences for certain crimes, levied by either the legislature or statewide public initiatives passed by voters, prevent the local community from determining whether certain offenders should be punished at a level lower than the standard, due to extenuating circumstances, ability to reform, contributions to society, and so forth.

Before *Blakely* was decided, the Court had exempted mandatory minimums from the *Apprendi* requirement, making judges the sole arbiter of punishment in *Harris v. United States*.[32] A four-justice plurality in *Harris* held that the jury need not play a role when an offender's sentence was enhanced beyond the minimum, because *Apprendi* technically involved a sentencing increase beyond the maximum. Moreover, despite the thin consensus agreeing to the preservation of mandatory minimums, the *Blakely* Court did not see fit to challenge *Harris* at that time.

Quite recently, however, the Court's consensus preserving mandatory minimums dissolved, once again ceding power to the community jury. In *Alleyne v. United States*,[33] the Court tackled a long-standing controversy regarding the method of proof that the Sixth Amendment requires to impose a mandatory minimum sentence. *Alleyne* involved a mandatory minimum sentence imposed by the court, above and beyond the offender's standard sentence, based on facts found by the judge, not the jury. Although the jury had acquitted Alleyne of brandishing a firearm during a robbery, the court held that the accused should have foreseen that his partner would do so and was therefore guilty of the additional offense. Accordingly, the trial court found that the mandatory minimum sentence for felony firearm possession must be imposed on top of Alleyne's existing sentence for the robbery itself. By imposing this additional punishment, the court usurped the jury's ability to decide for itself whether to punish Alleyne for his accomplice having brandished a gun.

Alleyne finally and decisively answered the mandatory minimum question by overruling *Harris*. In a 5-to-4 decision written by Justice Thomas, the Court held that the defendant's seven-year mandatory minimum sentence violated the Sixth Amendment right to trial by jury because the question of brandishing, which determination

[32] Harris v. United States, 536 U.S. 545 (2002).

[33] Alleyne 133 S. Ct. 2151.

increased the defendant's punishment, was never submitted to the jury. The *Alleyne* Court's opinion explained that the logic of *Apprendi* requires a jury to find all facts that fix the penalty range of a crime. *Alleyne*'s holding appropriately extended both *Apprendi-Blakely* and the community jury right, since the *Alleyne* trial court directly countermanded the decision of the community – as represented by the jury – not to punish an offender for a certain offense.

The Court's broad application of the *Apprendi-Blakely* community jury rule also emerges in *Cunningham v. California*,[34] which rejected California's attempt to evade *Blakely*'s requirements. California's sentencing guidelines required judicial fact-finding to elevate or mitigate a sentence beyond the "middle" range. The *Cunningham* Court found that this requirement violated the newly reaffirmed community jury trial right, of course, because any facts that alter punishment must be found by a jury.

The *Cunningham* majority clarified two important things. First, *any* judicial fact-finding that affects punishment presents constitutional problems. Second, the importance of the jury's role was paramount: it was constitutionally required for the jury to "find any fact necessary to the imposition of an elevated sentence."[35] In other words, any fact-finding that increases a sentence from the punishment arising from the guilty verdict must be found by the jury and the jury alone. *Cunningham* offers yet another sign that the Court considers the community's role in determining punishment essential for proper administration of criminal justice.

The Court's focus on community participation in criminal adjudication has not been limited to criminal trials. In *Southern Union v. United States*,[36] the Court reaffirmed the broad scope of *Apprendi-Blakely*, holding that any punishment rendered by the courts – including criminal fines – should have its facts determined by a jury beyond a reasonable doubt.[37] The *Southern Union* Court found that the criminal fine, although different in type from imprisonment, was not so different from it in substance, and therefore there was no principled basis to treat the two differently.[38]

[34] Cunningham v. California, 549 U.S. 270 (2007).
[35] *Id.*
[36] Southern Union Co. v. United States, 567 U.S. __, 132 S. Ct. 2344 (2012).
[37] *Id.*
[38] *Southern Union*, slip op. at 4.

Southern Union illustrated that a central concern of criminal justice is the jury's determination of facts that impose criminal punishment. This must include criminal fines because, as the Court reasoned, fines are just another form of state penalty for the commission of offenses. For the current Supreme Court, punishment is punishment is punishment, whether you call it "fines," "penalties," "sentences," or "punishment."

Notably, the *Southern Union* Court found support in historical antecedents, noting that criminal fines were by far the most common form of noncapital punishment in colonial America.[39] This reliance on the specific attributes of colonial criminal history was not an anomaly. The Court has repeatedly indicated in previous opinions that "the scope of the constitutional jury right must be informed by the historical role of the jury at common law."[40] Applied here, the Court clarified that in the case of criminal fines, as in the case of so many other areas of criminal justice, we must follow the prevailing practice from our colonial and Founding eras.[41]

In this way, the *Southern Union* Court reaffirmed that imposing punishment on offenders is solely the jury's province, no matter what kind of penalty. Ultimately, *Southern Union* helps bolster what we have already learned from our tour through colonial criminal justice: that the community must adjudicate punishment in all types of criminal procedures, from the front end to the back end.

Analyzing the Court's reasoning in its recent sentencing and punishment decisions, however, is not the end of the inquiry. To truly understand the Court's decisions and future direction, we must first determine a coherent jurisprudence of punishment – something that has been sorely lacking, for the most part, in the discussion of the reinvigoration of the community jury right. Accordingly, Chapters 4 and 5 begin an exploration of the jurisprudential currents animating this revolution in jury trial rights and how these trends should affect our use and potential expansion of the community voice in criminal justice.

39 *Id.*
40 Oregon v. Ice, 555 U.S. 160, 170 (2010).
41 *Southern Union*, slip op. at 14.

PART II

Old Becomes New: Sixth Amendment Jury Rights and Twenty-First-Century Criminal Procedure

4 RETRIBUTION, RESTORATIVE JUSTICE, AND THE SIXTH AMENDMENT JURY RIGHT

What are the jurisprudential underpinnings of the Court's recent jury trial right expansion? Over the past fifteen years, the Supreme Court has rethought its approach to the constitutional rights and requirements of the community jury. Despite this shift, however, it has left only a few clues as to why it has done so, apart from some historical references and incomplete sourcing. Thus the question remains: What, if any, theory of punishment underlies this major change to criminal justice?

In this chapter, I argue that the Court's championing of the criminal jury trial right is undergirded by a philosophy of punishment based on a type of expressive, restorative retribution. This theory of punishment is grounded both in the historical right of the community to decide all punishments and in the necessity of having community make decisions about blameworthiness. Expressive, restorative retribution not only helps clarify why the Court has become such a champion of the Sixth Amendment jury trial right at a time when most indictments are settled through guilty pleas, but also provides the best explanation of the Court's new jurisprudence of punishment.

Using expressive, restorative retribution as a blueprint allows us to predict and expand the use of the community as arbiter of punishment beyond trials to other forms of criminal process such as guilty pleas, bench trials, bail hearings, and ancillary sentencing – as I explore later in the book. In this chapter, I delve into the theory underlying both the Court's understanding of the Sixth Amendment jury trial right and the historical contours of colonial punishment and forgiveness upon which our criminal justice system is based.

FINDING A THEORY TO FIT

In the past several terms, the Court's decisions on sentencing have been nothing short of revolutionary. Indeed, courts, scholars, and practitioners are still attempting to come to terms with the new role for the jury in imposing criminal punishment. One area that has not been much explored, however, is the jurisprudential underpinnings of the Court's recent sentencing decisions. Although there is a general consensus that the Court's jurisprudence of punishment has changed, there is scant agreement as to how or why.

Exploring these unexamined aspects of the punishment philosophy underlying the *Apprendi-Blakely* line of cases is important for two reasons. First, exploring the details of such criminal theory helps us understand how and why the Court's sentencing jurisprudence has changed dramatically. Second, if we are successful in setting out the contours of the punishment philosophy envisioned by the Court, we will be better able to predict where this jurisprudence might ultimately lead. Although no one theory fits perfectly, an expressive, restorative, retributive theory of punishment best supports the Court's framework of constitutional criminal procedure.

PUNISHMENT PHILOSOPHY IN HISTORICAL PERSPECTIVE

Before exploring the new jurisprudence underlying the reasoning in *Apprendi-Blakely*, however, we must understand what punishment theory we are leaving behind. Over the past forty-five years, the philosophy underlying criminal punishment has been in flux. Although criminal justice proceedings have changed considerably, no coherent belief structure has been articulated, leading to inequity and inconsistency in sentencing and punishment procedures.

Historically, our tolerance of these relatively informal, nonadversarial punishment decisions was based on the demands of a discretionary and rehabilitative model of sentencing. The Court's approval of lax procedural rights in a discretionary sentencing system, as articulated in *Williams v. New York*, relied explicitly on a rehabilitative punishment model, a hallmark of the earlier part of the twentieth century.[1] By the 1980s, however, the underpinnings of punishment theory began to change as both state and federal legislatures began to reform their sentencing systems and do away with indeterminacy and discretion. Once rehabilitation theories of punishment went out of vogue, the *Williams* rationale supporting almost complete judicial and probationary discretion became untenable.

This change to a stricter, more regulated system was largely motivated by an increasing concern about sentencing arbitrariness and disparity, coupled with a loss of confidence in correctional rehabilitative programs. Instead of a rehabilitative theory of punishment, deterrence and incapacitation became the rule, as well as some consequentialist "communicative" theories of punishment; theories that argued that the aim of punishment was to communicate with the offender about her wrongdoing.

The sentencing reform movement rejected rehabilitation as a penal theory, in part because modern sentencing focused predominantly on incarceration and imposing punishment. This focus on punishment returned the focus to the local jury, which is the only body empowered to judge an offender and determine the proper penance.

There has been little thought about the philosophy that has replaced rehabilitation, however, and that itself is a problem. In this chapter, I aim to fill that gap. Accordingly, I propose that a theory of expressive, restorative retribution best supports the Court's rediscovery of the Sixth Amendment community trial right in sentencing and punishment.

EXPRESSIVE RETRIBUTION AND THE SIXTH AMENDMENT

Apprendi-Blakely and its progeny rely heavily on an unarticulated theory of community-based retribution that must inform our future understanding of the role of the jury in criminal punishment. Retributive theory, however, is often misunderstood and mischaracterized.

[1] Williams v. New York, 337 U.S. 241 (1949).

Although a retributivist must believe that imposition of deserved punishment is an intrinsic good, that is the only proposition to which she commits; she needn't believe it is the *only* intrinsic good. This view separates the retributivist from those, such as Jeremy Bentham, who believe punishment is an intrinsic evil.

In general, a retributivist believes in Immanuel Kant's "Justice of Punishment" and follows in his footsteps through a focus upon the moral appropriateness of individual punishments in relation to the offender's individual crime.[2] Moreover, many retributivists believe that wrongdoers should be punished only because and to the extent that they deserve it.[3] Generally, retributivists agree that the amount that a convicted offender deserves to be punished should be some combination of the wrong or harm caused (or attempted to cause) and the level of blameworthiness with which she caused it (or tried to cause it).

Unlike Kant, however, a retributivist need not argue that imposing just punishment is a "categorical imperative" nor agree with James Stephen that it is morally correct to hate criminals.[4] Neither must a retributivist stick to H. L. A. Hart's crude retributive model, which imposes suffering on those who voluntarily commit moral evil, believing that this is a moral positive. Instead, a retributivist can accept the goal of imposing the community's sanctions as an intrinsic good that expresses social disapproval, shapes norms, and creates moral education.

Additionally, many retributivists believe in a balancing of burdens as part of society's role in criminal punishment. This kind of consequential argument for retributivism can often turn on society's understanding of punishment rather than on the actual punishment itself. Thus, when there are conflicting perceptions of desert – or moral blameworthiness – democratic processes are most likely to provide a polity's best concept of moral guilt. Indeed, concepts of desert that emerge from democratic processes will generally be widely shared or respected.

[2] "The Penal Law is a Categorial Imperative; and woe to him who creeps through the serpent-windings of Utilitarianism to discover some advantage that may discharge him from the Justice of Punishment, or even from the due measure of it. . . ." IMMANUEL KANT, THE PHILOSOPHY OF LAW 195 (1887).

[3] *See* MICHAEL MOORE, PLACING BLAME: A GENERAL THEORY OF THE CRIMINAL LAW 91 (1997).

[4] *See* Kant, *supra* note 2, at 195; JAMES FITZJAMES STEPHEN, 2 A HISTORY OF THE CRIMINAL LAW OF ENGLAND 81 (Macmillan 1883).

We still justify criminal punishment and sentencing in terms of moral judgments. Accordingly, the level of punishment in retributive theory tends to be roughly equal to the seriousness of the wrong and the blameworthiness of the offender in committing it. In part, this is due to the central role of fairness and proportionality in retributive punishment.[5]

As a society, we value the proposition that only actual offenders can be punished. The Supreme Court's new punishment jurisprudence attempts to bolster this sentiment by ensuring that punishment is only imposed on offenders who have been found guilty of the charged offense by a jury. The jury's critical role in punishment reflects the importance the Court has placed on both the community and liberal democratic decision making in criminal justice procedures.

Historically, the jury has determined the blameworthiness of the offender. The Court's endorsement of the community jury trial right is equally an endorsement of the jury's right to determine who is blameworthy. Thus, retributive justice principles can be found in the Court's rediscovery and reaffirmation of the right of the jury – that is, the polity – to set out all criminal punishment, no matter what form it may take. This ideal is neither vengeful nor desirous of suffering, but instead allows the community to articulate blame for crimes that specifically affect it. We impose community standards of punishment with sadness, not "retributive hatred."[6]

Retribution is not only concerned with the offender's past wrongs, however. Retributivists require offenders to take responsibility for the reasonably foreseeable results of their actions. More specifically, when we punish an offender who knows or should have known his actions were illegal, he learns that his actions matter to the community – especially a community created by shared laws. This idea maps neatly into the Court's repeated arguments in recent decisions that the jury must decide on almost all facts that affect punishment, because only a decision made by a fair cross-section of the community imposes on the offender the responsibility of accepting moral blame.

[5] *See* Daniel T. Kobil, *The Quality of Mercy Strained: Wresting the Pardoning Power from the King*, 69 TEX. L. REV. 569, 581 (1991).

[6] *See* Jeffrie G. Murphy, *Hatred: A Qualified Defense*, *in* JEFFRIE G. MURPHY & JEAN HAMPTON, FORGIVENESS AND MERCY 88 (1988).

When the judge, instead of the jury, is primarily or solely responsible for doling out the moral blame of punishment, offenders may not feel responsible for their actions, because the kind and type of punishment is so far attenuated from the community. When the judge determines sentencing facts, the offender may very well attribute his punishment to the state, shrugging off the desired feelings of responsibility or awareness of his wrongdoing. In contrast, when the jury determines the facts leading to punishment, the wrongdoer has more difficulty avoiding the burden of criminal responsibility, because his fellow citizens, his community, and his peers have pronounced his blameworthiness – as signified by the weight and heft of his sentence.

As a distributive principle, retributive justice supports the Court's rediscovered community jury right jurisprudence, because every time the offender commits a crime, he undermines the sovereign will of the people by challenging their decision-making structure. Because criminal laws in liberal democracies reflect a democratic pedigree, committing a crime is a way of expressing superiority over the state and the local community. By involving the people's voice and will during the sentencing and punishment phase, the jury helps offset the imbalance in the community created by the offender.

In the Supreme Court's renewed allegiance to the criminal jury trial right, any attack against the will of the people through the commission of a crime is balanced by the requirement that the jury find all elements of the charged offense – in essence deciding on the punishment. If retribution communicates directly to offenders, then it is a communication from the local community to the wrongdoer.

Retribution, however, can be a rather blunt instrument to indiscriminately apply to all of modern punishment. Historically, there have been various objections to retribution, including its harshness, its focus on prisons, its supposed immorality, its impracticality, and its vagueness, among others. But this type of criticism overly simplifies modern interpretations of retribution, which have at their core at least three distinct conceptions of desert: vengeful, deontological, and empirical.[7] Thus, an

[7] *See generally* Paul H. Robinson, *Competing Conceptions of Modern Desert: Vengeful, Deontological, and Empirical*, 67 CAMBRIDGE L.J. 145 (2008).

accurate assessment of retribution as a distributive principle requires a discussion of each of these concepts.

A brief explanatory note is helpful here. Vengeful desert requires that the punishment be proportionate to the harm caused. In contrast, deontological desert focuses primarily on the blameworthiness of the offender. Finally, empirical desert also focuses on the blameworthiness of the offender but relies heavily on the community's intuitions of justice for punishment.

As applied to the Supreme Court's understanding of punishment, the concept of *empirical* desert proves most useful. Paul Robinson defines empirical retribution as a distributive principle focusing on the blameworthiness of the offender but assessing punishment based on the community intuitions of justice. The primary source of this principle derives from empirical research into what drives people's intuitions of blameworthiness.[8]

Notably, however, empirical retribution is not driven by the community's choice of punishment for a specific crime. Instead, it is a "set of liability and punishment rules" that apply identically to all defendants. Empirical desert does not seek to explore "true" moral culpability, but rather relies on the community's shared intuitions, or norms, about assigning blameworthiness.

There are practical benefits to empirical desert as well. When criminal law parallels the community's sense of justice in imposing punishment, the law gains legitimacy and promotes compliance by urging the populace to view it as a moral authority in uncertain situations. Moreover, having criminal law rely on the community's shared intuitions about punishment grants it the power to help influence powerful societal norms.[9]

If the criminal law best shapes societal norms when it commands moral respect, then using empirical desert as a framework for modern punishment simultaneously pays tribute to the Court's understanding of historical jury rights and the practical implications of locating the arbiters of moral blameworthiness within the offender's local community.

[8] *See* Robinson, *id.*
[9] *See id.*

Criminal law plays a key role in creating and sustaining the moral consensus needed for maintaining social norms in our diverse society. Accordingly, the jury, as representative of the community, must decide criminal punishment because the community determination of social norms "may be the only society-wide mechanism that transcends cultural and ethnic differences."[10]

Combined with this model of empirical desert, Jean Hampton's concept of retributive theory provides a strong normative framework that fits both the ideals and the doctrine of the Court's recent focus on the jury's proper role. Hampton's expressive theory of retribution, which explores the wrongfulness of negative public conduct and the retributive response, contends that although all wrongful actions violate a moral standard, some moral actions violate those standards in a way that also affronts the victim's value or dignity.[11] To say someone has value, Hampton argues, is to invoke a particular conception of human worth, specifically an egalitarian one.

Hampton finds people's worth related to their very humanity, a philosophy that allows each person an equal moral significance insofar as each person is an autonomous, rational being. In essence, Hampton posits a "democratic conception of value" underlying the "moral respect" crucial to her expressive retributive theory.[12] Simply put, to Hampton, and to those who follow her, punishment is a form of communication that "annuls" crime.[13] This type of expressive retribution is premised on respect for the moral autonomy of the offender and tries to make punishment literally express the wrongfulness of crime to the criminal offender.[14]

These Kantian, morally focused values, rooted in Judeo-Christian tradition, have been extremely influential in modern Western society and have played a key role in providing the blueprint for acceptable treatment of other individuals. Such an egalitarian theory of ethical

[10] *See id.*

[11] Jean Hampton, *Correcting Harms versus Righting Wrongs: The Goal of Retribution*, 39 UCLA L. Rev. 1659, 1659–69 (1992).

[12] *Id.*

[13] *See* Jean Hampton, *A New Theory of Retribution*, in Liability and Responsibility: Essays in Law and Morals 377 (R. G. Frey & Christopher W. Morris, eds., 1991).

[14] *See* Michael Tonry, *Rethinking Unthinkable Punishment Practices in America*, 46 UCLA L. Rev. 1451, 1464 (1999).

worth has always been implicit (and sometimes explicit) in American conceptions of the polity and the state, as we saw in Chapter 2's discussion of colonial era society and criminal punishment.

This undercurrent of democracy and egalitarianism makes Hampton's version of expressive retributivism particularly appropriate for our new jurisprudence of punishment, because the Court relies so heavily upon these democratic principles animating the institution of the criminal jury. Such an egalitarian philosophy of worth is, of course, part of a society's normative practices, motivating its belief system and its punishments.

We care about what people signal through their actions, good or bad, because we have deep concerns about whether our intrinsic value, and the intrinsic value of others, will garner our community's respect. When wrongful actions are committed, they not only misrepresent our value and reduce our entitlements resulting from that value, but also make more likely the community's acceptance of this incorrect valuation. It naturally follows, then, that a jury must impose sanctions and moral blame upon the wrongdoer, since the jury provides an egalitarian cross-section of the actual cultural community.

According to our historical ideals of criminal justice and equality, the jury must determine the scope of the punishment to be visited on the offender. It offends our bedrock notions of equality when a wrongdoer, by her actions, represents herself as superior to the rest of the community. This is not because she is a "free rider" and, in the words of Herbert Morris, "got something for nothing,"[15] but because she has gotten ahead in unfair and unequal ways, ways that are unequal and discourteous to the community. Thus, using the community-based jury to decide and determine punishment is the best way to restore corrective fairness and destroy inegalitarian belief systems that, if left intact, would undermine the community.

Restoring fairness and equalizing the community are also important components of restorative, redemptive justice, which in turn is an important part of the community's historical role as arbiter of punishment. Restorative justice envisions crime as an act that violates both

[15] HERBERT MORRIS, *Persons and Punishment, in* ON GUILT AND INNOCENCE, ESSAYS IN LEGAL PHILOSOPHY AND MORAL PSYCHOLOGY 31–58 (1976).

persons and relationships, requiring a mending of the created breach. The restorative theory of punishment conceptualizes justice as a process that incorporates both the community *and* the offender in an attempt to repair and reconcile the harm done.[16] This is an extremely important and sorely needed aspect of criminal justice. Even some retributivists have argued that the best forms of retribution focus on a convicted offender's remorse and ultimate reintegration back into the community.[17]

Moreover, there is a redemptive aspect of restorative justice that our current schema of criminal justice is lacking, one that fits with the historical understanding of the community's role. As important as imposing proper punishment on a wrongdoer was to our colonial forbearers, equally important was the role of redemption in the playing out of public morality.

This was particularly true in the case of the New England colonies. Viewed as a whole, the New England colonies had the most effective criminal justice systems in seventeenth-century America, because, with the exception of Rhode Island, they occupied a society highly intolerant of serious crime and were quick to punish.[18] Looking to scripture for legal models,[19] the law of the early New England colonies was deeply concerned with preventing sin.[20]

As quick to punish as early New England colonists may have been, however, there was a strong strain of restorative, redemptive justice within their retributive philosophy. Unlike today, the criminal offender was not viewed as a permanent outcast from the community, but instead as a community member who had sinned – an act that could happen to anyone.[21] Even the most zealous members of the community "spied more to save the sinner than to exalt the state."[22] This is a

[16] *See* David Dolinko, *The Theory and Jurisprudence of Restorative Justice*, 2003 UTAH L. REV. 319, 319 (2003).

[17] *See* Andrew Oldenquist, *An Explanation of Retribution*, 85 J. PHIL. 464, 470 (1988).

[18] *See* Douglas Greenberg, *Crime, Law Enforcement, and Social Control in Colonial America*, 26 AM. J. LEGAL HIST. 293, 300 (1982).

[19] *See* EDGAR J. MCMANUS, LAW AND LIBERTY IN EARLY NEW ENGLAND: CRIMINAL JUSTICE AND DUE PROCESS, 1620–1692, at 21, 29 (1993).

[20] *See* WILLIAM E. NELSON, AMERICANIZATION OF THE COMMON LAW: THE IMPACT OF LEGAL CHANGE ON MASSACHUSETTS SOCIETY, 1760–1830, at 39 (1975).

[21] *See* NELSON, AMERICANIZATION, *supra* note 20, at 39.

[22] *See* MCMANUS, *supra* note 19, at 71.

marked difference from the way we now treat convicted offenders in our culture – that is, as untouchables, permanent outcasts, with no role to play in conventional society once they have committed a crime.

Even by the beginning of the eighteenth century, a convicted offender was rarely imprisoned or permanently isolated from the community, as is our practice today. Instead, punishments for all but capital crimes were usually either fines, temporary excommunication,[23] or mild corporal punishments,[24] and offenses punishable by fine vastly outnumbered those punished by corporal means.[25] The punishment for theft, for example, was not capital punishment or dismemberment, but multiple restitution.[26]

Likewise, in the Quaker-Pennsylvania colony, punishment was more lenient, with much less attention paid to morals crimes.[27] In criminal cases, the punishments were usually either fines, whippings, or placement in the stocks.[28] Imprisonment was extremely rare, as the religious values of the Quakers placed strong emphasis on restoring the offender to the community after his or her wrongdoing.[29]

Although seemingly benevolent, the Quaker leadership still punished crime in a manner familiar to us today. Once punished, a convicted offender often had to pay a price both publicly and privately, until he or she was returned to the fold. In 1760, for example, a Philadelphia woman convicted of theft was whipped, fined, ordered to make restitution and pay the costs of prosecution, and required to give "security for herself" in the amount of 50 pounds and to find two sureties to put up 25 pounds each to guarantee her good behavior for the next twelve months.[30] So to translate that into our sentencing terms,

[23] *See* McManus, *supra* note 19, at 13.
[24] *See* Nelson, Americanization, *supra* note 20, at 20.
[25] *See* McManus, *supra* note 19, at 171. This was true in early New England as well. *Id.*
[26] *See* Kathryn Preyer, *Penal Measures in the American Colonies – An Overview*, in Colonial British America: Essays in the New History of the Early Modern Era 63 (Jack P. Greene & J. R. Pole, eds., 1984).
[27] *See* Greenberg, *Crime, Law Enforcement and Social Control*, *supra* note 18, at 301.
[28] *See* William H. Loyd, The Early Courts of Pennsylvania 56 (1910).
[29] Notably, in the late seventeenth century, Pennsylvania was reportedly "ye greatest refuge & shelter for pirates & Rogues in America," in part due to the humanity and mercy of the Quakers. Loyd, *supra* note 28, at 69.
[30] *See* Lawrence M. Friedman, Crime and Punishment in American History 38–39 (1993).

the woman was publicly shamed, fined, required to pay back her victim and pay for court costs, released on her own recognizance with a bail of 50 pounds, and required to have two guarantors to ensure her good behavior during her probation of one year. This punishment exemplified, in other words, what can be called an expressive, restorative, redemptive, and retributive philosophy of punishment.

Redemption and restoration are missing pieces of our modern criminal philosophy, pieces sorely needed to help reintegrate the segment of our population returning from prison. Released convicts are kept at a distance from full membership in the civil life of the community. In contrast, the redemptive perspective sees punishment in terms of its potential to transform the offender.[31] Indeed, the reparation of harm and community empowerment are two distinct goals of restorative justice.[32] At best, those community members involved in restorative processes jointly and actively make decisions concerning the harm, its implications, and the community's proper responses.[33]

Restorative justice also contains aspects of expressive philosophy, because expressive theories help publicize the negative aspects of the crime and convey punishment's condemning message.[34] Restorative justice processes promote social disapproval of crime by the very expression of condemnation handed down by the community, which is far more meaningful than a sentence and punishment simply dictated by the state. In the restorative justice paradigm, community disapproval is the predominant deterrence to misconduct,[35] and thus the stronger the community involvement, the safer the community. Restorative justice is not private justice,[36] and integrating its tenets into our standard understanding of traditional crime and punishment processes helps create a stronger and safer community.

[31] *See* Elizabeth Rapaport, *Retribution and Redemption in the Operation of Executive Clemency*, 74 CHI.-KENT L. REV. 1501, 1503 (2000).

[32] *See* Hadar Dancig-Rosenberg & Tali Gal, *Restorative Criminal Justice*, 34 CARDOZO L. REV. 2313, 2316 (2013).

[33] *See id.* at 2319.

[34] *See id.* at 2330.

[35] *See* John O. Haley, *Beyond Retribution: An Integrated Approach to Restorative* Justice, 36 WASH. U. L & POL'Y 1, 5 (2011).

[36] *See* Rosenberg & Gal, *supra* note 32, at 2335.

Redemptive goals of criminal justice include reintegration and reconciliation of the offender, the victim, and the community. Redemption provides the opportunity for people to rebuild their lives and take full responsibility for their actions after mistakes or wrongdoing. Most people, including convicted offenders, grow and change over time in response to their circumstances, and those who falter or break societal rules should warrant the chance for some restorative justice and a new start after retribution has been served.

Redemptive justice fits in well with expressive retribution in that one can agree or insist that just punishment or restitution be exacted and yet still forgive the offender working for his redemption at the end of the punishment. To be complete, to be true to historical origins, our criminal justice must have a redemptive quality as well as an expressive, retributive one.

Another way to look at a redemptive theory of criminal justice is as a form of atonement. Essentially, atonement tries to reconcile the criminal offender and the victim and reintegrate the offender back into the community as a valued member.[37] Following Stephen Garvey's theory, "the atonement model provides punishment with an end – the atonement of the wrongdoer and his victim and the restoration of the relationship that existed between them before the wrong – but treats punishment as an intrinsically appropriate way in which to pursue and achieve that end."[38] If, as Garvey contends, crime and punishment are expressive, altering the material world,[39] then these breaches must be repaired through the criminal offender's atonement, redemption, and reintegration. Atonement, or redemptive justice, works because atonement posits a stopping place for punishment beyond the punishment itself,[40] something that most retributive theories fail to address.

[37] *See* Stephen P. Garvey, *Punishment as Atonement*, 46 UCLA L. REV. 1801, 1804 (1999).

[38] *Id.* at 1806.

[39] *See Id.* at 1819–20. Echoing Hampton, Garvey argues that "a crime changes not only the material relationship between [a wrongdoer] and his victim, but also their moral relationship. Crime degrades, demeans, diminishes, and dishonors the victim, in addition to whatever material damage it may cause." *Id.* at 1821.

[40] *See* Stephen P. Garvey, *Is It Wrong to Commute Death Row? Retribution, Atonement and Mercy*, 82 N. Carolina L. Rev. 1319, 1336 (2004). As Garvey further explains, "[Atonement] holds that deserved punishment is justified because it forms a necessary part of a larger process through which an offender atones for his offense, a process leading

Most critically, redemptive justice or atonement provides an understanding of how punishment functions in a working community, one in which both the offender and the victim have some degree of mutual respect and collective interest, upon which communal existence depends.[41] Although very large and/or divided communities may have more trouble coalescing around an offender who has served his punishment, there are many ways to redeem and reintegrate an offender without a wholesale forgiveness from the local community. Ultimately, a community that understands punishment only as a way to control and incarcerate will remain a community of strangers. Alternately, a community that envisions punishment as way of bringing the community together is a very different kind of community, a "community of citizens."[42]

Redemptive and reintegrative policies work in a variety of practical ways in today's criminal justice system. One set of redemptive policies treats problems of drug addiction and mental illness through public health responses and institutions such as drug courts and halfway houses, as opposed to simply imprisonment with no treatment. Another set of policies tries to reduce recidivism by building the social and economic skills of released offenders, helping them reintegrate back into working society. These policies consider the impact of crime and punishment on individuals, families, and communities. Redemptive philosophy also holds that denying the fundamental rights to vote, to housing, and to education thwarts the goal of returning to productive citizenship.

Today, many criminal justice policies and practices have made redemption and reintegration into society almost impossible. The stigma of incarceration damages employment prospects, and entire communities – almost invariably the economically poorer ones – suffer opportunity costs when large segments of residents revolve in and out of the criminal

ideally to the reconciliation of the offender and those he wronged. Reconciliation or atonement is the end toward which punishment is a means." *Id.*

41 *See* Garvey, *Retribution, Atonement and Mercy, supra* note 40, at 1336.

42 *See* Garvey, *Punishment as Atonement, supra* note 37, at 1854. As Garvey notes, "the meaning of punishment within a particular community undoubtedly reflects the underlying nature of the community, but the underlying nature of the community is also a function of the meaning the community attaches to punishment." *Id.* I will discuss the different types of community in greater detail in Chapter 5.

justice system. In contrast, a proper reabsorption of released offenders back into the local community has the possibility of reducing crime rates, recidivism rates, and crime control costs. "At the community level, especially in black and other poor minority communities where the rates of incarceration are catastrophic, the absent are needed to cope with the ordinary, essential, economic, and social tasks of life."[43] The more extreme and inhumane our punishments, the more damaged our communities become.

Moreover, victims of crimes sometimes want an offender's contrition as much as his punishment, craving recognition of their undeserved suffering and acknowledgement of responsibility.[44] One excellent way to improve and bolster a modern theory of expressive retribution is by adding a redemptive view of the relationship between transgressor and society that has a strong focus on reconciliation and reintegration.[45] Under a scheme of expressive, redemptive (or restorative) retribution, completing a term of punishment enables an offender to atone for his crime, redeem himself, and restore his membership in the community from which his wrongdoing had separated him.[46]

Our original, historical criminal law, while enforcing strong religious and moral values, also had a robust tradition of reintegrating offenders back into society[47] – something we have seemingly forgotten. In other words, although a strong retributive strain, tinged with religion, imbued the colonists' understanding of punishment, so too did a sense of restorative, redemptive justice. It was this mix that helped shape the creation of the community jury trial right.

Although many have characterized restorative and retributive theories of justice as polar opposites, the theories have much in common, including a need to offset the offender's crime by some type of punitive response and a desire to have punishment for crimes be proportional. In fact, an expressive, restorative, retributive theory of punishment, such as I elucidate here, borrows from restorative justice in that it is deeply

[43] Rapaport, *supra* note 31, at 1530.
[44] *See id.* at 1527.
[45] *See, e.g.*, Garvey, *Punishment as Atonement*, *supra* note 37, at 1830–34 (arguing that many retributivists neglect the roles of redemption and reconciliation, while focusing entirely on the moral requirements of punishment).
[46] *See id.* at 1838.
[47] *See* NELSON, AMERICANIZATION, *supra* note 20, at 40.

concerned with the mending of any material or emotional harm that specific criminal behavior inflicts. By using the jury as the adjudicator of the harm and determinant of punishment, expressive restorative retribution focuses on the community's role in maintaining the fairness of our society, something juries have done on American soil since the colonies were established.

American normative theories of democracy and democratic deliberation have always included the participation of the jury in our system of criminal justice. If you accept that conceptions of egalitarian moral worth are part of our culture's normative values and have therefore set the standards for acceptable treatment of people in our society, then juries must be part of the determination of punishment.

This is particularly resonant because the jury is the most effective tool with which to impose the normative judgment of the community. Our Kantian, egalitarian theory of worth, which undergirds the values of the American polity, is best implemented through the jury, the most egalitarian representation of the community and the state.

Following the *Apprendi-Blakely* line of cases, the Supreme Court's interest in and dedication to the jury's right to determine punishment is, in many ways, an expressive approach to the rights and needs of the community. This is in large part because the Court relies upon the people's moral agent – the jury – to express the community's condemnation and to reestablish the victim's unfairly diminished sense of worth.

Expressive, restorative retribution serves not only to give the community a voice and help foster egalitarian and democratic ideals. If fully implemented, ERR also requires offenders to take more responsibility for their wrongdoings, since the community is involved in the imposition of punishment and restoring the balance. Although retributivism works well in forcefully condemning the convicted offender's crime in the name of justice, it is unconcerned about reconstituting communal bonds with the offender after she has served her punishment.[48] Community involvement is the much-needed step that has long been missing from our current regime of criminal punishment.

From the beginning of the American colonial experiment, then, the community right to a public trial was deeply intertwined with an

[48] *See* Garvey, *Punishment as Atonement*, *supra* note 37, at 1830.

expressive, retributive, and restorative understanding of punishment. The colonists' philosophy was one closely tied to the sovereign will of the people, the community's traditional role in determining moral blameworthiness, the importance of popular authority, the public right to trial, and the community's willingness to forgive wrongdoers and eventually restore their rights. As I have shown, the use of expressive, restorative retribution was inexorably tied to the community's right to determine punishment for wrongdoers. This theory of criminal justice is just as powerful today as it was in the colonial era.

Ultimately, a framework of expressive, restorative retribution encompasses both the historical antecedents of the Sixth Amendment jury right and modern ideals of punishment. Revisiting retributive theory with an awareness of its contours shows that it is the best model to balance the needs of both the community and the individual within the arena of criminal justice. Furthermore, it is the best suited to explain, on a philosophical level, the Court's recent reforms incorporating the jury.

5 DEFINING COMMUNITY IN THE TWENTY-FIRST CENTURY: CITIES, COUNTIES, AND COLLECTIVE ACTION

What does it mean to be part of a community? In the twenty-first-century digital world, this is a difficult question. Though used routinely within the world of criminal justice, the term "community" has been underinvestigated. The greater significance, the wider scope, and the broader meaning of the term community have remained unexplored. In response, this chapter evaluates the various meanings and understandings of the community as it exists today.

The criminal jury setting has long defined notions of "the community" in geographical and corporeal terms, focusing on the local, physically present peers of the defendant as the community's primary representative. However, in the modern world, which now has both multiple overlapping online communities (ranging from Facebook to Twitter to Instagram) as well as online crimes, the notion of "community rights" and the means of incorporating the community into criminal justice decision-making needs to be premised on more than traditional conceptions of the community. Accordingly, Chapter 5 charts the various forms that community can take in today's criminal justice system, discussing the various problems that can arise from relying on a modern, amorphous "community" to dispense justice.

Generally, those who argue that the community has a right and a need to participate in all major criminal justice procedures assume that the community is a defined entity. The phrase "the community," however, can mean a variety of things, often simultaneously. It is this multiplicity of meaning that I seek to explore throughout the rest of this chapter.

Relying on the community to adjudicate crime and punishment can be appealing because the concept is woven deep within the American psyche. As William Stuntz offered, "Make criminal justice more locally democratic, and justice will be both more moderate and more egalitarian."[1] Moderation emerges because criminal justice creates its value by generating societal opinions of how best to apply legal rules and adjudicate offenses.[2] More specifically, the community's shared principles of justice, or "empirical desert,"[3] make the rule of law both workable and legitimate.

The power of moral credibility and the pressure of social norms also lend a hand in obtaining compliance with society's rules of conduct, by using the influence of the forces of social and individual moral control.[4] Local community-level social processes, including the petit jury, have much more of an effect on the prevention and promotion of crime and delinquency than do individual offender characteristics.[5] In our culture, criminal law may be the only society-wide process that rises above cultural and ethnic differences.[6] In addition, the "human consequences and articulated explanations" of crime are mostly local.[7]

But what does "local democracy" mean? How best to implement it? As Albert Alschuler and Stephen Schulhofer argued, we must be "on guard against the appealing but highly manipulable rhetoric of 'community,' a rhetoric that is increasingly prevalent in contemporary discourse."[8] This is particularly true in the criminal justice arena, which can have an overwhelming effect on both defendants and crime victims. Accordingly, we must exercise particular care in relying on the community to judge crime, as notions of "community" have enormous symbolic and emotive appeal without any strict definition of the term.[9]

1 William Stuntz, *Unequal Justice*, 121 HARV. L. REV. 1969, 1974 (2008).

2 *See* Josh Bowers & Paul H. Robinson, *Perceptions of Fairness and Justice: The Shared Aims and Occasional Conflicts of Legitimacy and Moral Credibility*, 47 WAKE FOREST L. REV. 211, 211 (2012).

3 *See id.* at 216.

4 *See id.* at 217.

5 *See* Tracy Meares & Dan Kahan, at 810 (citing a 1969 study by Clifford Shaw and Henry McKay).

6 *See* Paul H. Robinson, *Competing Conceptions of Modern Desert: Vengeful, Deontological, and Empirical*, 67 CAMBRIDGE L.J. 145, 154 (2008).

7 See Wayne A. Logan, *The Shadow Criminal Law of Municipal Governance*, 62 OHIO ST. L.J. 1409, 1419 (2001).

8 Albert W. Alschuler & Stephen J. Schulhofer, *Antiquated Procedures or Bedrock Rights? A Response to Professors Meares and Kahan*, 1998 U. CHI. LEGAL F. 215, 216 (1998).

9 *See* Logan, *supra* note 7, at 1412.

Scholars have repeatedly debated whether the prosecution of crime should be federal, state, or local,[10] because the community that judges an offender can make a huge difference to the adjudication of the case.

Community decision-making and community justice are heavily rooted in a more local approach to crime and punishment. This includes advocacy of neighborhood initiatives promulgated through robust citizen participation. At its best, community justice provides for strong local, popular participation within existing criminal justice institutions. This form of local democracy is essential to our original, historical vision of criminal process,[11] where the public citizenry is involved in adjudicatory justice.

Social science research shows that there is great practical value in having the criminal law reflect community views, because it supports effective crime control. A criminal law that distributes criminal liability and punishment in community-supported ways accrues moral credibility, which translates into greater deference to, support for, and cooperation with the criminal justice system. As Paul Robinson contends, the stronger the system's moral credibility, the greater its ability to gain deference, influence, and cooperation.[12]

One version of community, and the one most generally used when discussing jury rights, is a definable social entity, one to which we apply judicial procedures and behavioral norms.[13] But "community" can also simply be a floating normative concept, signifying much but referring to nothing in particular.

Great legal power results from characterizing any specific place as a community, as doing so raises issues of authority, responsibility, and the exercise of sovereignty. Proponents of community self-determination and power have often based their arguments on a distinct understanding of the neighborhood or local community as a place that fosters

[10] *See* Rachel E. Barkow, *Federalism and Criminal Law: What the Feds Can Learn from the States*, 109 MICH. L. REV. 519, 521 (2011).

[11] *See* WILLIAM STUNTZ, THE COLLAPSE OF AMERICAN CRIMINAL JUSTICE 9 (Oxford 2011).

[12] *See* Paul H. Robinson, *The Proper Role of the Community in Determining Criminal Liability and Punishment*, in POPULAR PUNISHMENT: ON THE NORMATIVE SIGNIFICANCE OF PUBLIC OPINION 55 (Jesper Ryberg & Julian A. Roberts, eds., 2014).

[13] *See* Robert Weisberg, *Restorative Justice & the Dangers of Community*, 2003 UTAH L. REV. 343, 347 (2003).

individual freedoms, balances liberty and order, and commands moral respect.[14] In addition, the word *community* evokes an appealing sense of place, shared values, and neighborhood empowerment – all of which is appealing.[15]

Recently we have seen increased interest in local control over local environments, which dovetails nicely with a renewed focus on the role of the community in criminal justice. Various advocates of localism argue that local governments respond better to the particular requirements of specific communities and that local institutions can provide improved amenities for those communities.[16] These arguments are parallel to ones that can be made for the criminal justice system: that the local governments are critical in implementing punishment, for both constitutional and civic reasons. Additionally, local governance possesses the basic power to enact criminal laws overseen only weakly by state and federal courts.[17]

Defining community, however, can be quite difficult. The rhetoric of community often covers a variety of different meanings, some of which are contradictory. So let us start at the beginning. One very basic definition of *community* is "a group of people who share things in common – a sense of identity or history or values – and who seek to foster the bonds they have with each other."[18]

Granted, this interpretation proves too simplistic for complete reliance. My vision of community, at least for the purposes of the criminal justice system, can be classified as a combination of a deep and a dualist account, following in the steps of Richard Schragger.[19] A deep account of community, an affective community, can be described as having the mutual awareness of shared values, based on the existence

[14] *See, e.g.*, Tracey L. Meares & Dan M. Kahan, *Black, White and Gray: A Reply to Alschuler and Schulhofer*, 1998 U. CHI. LEGAL F. 245, 258–59 (1998).

[15] Alschuler & Schulhofer, *Antiquated Procedures*, *supra* note 8, at 216.

[16] *See* Richard C. Schragger, *The Limits of Localism*, 100 MICH. L. REV. 371, 372–73 (2001).

[17] *See* Logan, *Shadow Criminal Law of Municipal Governance*, *supra* note 7, at 1416–17. Logan argues that this has "resulted in the creation of a shadow criminal law that has significantly expanded the range of behaviors that can be targeted by law enforcement, created unique procedural regimes, and diversified the range of sanctions attaching to criminal behavior, including the use of forfeiture." *Id.*

[18] Jerry Frug, *The Geography of Community*, 48 STANFORD L. REV. 1047, 1049 (1996).

[19] *See* Schragger, *supra* note 16, at 372–74.

and quality of social connections, shared experience, mutuality, and common fate. Relatedly, a dualist account of community is defined by deliberation – a participatory practice in which shared principles are crafted by discussion and compromise. In other words, the dualist vision depends on the idea that local engagement occurs only in assemblies where community members can meet in person, through participation in small-scale democratic governance.[20] My understanding of community relies on a combination of both.

To add to this understanding, I draw on a definition that looks at communities as people "bound to one another, in what should be and sometimes is a single polity . . . entail[ing] some common problems and common interests, but [not necessarily] sharing final ends, . . . mutual identification and reciprocity."[21]

But what comprises a community when focusing on the task of adjudicating criminal justice? The venire, or geographical area, from which the petit jury is drawn is sometimes considered a community, although no jurisdiction constitutes a true community. Indeed, each jurisdiction is an amalgamation of numerous communities, whether defined along geographic, occupational, social, religious, or other lines. If different communities in each jurisdiction have different views, then which community view should criminal punishment follow?

Some punishment scholars have contended that the answer is as simple as looking to the community that will be governed by the law at issue. For example, they argue that if the question is the formulation of a provision of the state's criminal code, then you must look to the state as the relevant community; if the question is the sentencing practice in a particular city, look to that city's residents.[22] But this oversimplifies the matter, particularly with larger or more metropolitan jurisdictions, which contain a multiplicity of communities within the greater geographical one.

Defining who comprises the community is a particularly thorny problem when trying to determine a law's legitimacy, because this turns on how the relevant community is delineated. It is unclear how

[20] *See* Schragger, *supra* note 16, at 393.

[21] Frug, *Geography of Community*, *supra* note 18, at 1048–49 (quoting from Iris Marion Young, Justice and the Politics of Difference 237–38 (1990)).

[22] *See* Robinson, *Proper Role of Community*, *supra* note 12, at 74.

to comprehensively define community down to some subset of the sovereign whole,[23] especially in the context of legitimacy. Many scholars believe that the pertinent community is the local community, since the practice of criminal law is a local concern and, accordingly, should remain reactive to neighborhood issues. To build moral credibility, they argue, the criminal law must avoid conflict with the community's principles of justice.[24]

This problem of defining community has also plagued official governmental agencies. As one Department of Justice roundtable noted, it is difficult to think of two words that have more freighted meaning than "community" and "justice," independently and together.[25] Moreover, there is no such thing as one distinct community, and we must learn to distinguish between the identities of different communities and query who they are and what they might need.[26]

Most practitioners and scholars agree, however, that the criminal justice system should involve the community in a more concrete way, also playing the role as a convener of community. In other words, the ever-present problem of crime can be used as an opportunity to gather people to build stronger communities.[27] As a rule, once given the opportunity to participate in the criminal justice system, most communities do not want to fundamentally change the system. Instead, most communities tend to request only marginal changes, such as allowing defendants, even offenders with long records, to be given an opportunity to use community services.[28]

Another, more recent issue with relying on community in the criminal justice context is our tendency to belong to multiple communities by virtue of our distinct work and home locations, and, for some, differing real-life and online communities. Unpacking these various communities reveals problems in the legal definition of each. First, local governance based solely on residence, which is what we have

23 *See* Bowers & Robinson, *Perceptions of Fairness and Justice*, *supra* note 2, at 233.
24 *See id.* at 241.
25 *See* Greg Berman & Audrey Fox, *From the Margins to the Mainstream: Community Justice at the Crossroads*, 22 Jus. Sys. J. 189, 190 (2001).
26 *See id.* at 205.
27 *See id.* at 197.
28 *See id.* at 198.

now, ignores the complex realities of metropolitan life. Individuals often work, live, and go to school in completely different localities. And many people have an equally strong interest in affecting criminal justice in each of those areas.

Furthermore, selecting the jury only from citizens with fixed residences may exclude the poor, the homeless, and the young – many of whom do not have permanent addresses. Those citizens who are disadvantaged, transient, or homeless are all part of the community, but they are shut out from participation in the criminal justice system due to their temporary residential status. Jerry Frug addressed this problem by suggesting that we lessen the significance of the boundaries that demarcate the localities in a metropolitan area. He argued that this type of a "postmodern city identity" would enable citizens to utilize various connections to nonresidential localities – for example, places of work, schools, and family ties[29] – to be counted in determining who comprises part of a community. This innovation, although potentially complicated to implement, would broaden jury rolls from their currently limited status.

Next we confront the ongoing problem of finding the correct community to adjudicate online crimes. Effectively regulating online crimes is a daunting task, because the traditional model of law enforcement was not designed to manage cybercrime. The internet community is enormous, even when just considering the United States.[30] In part, this is because online crime possesses very few of the normal characteristics of real-world crime.[31] Cybercrime lacks the proximity, scale, and physical constraints of real-world crime – it is essentially unbounded and borderless.[32] The problems resulting from scale become particularly tricky when trying to determine the location of a cybercrime (to best assess the community that should adjudicate it). In cyberspace there is usually no traditional, physical crime scene, but rather a scattering of evidence over disparate locations, including the computer used by the

[29] *See* Jerry Frug, *Decentering Decentralization*, 60 U. Chi. L. Rev. 253, 304–38 (1993).

[30] *See* Philip A. Wells, *Shrinking the Internet*, 5 N.Y.U. J.L. & Liberty 531, 552 (2010). As the author points out, "There are already over 1.8 billion Internet users worldwide, and over one billion 'publicly readable web pages.'" *Id.*

[31] *See* Susan W. Brenner, *Towards a Criminal Law for Cyberspace: Distributed Security*, 10 Boston U. J. of Science & Tech. L. 1, 65 (2004).

[32] *See id.* at 65.

perpetrator, the victim's computer, and intervening computers and computer servers the perpetrator used in the offense.[33]

Cyberspace "communities" are usually defined by interests, not territory,[34] thus defying the place-based assumptions that are a traditional part of criminal adjudication.[35] Thus, drawing together a jury pool of cyberspace community members when those individuals might be scattered among various states and geographies would be extremely complex and expensive. This task is further complicated by the multi-jurisdictional aspect of most cybercrime, involving more than one state at a time and often implicating both federal and state laws. Every criminal encounter in cyberspace, therefore, raises the possibility that diverse laws and multiple communities will be engaged.[36]

Further complicating matters, the social norms that usually help regulate crimes in communities are not as easily enforced and reiterated on the internet. On the contrary, cyberspace can often create and breed feelings of remoteness and anonymity.[37] Wherever social norms struggle to grow spontaneously, such as in cyberspace, policy makers may lose a useful crime-fighting device.[38] Because anonymity removes from communities the traditional tools for detecting deviance, many traditional social sanctions that limit crime are disabled in this venue.[39]

Online crime has become a continuing concern, since as the internet matures, so do the types and degrees of crimes committed. Because unarticulated social norms essentially reduce the cost of committing crimes on the internet, "law enforcement must punish, rapidly and powerfully, those crimes that produce the most visible social disorder in cyberspace."[40]

Yet another problem inherent in relying on community norms to order criminal justice is the lack of jury diversity. An obvious difference

[33] *See* Brenner, *Criminal Law for Cyberspace*, *supra* note 31, at 75.

[34] *See, e.g.*, PETER KOLLOCK & MARC A. SMITH, COMMUNITIES IN CYBERSPACE 3–28 (1998).

[35] *See* Brenner, *supra* note 31, at 83.

[36] Peter P. Swire, *Elephants and Mice Revisited: Law and Choice of Law on the Internet*, 153 U. PA. L. REV. 1975, 1976 (2005).

[37] *See* Wells, *supra* note 30, at 532.

[38] *See id.*

[39] *See id.* at 556.

[40] Neal K. Katyal, *Criminal Law in Cyberspace*, 149 U. PA. L. REV. 1003, 1110 (2001).

between the Revolutionary jury and juries today is the inclusiveness of the juries and the diversity of the communities they are supposed to represent. Ironically, early American juries represented their communities better than modern juries, in part because the role of an official community member, for the purposes of serving on a jury, was very narrowly limited to white male property owners. Moreover, these early juries represented communities that were themselves homogeneous and exclusive.[41]

Contrast this notion of community with that of today, when the American public is much more diverse. Although the United States has become more polyglot, however, many communities have not become more integrated. Individual communities in the United States have tended to remain, by many measures, segregated according to race, ethnicity, and class – therefore rendering localized communities more homogeneous.[42]

In our divided society, the communities of the defendant and the victim may be different. If different, the two communities may clash in any legal procedure, no matter how much involvement given to the public. The healing balm of community does not necessarily soothe when different factions compete within a given district or jurisdiction. Some localities punish in similar or lesser measures than do concurrent state criminal laws,[43] which can also fracture community consensus.

In addition, even if we attempt to break up the larger community into smaller, more homogenous subsections, definitional questions still plague us. For example, if we are discussing the "minority" community, are we including all nonwhite citizens? Or must we then further subdivide into different racial and ethnic phenotypes? If we are talking about local crime, should we only focus on certain higher-crime neighborhoods, minority or not? Moreover, how do we decide which communities have the higher priority in terms of criminal adjudication? Race, ethnicity, gender, and geography do not exclusively define a person's various communities. Community identity is likely to rely on multiple combinations of differing characteristics, including the characteristics of religion,

[41] *See* Kevin Washburn, *Restoring the Grand Jury*, 76 FORDHAM L. REV. 2333, 2372 (2008).

[42] *See id.* at 2373.

[43] *See* Logan, *supra* note 7, at 1433.

race, ethnicity, residence, wealth, gender, sexual orientation, occupation, physical disability, age, and political values, to name just a few.[44] In this way, "the concept of community ... provides almost limitless opportunities for creative redefinition and manipulation."[45]

These complex issues naturally defy easy answers. Defining communities (or at least jury roll lists) by racial and ethnic lines might run afoul of equal protection. And yet standard juries are not always representative of the community. This is notably true when felon exclusion, peremptory and for-cause challenges, homelessness, transience, and voter apathy are taken into account.

To address some of these problems, some have called for the creation of legislative districts that have been further divided into "communities of interest."[46] Although these proposals offer a promising beginning, better yet would be selection of jurors from even smaller communities – those created by townships, municipalities, and villages. Criminal justice runs more smoothly when the members of the community, however jurisdictionally defined, are at least marginally familiar with each other.

Local governments can perform a unique function in fashioning a communal political life.[47] Thus, a venire drawn from each local or micro-community would ensure that more citizens would be able to participate meaningfully in criminal justice. The educative value of the increased volume of citizen participation would be realized, and the substance of the education would be improved as well. Because jury members would learn about crime in their own community, their participation might encourage more focus on realistic solutions to crime issues. As our world becomes more fragmented and remote, local jury service can be a way of reconnecting members of a community around specific problems of crime and punishment.[48]

[44] *See* Alschuler & Schulhofer, *Antiquated Procedures*, *supra* note 8, at 241.

[45] *See id.* at 242.

[46] *See* Kim Forde-Mazrui, *Jural Districting: Selecting Impartial Juries Through Community Representation*, 52 VAND. L. REV. 353, 386 (1999).

[47] *See* David Barron, *The Promise of Cooley's City: Traces of Local Constitutionalism*, 147 U. PA. L. REV. 487, 491 (1999).

[48] Kevin Washburn has made a similar argument for localizing grand jury service. *See Restoring the Grand Jury*, *supra* note 41, at 2380.

In addition, communities would be far better served if local citizens became more comprehensively informed about the crime in their own backyards. Following jury service, those participating members of the public would be both better positioned and better inspired to address local crime. Through the local determination of public politics, via their service on a jury, citizens would be required, in a direct and immediate way, to determine for themselves which criminal justice decisions would best serve the community interests and which would not.[49]

The criminal justice system will best achieve legitimacy when each voice in the criminal jurisdiction is heard.[50] Legitimacy is better served when the community is invested in fair criminal justice processes. In turn, community interest strengthens the rule of law, because engaged citizens are more likely to comply with the law and trust it as fair.

The most dangerous legitimacy problems in criminal justice come from distrust of government. One way to tackle this is to give all citizens a say in the governance of the criminal process. If taking part in decision-making creates a sense of trust, however fledgling or fragile, then policy makers should seek to increase participation among those communities that have the lowest levels of trust.[51] Indeed, "constitutional freedom can be secured only if diverse communities, organized in various towns and cities across the Nation, are encouraged (and permitted) to govern themselves in accordance with a set of common principles that they know to be more enduring than the preferences of any temporary majority."[52] Local governments "provide citizens with opportunities for political participation, to reflect diversity, to increase the likelihood of innovation and experimentation, and to engage in the kind of competition that constrains governmental behavior."[53]

[49] *See* Barron, *Local Constitutionalism*, supra note 47, at 517.

[50] *See, e.g.*, Daniel D. Blinka, *Jefferson and Juries: The Problem of Law, Reason, and Politics in the New Republic*, 47 AM. J. OF LEGAL HIST. 35, 100 (2005) (noting that Thomas Jefferson once famously proposed that trial jurors be elected by voters from small districts). *See also* Washburn, *Restoring the Grand Jury*, *supra* note 41, at 3281.

[51] *See* Washburn, *Restoring the Grand Jury*, *supra* note 41, at 2381–82.

[52] *See* David Barron, *Local Constitutionalism*, *supra* note 47, at 495. Barron is discussing civil decisions by local majorities, but the concern rings even louder within the criminal justice sphere.

[53] Barkow, *supra* note 10, at 533 (quoting Richard Briffault, *"What About the 'Ism'?" Normative and Formal Concerns in Contemporary Federalism*, 47 VAND. L. REV. 1303,

One further boost to the legitimizing nature of increased community involvement upon the criminal justice system is the empirical support showing a surprising amount of community consensus in ranking different offenders' punishments.[54] People tend to grade the seriousness of various crimes very similarly, despite many cultural and other differences. These empirical findings, of note to those concerned about community differentiation, illustrate a bedrock conception of retributive justice – or just deserts – that reaches across communities, no matter how different they might be.

Furthermore, even our modern flawed juries have often served as an escape valve for addressing issues of fairness and ensuring system legitimacy, focusing in on the racial issues that have plagued criminal justice in the United States and created much deep mistrust in certain communities.[55] This is particularly true when jury nullification comes into play, an occurrence that I discuss in greater detail in Chapter 11.

Localizing criminal justice, however, does not come without costs. To the extent that the purpose is to permit the local public, as represented by the neighborhood or community jury, to follow its own normative policy judgments over those of a broader district, there may be certain circumstances in which the local jury would behave in a manner inconsistent with contemporary legal values.[56] For example, a local jury might either fail to convict a member of the community who has committed a crime or unfairly convict an outsider of crimes he did not commit, either to prove a point or to reject certain governmental policies.[57] Most dangerous, of course, is when these normative judgments are motivated by negative, extralegal belief systems.

1348 (1994)). Barkow's survey of state practice highlights the importance of localism and community: "In almost every state, a conscious choice has been made to defer to local prosecutors. States have centralized authority in a statewide prosecutor in a handful of areas, ... [b]ut outside these contexts, local prosecutors are responsible for the vast bulk of criminal law enforcement within a state. And these local prosecutors are operating in most states with little centralized supervision by a state-level actor." *Id.* at 545.

54 *See* Paul H. Robinson & Robert Kurzban, *Concordance and Conflict in Intuitions of Justice*, 91 MINN. L. REV. 1829, 1846–92 (2007) (finding that, based on empirical studies, there is strong agreement across groups and cultures on the relative seriousness of violent, property, and deception crimes, and lesser – but still important – agreement about drug and sex offenses).

55 *See* Washburn, *Restoring the Grand Jury*, *supra* note 41, at 2347.

56 *See id.* at 2383.

57 This kind of jury nullification still happens in certain communities such as the Bronx, where it is very hard to get a low-level drug dealer convicted by a jury, since many of the

Similarly, when a crime is shocking or notorious, the concern emerges that the community will decide punishment based on views formed in passion and emotion that will later be seen as unjust, after the heat of the moment passes.[58] To this end, there is some danger of allowing the community to take too much control, if we presume that the inflamed local majority is not always likely to keep constitutional obligations in mind while making decisions.[59]

Ultimately, to rely on community participation as a means of improving criminal justice decision-making is to presume that the community is sufficiently democratic, informed, and thoughtful to ensure that community adjudication will serve the larger community interest as well as legitimacy and general moral values.[60] When these assumptions are challenged, as when the community in question is itself morally compromised or flawed, then the entire project of democratic participation and legitimacy in criminal justice is imperiled. Although hopefully this particular problem would not occur frequently, it is always a possibility.

Turning over criminal justice to the community exposes the risk that emotion, as opposed to logic and rule of law, will undergird decisions. Fear and violence are often part of the deep nature of humanity.[61] The possibility always persists that an unjust society would believe its unfair procedures and rules to be just – even where these beliefs merely reproduce that society's incorrect worldview.[62]

Perhaps the best way to address the many issues associated with defining community in the criminal justice system would be to preserve the option of county-wide and federal juries for some offenses and to use community juries largely for local offenses with local suspects and local victims. This measure would merely add another level of criminal

community members do not agree with the harsh state and federal sentencing guidelines that require long sentences imposed on even minor players in the drug-dealing system.

[58] *See* Robinson, *Proper Role of the Community*, *supra* note 12, at 18.

[59] *See* David Barron, *Local Constitutionalism*, *supra* note 47, at 554. Barron is discussing civil decisions by local majorities, but the concern rings even louder within the criminal justice sphere.

[60] Alafair Burke & Bruce Green make a similar point in their article about community prosecution. *See* Alafair Burke & Bruce Green, *The Community Prosecutor: Questions of Professional Discretion*, 47 WAKE FOREST L. REV. 285, 305 (2012).

[61] *See* Berman & Fox, *Margins to Mainstream*, *supra* note 25, at 199.

[62] *See* Bowers & Robinson, *Perceptions of Fairness and Justice*, *supra* note 2, at 251.

jury service to our system; instead of having state and federal criminal juries, we would also have neighborhood juries, for neighborhood crimes. This scheme would work effectively because of the varying levels of interest in specific crimes. For local offenses, like most violent offenses and low-level drug and property crimes, the local community's interest in the crime is high and the state and federal interest is low. Thus, the state or federal government has a much lesser claim to legitimate concern. On the other hand, for offenses with greater, potentially state or national impact or those that cross jurisdictional boundaries, the larger jury venires would have greater legitimacy, and a jury with a wider reach might be best suited to address the crime.[63]

Because criminal justice is a largely local process with primarily local effects, the local community must be involved much more substantially in its application. Citizens need to participate in criminal justice decisions, preferably without extinguishing the voices of minority communities. The petit jury should be a body where local neighborhood residents can make themselves heard.[64]

Another, more limited way to engage the community in criminal justice would be to use community views to set the rules for criminal liability and punishment, but not to decide individual cases.[65] This would certainly eliminate most risks that involving the community in criminal punishment decisions would entail, as the community would only be part of creating legal rules, which would obviously be decided at a remove, discouraging decisions dictated by passion. This plan has the drawback, however, that it would not involve the community as much as would a more long-term, consistent participation in criminal justice decision-making.

Communities have their best chance at promoting positive values when they govern themselves. Some scholars have even argued that constitutional freedom can only arrive when diverse communities are allowed to govern themselves in accordance with a set of common principles.[66]

[63] *See* Washburn, *Restoring the Grand Jury*, *supra* note 41, at 2384.

[64] Washburn makes a similar point regarding the role of grand juries in the community. *See* Washburn, *Restoring the Grand Jury*, *supra* note 41, at 2388.

[65] *See* Robinson, *The Proper Role of Communities*, *supra* note 12, at 18.

[66] *See* Barron, *Traces of Local Constitutionalism*, *supra* note 47, at 495.

If, as the line of argument goes, local governments are critical components of the federal constitutional structure,[67] then using local community-based juries in the practice of criminal justice is necessary to vindicate the requirements of the Sixth Amendment jury trial right, for all aspects of criminal adjudication.

Criminal adjudication has always been a local process, and differences will always persist between one community and the next. Punishment is often determined by geography. This is because jurisdictions often have differing laws, penalties, resources, enforcement priorities, and prosecutorial and sentencing rules and guidelines. Such differences create outcome-determinative effects.[68]

"The most important benefit of localism in criminal justice is its tendency to make the enforcement of criminal law more responsive to the values, priorities, and felt needs of local communities."[69] This is positive, and a particular hallmark of our criminal justice system, because crime has always been specifically envisioned as an offense against the local community. Put another way, localism is inherent in the American conception of crime – indeed, it is hardwired into our historical and constitutional understanding of criminal justice.[70]

This understanding is supported by the idea that the local community can serve as the formal apparatus by which the contours of constitutional principles themselves would become known, as was contended by nineteenth-century scholar Thomas Cooley.[71] In other words, criminal justice principles embodying substantive constitutional norms are only defined through community interactions at the local level.[72] For

[67] *See id.* at 495 n.18.

[68] *See* Stephen Smith, *Localism and Capital Punishment*, 64 VAND. L. REV. EN BANC 105, 107 (2011). As Smith notes, "Crimes that, in one place, might not even result in charges may end in arrest and prosecution if committed elsewhere, and even serious crimes might be graded or punished very differently in different jurisdictions." *Id.*

[69] *Id.* at 110.

[70] *See id.* at 110.

[71] *See* Barron, *Local Constitutionalism*, *supra* note 47, at 556, discussing Cooley's scholarship. *See, e.g.*, Thomas M. Cooley, *Comparative Merits of Written and Prescriptive Constitutions*, 2 HARV. L. REV. 341, 349 (1889) (noting local governments' place in realizing constitutional values). Broadly, Cooley argued that constitutional principles could not be divined solely from the written text. Their meanings and scopes acquired their shapes through the habits and customs of the people as they developed over time. *See id.*

[72] *See* Barron, *Local Constitutionalism*, *supra* note 47, at 519.

Cooley, and for modern-day supporters of localism, the practice of public participation helps serve the public interest.[73]

Local representation within the criminal justice system would be greatly improved if it is broadened from the more limited nature of the traditional criminal jury, with its well-known tendency to exclude a variety of groups, including felons, minorities, students, recent immigrants, and many others.[74] One of the positive aspects of drawing on the venire rolls to comprise alternate jury-like bodies, as I discuss in Part III of this book, is that the Sixth Amendment's fair cross-section requirement applies to the jury venire,[75] as opposed to the seated jury. Thus if there are no peremptory challenges to these jury-like bodies, as in the grand jury, then the local representation of the community is greater than in the standard criminal petit jury, which is subject to various cause and peremptory challenges.

The juror's role as constitutional actor[76] provides another reason to concentrate on the local community. By focusing on the constant potential of most local citizens to be jurors, jury service is framed along an active continuum, encouraging community members to view their interaction with the criminal justice as an ongoing project, not just an isolated, one-time role.[77] The importance of being invited to participate equally in the constitutional system is one of the reasons jury service has always been such a contested enterprise.[78] Thus, involving the full community in jury service as a continuing duty of citizenry is one way of empowering more individuals within the polity.

Of course, broadening the definition of jury service to better involve the local community is not quite as simple as informing said jurors that

[73] *See* Barron, *Local Constitutionalism*, *supra* note 47, at 519.

[74] *See, e.g.*, Sanjay K. Chablani, *Re-Framing the 'Fair Cross-Section' Requirement*, 13 U. Pa. J. Const. L. 931, 947–48 (2011)(noting that the "fair-cross section" requirement excludes "[Y]oung people, old people, poor people, deaf people, less educated people, college students, resident aliens, blue-collar workers, professional workers, felons, juvenile offenders, those not registered to vote, those opposed to the death penalty, those affiliated with the National Rifle Association, city residents, and residents of Minneapolis." *Id.*

[75] *See id.* at 959.

[76] *See* Andrew G. Ferguson, *The Jury as Constitutional Identity*, 47 U.C. Davis 1105, 1108 (2014).

[77] *See id.* at 1111–12.

[78] *See id.* at 1131.

they are an essential part of the constitutional structure. Most jurors – and citizens in general – are entirely innocent of both the role formerly played by jurors in the founding of the Republic as well as the potential role they could play now. So the first step would be to educate citizens on the history of the jury and the larger role it should play again.[79]

Perhaps most critically, potential jurors need to understand that jury service, in all its forms, is the way of meaningfully connecting to the larger constitutional system[80] and, even more broadly, the polity. Jurors need to learn that they can be a formidable aspect of the criminal justice system with significant constitutional power; specifically, that they can be a distinct body that provides a strong voice against government oppression.[81] This would also have the added benefit of empowering those jurors who are more reluctant to participate, due to unfamiliarity, confusion, or showing ignorance before other community members.[82]

Finally, envisioning jury service as part of a more integrated, constitutionally focused continuum[83] has the advantage of helping community members feel connected to both the inner workings of the criminal justice system and the larger civic structure. Noting and preserving the use of the juror's public voice, through this expanded vision of community service as jury service, will help preserve the positive experiences that jurors often undergo, inform the wider community about the service given, and link said service to involvement in other democratic responsibilities.[84] In this way, jury service transforms from an isolated undertaking by an individual to an act of civic participation where people in a local community see how constitutional ideals and the promise of criminal justice are made real.

The vexing questions concerning "what comprises a local community" will not likely be easily solved with a few changes in the jury rolls. However, integrating loose, jury-like bodies into various criminal

[79] As Ferguson aptly notes, "The first step then is to make jurors aware of the value of jury service by reminding them of this past constitutional connection. This is not a mere history lesson, but a linkage to the constitutional mythology of America. If citizens see jury duty as constitutional duty, it becomes of elevated importance." *Id.* at 1153.

[80] *See id.* at 1153.

[81] *See id.* at 1156.

[82] *See id.* at 1159.

[83] *See id.* at 1162.

[84] *See id.* at 1165.

procedures would at least permit some greater representation of the heterogeneity that makes up a modern community. In the next few chapters, I discuss specifically how to implement greater community participation in several critical criminal procedures, including the guilty plea, the bail hearing, and ancillary criminal sentencing.

PART III

Theory into Practice: Origins and Community in Modern Criminal Procedure

6 BAIL, JAIL, AND THE COMMUNITY VOICE

Our current framework of criminal justice has focused primarily on either a criminal offender's fate once the trial or plea proceeding has begun or, to a lesser extent, his fate once he has been convicted and imprisoned. Until very recently, however, little attention was paid to those pretrial defendants languishing in the netherworld of *jails*. In part, this is due to our classification of a pretrial offender's incarceration as "detention" as opposed to "punishment." This chapter contends that the conditions of most pretrial detention differ little from punitive incarceration, subjecting these offenders to the worst of conditions without even a guilty verdict.

Accordingly, pretrial detainees can claim the denial of their Sixth Amendment jury trial right, which, at its broadest, forbids punishment for any crime unless a cross-section of the offender's community adjudicates a crime and finds guilt. This chapter explores how the animating principles of the community jury trial right applies to criminal defendants who are held in pretrial detention. In doing so, I look specifically at the procedures surrounding indicted offenders who are denied bail and confined in jail.

As we explored in Chapter 3, the Supreme Court reaffirmed, in *Blakely v. Washington*,[1] that a jury must determine any imposition of punishment that increases the maximum.[2] The realities of bail and jail in

[1] *See* Blakely v. Washington, 542 U.S. 296, 305 (2004) (holding that a state trial court's sentence of more than three years about the statutory maximum "did not comply with the Sixth Amendment").

[2] *See id.* at 304 ("When a judge inflicts punishment that the jury's verdict alone does not allow, the jury has not found all the facts 'which the law makes essential to punishment.'").

today's criminal justice system, however, dictate that punishment is often imposed by nonjury, nonjudicial, and even private actors, such as bail bondsmen, probation officers, and correction officials. In other words, conditions tantamount to punishment are imposed far from any constitutional oversight. This violates the true spirit of the Sixth Amendment jury trial right, which only permits members of the community to arbitrate punishment.

PRETRIAL DETENTION AS PUNISHMENT

Pretrial detention in the twenty-first century has evolved from brief containment for a few exceptionally dangerous criminal offenders to standard incarceration for large numbers of the accused awaiting trial. The combination of inhumane and degrading conditions, a corrupt and unregulated system of bail surety, bail bondsmen and bounty hunters, and rising numbers of detainees – coupled with the general absence of criminal due process in the pretrial realm – has resulted in a criminal justice system that punishes before it convicts. Even worse, this pretrial punishment decision is made by administrative and corrections officials instead of the community.

The current procedures for those accused offenders contradicts the requirements of even our minimal pretrial protection for all defendants, which requires that punishment can only be imposed after a conviction.[3] Punishing the accused before she is proven guilty violates every theory of punishment, but particularly that of retributive justice, which requires that punishment can only be imposed after a cross-section of the community has pronounced guilt – a far cry from the pretrial detention system we have now.

Our current bail system is by and large unregulated and plagued with corruption. First, numerous offenders languish in local jails for weeks for committing mere misdemeanors, simply because they lack funds to post bail.[4] In fact, the overwhelming majority of criminal

[3] *See* Bell v. Wolfish, 447 U.S. 520, 536–37 (1979) (holding that due process requires that pretrial detainees be free from "punishment").

[4] Mosi Secret, *N.Y.C. Misdemeanor Defendants Lack Bail Money*, N.Y. TIMES, Dec. 3, 2010, at A27.

defendants who are granted bail for nonviolent offenses are unable to muster funds and are sent to jail, often remaining there for over two weeks.[5] In a 2010 study, 87 percent of the low-income defendants who were not released on their own recognizance were unable to post bail and went to jail to await guilty pleas or trial.[6] In addition, pretrial detainees, who often have long incarceration periods, tend to miss work or forfeit their jobs entirely during detention, leaving any children and other dependents to fend for themselves.[7]

Equally disturbing is that that many of the poorer defendants plead guilty at arraignment for sentences with no jail time, simply to avoid being behind bars while awaiting trial.[8] Even innocent defendants will often accept a guilty plea in order to gain release from pretrial detention, even if this injures their long-term prospects.[9] These kinds of pressures create a situation in which criminal defendants, indicted but not yet convicted, are punished by nonjury actors before they are even convicted. In the unregulated arena of pretrial detention, there are few controls on who imposes punishment.

One of the most disturbing players in the pretrial detention scene is the bail bondsman. Even if an indicted defendant is fortunate enough to be granted bail, often he is held at the mercy of these commercial money granters. Bail bondsmen hold an immense amount of power over freed arrestees, despite the bondsmen's lack of legal, political, or police authority. Far from having a jury or a judge decide whether an indicted defendant should be incarcerated and punished, bail bondsmen make such decisions in a completely unstructured universe, where they are both judge and jury. This kind of unauthorized decision-making surely violates the spirit of the Sixth Amendment, which at its very core requires legal conviction by a cross-section of the community before punishment.

[5] *See id.* (finding that 87% of defendants whose bail was set at $1,000 or less did not post bail).

[6] Human Rights Watch, The Price of Freedom: Bail and Pretrial Detention of Nonfelony Low-Income Defendants in New York City, 2 (2010), *available at* http://www.hrw.org/sites/default/files/reports/us1210web wcover_0.pdf.

[7] See Samuel Wiseman, *The Right to Be Monitored*, 123 Yale L.J. 1344, 1348 (2013).

[8] See *id.* at 1345–46: "Most persons accused of low level offenses when faced with a bail amount they cannot make will accept a guilty plea; if they do not plea at arraignment, they will do so after having been in detention a week or two."

[9] Laura Sullivan, *Bail Burden Keeps U.S. Jails Stuffed with Inmates*, NPR, Jan. 22, 2010, *available at* http://www.npr.org/2010/01/21/122725771/Bail-Burden-Keeps-U-S-Jails-Stuffed-With-Inmates.

Similarly troubling are the vast amounts, sometimes thousands of dollars, that a bail bondsman may charge if he makes the decision to revoke bail and return the defendant to jail.[10] This kind of revocation decision, made entirely on the bondsman's own accord – with no regulation from any judicial, police, or legal authority – ends up not only returning the defendant to jail but also costing him and his family a large percentage of the deposited bond, which is forfeited when the defendant is surrendered.

There are few state laws regulating when it is permissible for a bondsman to surrender a defendant, which leaves the bail system open to manipulation. Some states, such as Oregon, ban commercial bondsmen altogether, but most leave the area entirely unregulated. New York bondsmen, among others, have been returning defendants to jail for questionable or unspecified reasons and then withholding thousands of dollars to which the bondsmen may not be entitled.[11]

Because most state laws allow bondsmen to enter into private contracts with indicted offenders, it is hard for judges to regulate their behavior. And even in states that afford some regulatory supervision, judges rarely take advantage of it. For example, in New York, although state law allows judicial consideration of the bondsman's background, character, and reputation when deciding whether to accept a bond, a judge rarely denies bond because of improper bondsman behavior.[12]

Equally troubling, instead of helping defendants stay out of jail (as they are paid to do), some bail bondsmen take advantage of the situation and exploit defendants by manipulating the pretrial detention process for further profit.[13] In other words, as described by a New York attorney familiar with these sorts of abuses, an indicted offender "can be ordered imprisoned by a court based solely on the unsworn, untested word of a non-law-enforcement civilian, a civilian who stands to profit financially

[10] *See id.* (noting that one bondsman returned eighty-nine bailees over a four-month period and pocketed 15% of the bail when doing so).

[11] *See id.*

[12] *See* John Eligon, *New York Is Owed More than 2 Million Dollars in Delinquent Forfeitures*, N.Y. Times, Jan. 10, 2011, at A18.

[13] *See* John Eligon, *For Poor, Bail System Can Be an Obstacle to Freedom*, N.Y. Times, Jan. 10, 2011, at A15 (hereinafter Eligon, *Bail System*) (recounting abuses of N.Y.C. bail bondsmen that have been investigated by the New York State Insurance Department).

if the defendant is incarcerated."[14] This type of entirely unregulated, potentially improper bond revocation, requiring the defendant to return to jail on the whims of a private actor, is yet another example of how the world of pretrial detention violates the spirit and the meaning of the Sixth Amendment jury trial right.

If bailees fail to appear for their hearings, the bondsman owes the entire bail amount to the court.[15] This kind of financial liability has led to many bondsmen employing recovery agents, usually known as bounty hunters, to ensure that indicted defendants appear for their court dates.[16] The last time the Supreme Court addressed the role of bounty hunters and bondsmen – approximately one hundred fifty years ago[17] – it acknowledged the historical common law privileges of both bondsmen and bounty hunters, holding that the right to apprehend a fleeing defendant originates from the contract relationship between bondsmen and their clients.[18] And despite vast changes in both criminal law and procedure, the Court has not addressed the topic since.

Bounty hunters do have a few, minor regulations on their behavior, mostly codified in state law, though they vary widely from state to state.[19] Despite persistent effort, however, attempts to control bounty hunters through federal legislation have failed.[20] As should not be

[14] *Id.*

[15] See Stephen N. Freeland, Note, *The Invisible Badge: Why Bounty Hunters Should Be Regarded as State Actors Under the Symbiotic Relationship Test*, 49 WASHBURN L.J. 201, 207 (2010).

[16] *See id.*

[17] Taylor v. Taintor, 83 U.S. (16 Wall.) 366, 371 (1872).

[18] *See id.* at 370–71. The *Taylor* Court noted that bounty hunters could "seize [the delinquent defendant] at any time, detain them until trial, pursue them across state lines, and even break into their homes if necessary." *Id.* at 371. Some scholars, however, have argued that this statement by the *Taylor* Court is only dicta, and not binding on modern-day courts; *see, e.g.*, Todd Barsumian, Note, *Bail Bondsmen and Bounty Hunters: Re-Examining the Right to Recapture*, 47 DRAKE L. REV. 877, 887–88 (1999) (citing Landry v. A-Able Bonding, Inc., 1994 WL 575480 (E.D. Tex. May 9, 1994), *aff'd in part, rev'd in part*, 75 F.3d 200 (5th Cir. 1996)).

[19] Forty-seven states have some sort of statute regulating bounty hunting. *See* Freeland, *supra* note 15, at 210 n.70. For example, in 1997, Indiana, Nevada, and North Carolina started licensing bounty hunters, and Texas began to require warrants for bounty hunters as well as the assistance of licensed private investigators/security guards. In addition, Florida, Illinois, Kentucky, and Oregon have banned commercial bail bonds systems, and hence have no bounty hunters. *See id.* at 210 nn. 66, 70.

[20] *See id.* at 211–12 (noting that two bills that would have made bounty hunters subject to the same laws and constitutional constraints as police failed in the House of Representatives).

surprising in such a "wild West" situation, behavior of some bounty hunters can be reprehensible. Beyond the show of brutality spotlighted in such reality shows as "Dog the Bounty Hunter,"[21] the rules and prohibitions that constrain the police do not generally apply to bounty hunters.[22] As a result, misconduct often occurs as bounty hunters take advantage of their legal privileges.[23]

Bounty hunters look and act like police but lack the screening and training that law enforcement provides its recruits.[24] Recovery agents often use dangerous and sometimes illegal tactics to retrieve defendants, property, or both, including confrontations at gunpoint, forced entries into homes without a search warrant, and the commandeering of vehicles on public roadways.[25] Indeed, in states where they are allowed to practice, bounty hunters can legally use stun guns, mace, and firearms while apprehending bailees. As a result, in the process of "recovering" the bailee, bounty hunters often complicate and endanger public safety.[26] Moreover, although bounty hunters play a police-like role, there is little constitutional protection against poor behavior because they are usually not considered state actors.[27]

In sum, the unregulated private actors, unsupervised and unaccountable bail bonding companies, complex and unfair fee structures, tremendous pressure to plead guilty, overincarceration for minor offenses, and disproportionately high bail all combine to make our system of pretrial detention both a navigational nightmare and constitutionally questionable under the Sixth Amendment.

[21] *Dog the Bounty Hunter* is a reality television show on A&E, which follows Duane Chapman as he hunts down defendants who have missed court appearances. *See* DOG THE BOUNTY HUNTER, www.dogthebounty hunter.com/. The website for the show proclaims, "Consi dered the greatest bounty hunter in the world, Duane 'Dog' Chapman has made more than 6,000 captures in his twenty-seven-year career." *Id.*

[22] See JACQUELINE POPE, BOUNTY HUNTERS, MARSHALS, AND SHERIFFS: FORWARD TO THE PAST 4 (1998) ("Rules of law and conduct under which police function have no relevance for bounty hunters.").

[23] See Freeland, *supra* note 15, at 212 (collecting stories of incidents).

[24] Daniel Stanton, *Bondsmen Pose Danger to Public*, PORTLAND TRIB., May 12, 2011, *available at* http://portlandtribune.com/component/content/article?id=6639.

[25] *Id.*

[26] *Id.*

[27] *See* Freeland, *supra* note 15, at 228 (discussing the inadequacy of the logic behind distinguishing police officers and bounty hunters).

Pretrial Detention as Punishment

At any given moment, a large proportion of jail dwellers consist of felony and nonfelony pretrial detainees who are in jail because they have not posted bail. Fully 60.2 percent of the nation's jail population consists of detainees awaiting trial.[28] Nationally, taxpayers spend $9 billion annually to incarcerate defendants held on bail.[29]

The rate of pretrial incarceration (and incarceration in jails and other nonprison detention centers in general) has continued to rise over the past ten years even though prison growth rates have been leveling off.[30] Indicted offenders are much less likely to be released pretrial today than they were in the past.[31] These jailed offenders include not only alleged violent offenders but also those who are awaiting trial for property, drug, and public-order-related charges.[32] In addition, fewer indicted offenders are being released from jail on their own recognizance, and those who have been granted bail are often unable to afford it.[33] These types of challenging bail requirements make it quite difficult for indicted defendants to obtain pretrial release, despite the fact that the vast majority have been arrested for low-level, nonviolent offenses.[34]

Despite this increasing reliance on incarcerating indicted defendants before trial, American communities are not necessarily any safer. The places with the highest incarceration rates have not seen violent crime rates fall.[35] In fact, quite to the contrary, New York City decreased its jail population and experienced a drastic reduction in crime rates.[36]

28 Todd D. Minton, U.S. Dep't of Justice, Jail Inmates at Midyear 2011 – Statistical Tables 1 (2011).

29 Pretrial Justice Institute, January–December 2011 Annual Report 3 (2011).

30 Amanda Petteruti & Nastassia Walsh, Jailing Communities: The Impact of Jail Expansion and Expansive Public Safety Strategies 2 (Justice Policy Institute 2008).

31 *Id.* at 3.

32 *Id.* Indeed, as the report notes, three-quarters of those pretrial detainees charged with property, drug, and public order–related charges are "significantly less likely" to be released. *Id.*

33 *Id.* As the report explains: "Once, more than half of those jailed received bail amounts of $5,000 or less; today, just about half of the people in jail receive the highest bail amounts ($10,000 to the maximum)." *Id.*

34 *Id.*

35 See Human Rights Watch, *supra* note 6, at 4.

36 *See id.* at 4.

These increasing rates of pretrial detention are worrying in part due to the conditions of the actual detention centers housing pretrial defendants. Although state and federal prisons are not generally known for their plush accommodations, the general state of the jails that hold pretrial detainees are so bad that simply to be incarcerated in them rises to a punitive experience.

The substandard conditions of today's pretrial detention centers – halfway houses and local and municipal jails – have transformed the detainee's experience into a form of punishment. It is a little-known but unfortunate truth that pretrial detainees often undergo harsher conditions of confinement than those defendants who are convicted.[37] Although state and federal prisons house most convicted prisoners, jails and county lockups house the accused who have either been denied bail or cannot afford to pay it.

In addition, pretrial detainees are often incarcerated alongside the 10 percent of convicted criminals who are housed in jails rather than prisons.[38] This indicates that the holding conditions for pretrial detainees are, at minimum, punishment-like, as the conditions are precisely the same for some convicted offenders. The lines between prison and jail are becoming increasingly blurred.[39] This situation is worrisome because pretrial detainees should not undergo any type of punishment before conviction or a guilty plea, no matter who or what imposes it.

The Supreme Court has held that determining whether certain conditions rise to the level of punishment can be measured by objective indicia.[40] In the case of pretrial detainees, their confinement often meets this level, and there are many well-substantiated examples of this. By far the most concerning – but not isolated – cases come from Rikers Island in New York: the municipal lockup for those arrested and held over for

[37] *See* David Gorlin, Note, *Evaluating Punishment in Purgatory: The Need to Separate Pretrial Detainees' Conditions-of-Confinement Claims from Inadequate Eighth Amendment Analysis*, 108 Mich. L. Rev. 417, 419 (2009)

[38] Petteruti & Walsh, *supra* note 30, at 3.

[39] *See id.* (noting that convicted criminal defendants are increasingly sent to jail, not prison).

[40] *See, e.g.*, Youngberg v. Romeo, 457 U.S. 307 (1982) (holding that a mentally handicapped prisoner had "constitutionally protected liberty interests under the Due Process Clause of the Fourteenth Amendment to reasonably safe conditions of confinement, freedom from unreasonable bodily restraints, and such minimally adequate training as reasonably may be required by these interests"); Bell v. Wolfish, 441 U.S. 520, 537 (1979) (holding that courts may decide "whether [the detainee's condition] has historically been regarded as punishment").

trial, as well as the detention area for immigrants, juveniles, and any prisoner subject to rehearing or resentencing.[41] The jail on Rikers Island has recently been sued over its "startling culture of violence"[42] by more than a half-dozen Rikers inmates, all claiming to have been the victims of beatings by prisoners while guards ignored it or, worse, ordered the attacks.[43] Likewise, the Baltimore City Detention Center was found to be controlled by violent gangs and complicit female guards, with the power of life-and-death decisions over other inmates.[44]

Jails in other major metropolitan areas are rife with similar abuses. The Los Angeles County Men's Central Jail is notorious for overcrowding, forcing inmates to sleep on dirty floors, live devoid of natural light, and receive only a two-hour outdoor recreation session per week on the jail's roof.[45] California prisons, which have been under a federal consent decree since 2009 for violating health codes in prison and jail housing,[46] have recently been forced to move inmates due to the threat of "valley fever," a sometimes-deadly fungal disease infecting the San Joaquin Valley correctional facilities.[47] In Maricopa County's Tent City Jail, in Phoenix, Arizona, inmates are housed outdoors in military tents without

[41] See N.Y. DEP'T OF CORRECTION, AN OVERVIEW OF NEW YORK CITY DEPARTMENT OF CORRECTION FACILITIES, *available at* http://www.nyc.gov/html/doc/html/about/facilities-overview.shtml. The Rikers Island complex contains nine separate cen ters for both sentenced defendants and pretrial detainees, including an adolescent male unit, detox and mental health unit, hospital, women and babies unit, misdemeanor unit, maximum security, extreme protective custody, and detainees unit. *Id.*

[42] *See* Editorial Board, *The Shake-Up at Rikers Island*, N.Y. TIMES, Nov. 3, 2014, at A22.

[43] Benjamin Weiser, *Lawsuits Suggest Pattern of Rikers Guards Looking Other Way*, N.Y. TIMES, Feb. 4, 2009, at A21.

[44] *See* Jeffrey Toobin, *This Is My Jail*, THE NEW YORKER 26 (April 14, 2014). As Toobin notes, the majority of the inmates housed in Baltimore City Detention Center were being held on bail and awaited trial. *Id.* at 27.

[45] PETTERUTI & WALSH, *supra* note 30, at 19.

[46] *See* Brown v. Plata, 131 S. Ct. 1910 (2011) (ordering California to reduce its prison population by 37,000 inmates). The plaintiffs claimed that California state prisons failed to provide adequate healthcare to its prisoners in violation of their Eighth Amendment constitutional rights and the American with Disabilities Act. *See id.* They also argued – and the Court agreed – that a remedy for unconstitutional medical and mental health care could not be achieved without reducing prison overcrowding. *See id.*

[47] *See* Laila Kearney, *California agrees to move inmates at risk of Valley Fever*, REUTERS.COM, *available at* http://www.reuters.com/article/2013/07/03/us-usa-california-prisons-idUSBRE96201N20130703. As the article notes, "Valley Fever is rarely fatal in otherwise healthy people. But it has killed 52 California inmates since 2006, said Warren George, an attorney with the Prison Law Office, a nonprofit law firm representing the at-risk inmates."

air conditioning (despite over 100-degree temperatures in the summers), fed 15-cent meals only twice a day to cut costs, are forced to wear humiliating prison gear, and have very few amenities.[48] And in Washington, DC's Central Detention Facility, there has repeatedly been overcrowding, serious health and sanitation issues (including broken showers, no running water in cells, and animal feces throughout the facility), and inadequate healthcare.[49] All this is in addition to the abuse that pretrial detainees can be subjected to in jails, ranging from violent treatment by other prisoners to more institutionalized practices.

The Harm of Pretrial Incarceration

Jails in and of themselves can be dangerous and unhealthy environments, even more so than prisons. First, jail buildings are often old and decaying.[50] These old buildings frequently have various dangers associated with them, including mold, poor ventilation, lead pipes, and asbestos, all of which can be detrimental to the health of pretrial detainees.[51]

Moreover, the concentration of prisoners, wardens, and visitors in a jail make it a vector of contagious diseases.[52] This is in large part because serious infections and sexually transmitted diseases are highly concentrated and can easily spread in jails,[53] and an ever-changing detainee population means that the residents are constantly in flux.[54] For example, the MRSA drug-resistant superbug has been thriving in jails, with the potential to infect those detainees who are there even for only a short time.[55] Many jails are not properly equipped to treat serious

[48] *Id.*

[49] *Id.*

[50] See PETTERUTI & WALSH, *supra* note 30, at 15 (citing studies from the 1990s that show that 700 jails in the United States are older than 50 years old and 140 jails were more than 100 years old).

[51] *See id.*

[52] *See id.*

[53] For example, HIV, antibiotic-resistant TB, and bacterial infections all exist at much higher rates in jails than in the general population. *See id.*

[54] *See id.*

[55] *See* Silja J. A. Talvi, *Deadly Staph Infection 'Superbug' Has a Dangerous Foothold in U.S. Jails*, ALTERNET.COM (Dec. 4, 2007), *available at* http://www.alternet.org/story/69576 (last visited July 30, 2012) (detailing how Superbug spreads all too easily in jails because of problems like poorly ventilated living and sleeping quarters; overcrowded rooms;

health problems in their detainees, and what healthcare is available is not easily provided to a jail's often short-term visitors.[56]

Being detained in jail prior to trial also augments the possibility of conviction.[57] Defendants incarcerated before trial are more likely to be found or to plead guilty and serve prison time than those released pretrial.[58] The mere possibility of pretrial imprisonment often compels defendants to plead guilty and give up their right to trial.[59] The prospect of being incarcerated, even for a short time, can be ruinous for poor defendants, as this often means the loss of their livelihood, severe disruptions to their family lives, or both. Accordingly, when confronted with an unaffordable bail, a large number of pretrial detainees simply plead guilty.[60]

Moreover, the simple fact of being detained pretrial increases the defendant's potential of committing future crimes and injures the quality of an offender's defense, making it more likely that the detainee will be convicted, imprisoned, and subjected to prolonged deprivation of liberty, privacy, and other fundamental elements of human existence.

Finally, pretrial detention can, in some cases, be literally deadly. The privatization of jails, prisons, and halfway houses in states such as New Jersey has resulted in the housing of violent convicted offenders with nonviolent pretrial detainees.[61] This mixture of low-level detainees with dangerous convicted felons has repeatedly resulted in injury or death for those who cannot make bail for misdemeanor charges.[62]

shared mattresses, toilets, and showers; and a preponderance of people who arrive with poor health, drug problems, and severely compromised immune systems).

56 PETTERUTI & WALSH, *supra* note 30, at 15.

57 HUMAN RIGHTS WATCH, *supra* note 6, at 2.

58 *See* Shima Baradaran & Frank McIntyre, *Predicting Violence*, 90 TEX. L. REV. 497, 555 (2012). As the authors expound, "Detention leads to the loss of employment and other negative financial conditions, less likelihood to obtain private counsel, which harms defendant's chances to be acquitted or at sentencing." *Id.*

59 HUMAN RIGHTS WATCH, *supra* note 6, at 3. *See also* Baradaran & McIntyre, *supra* note 58, at 555 ("[L]iving conditions in jail are often poor and have been shown to have a negative influence on defendant's trial demeanor.").

60 HUMAN RIGHTS WATCH, *supra* note 6, at 3. For example, guilty pleas account for 99.6% of all convictions of New York City misdemeanor defendants. *Id.*

61 *See* Sam Dolnick, *At Penal Unit, Volatile Mix Fuels a Murder*, N.Y.TIMES, June 18, 2012, at A1.

62 *See id.*

All of these practices are transforming our imposition of pretrial detention from its original incarnation as brief confinement based on risk of flight to a punitive incarceration decided by a fragmented and inconsistent variety of private and public actors. This transformation creates two major problems: not only do our procedures for imposing jail and denying bail disproportionately punish the poor and disenfranchised, but, as I contend below, they also violate the spirit of the Sixth Amendment jury trial right. Taken together, these practices have created an unregulated shadowland where the normal promises of substantive and procedural criminal justice do not apply.

Violating the Spirit of the Sixth Amendment

Prolonged pretrial incarceration feels wrong because it punishes indicted offenders before conviction without any say by members of the community, violating the very spirit of our criminal justice system. Despite popular sentiment, these offenders are innocent at this phase of the criminal process. Thus, some of the discomfort we feel with such practices logically stems from the Sixth Amendment jury trial right, which holds that the accused "shall enjoy the right to a speedy and public trial, by an impartial jury of the state and district wherein the crime shall have been committed."[63]

Our current pretrial detention practices violate the very tenets of the Sixth Amendment: the accused are incarcerated for lengthy periods, suffering punitive and dangerous conditions in jails and county lockups, based on decisions made by either unaccountable private actors, harried magistrates, or line prosecutors. Punishment, in other words, is being imposed on those not yet convicted, without the imprimatur of the community.

As we have seen, bail and jail determinations take place far from the community and the jury room, in the barrens of procedural justice. This is particularly important with our recent understanding of the Sixth Amendment jury trial right, where the Court's focus on community participation in criminal adjudication was not limited to criminal trials.[64]

63 U.S. Const.Amend. VI.
64 *Southern Union v. United States*, 132 S.Ct. 2344 (2012), held that a jury must decide about the imposition of a criminal fine.

The Court's refusal to limit *Apprendi-Blakely* to jury trials leaves space for integrating the community jury right into the pretrial detention sphere. If the Supreme Court has focused on the jury as the only appropriate community body to impose punishment on a convicted offender, then how much more important is it that the community determine whether punitive conditions may be imposed upon an arrested detainee? The *Apprendi-Blakely* line of decisions forbidding imposition of punishment until the jury has decided guilt or innocence must inform our practices governing pretrial detention.

Whenever detention turns from regulatory to punitive, the community must have a say in the punishment imposed. There is convincing evidence that modern-day bail and jail practices result in punishment for an indicted defendant incarcerated before trial. Although usually the underlying reasoning for imposing pretrial detention is not based on a punishment rationale, the consequences of such decisions are often so severe that the end results are the same.

This punishment before conviction creates numerous problems for our current framework of bail and jail. First, many offenders are denied bail based on the relatively new field of preventative detention, one riddled with errors, both in theory and in practice. Second, although the Supreme Court, in *United States v. Salerno*,[65] has seemingly closed off both due process and Eighth Amendment attacks against the 1984 Bail Act, which permits pretrial detention based on "community safety," there have not yet been any challenges based on the Sixth Amendment ban on punishment imposed before a conviction and without a jury's sanction. Third, and relatedly, if we follow the dictates of the Sixth Amendment jury trial right, the community must take part if any punishment is to be imposed on an offender.

Given the changes made to the historical right to bail, our newfound reliance on preventative incarceration, and the Supreme Court's recent focus on the Sixth Amendment's jury trial right, our current pretrial detention procedures may require some substantive changes. Below I explore how these factors – the mistaken reliance on preventative detention, the holes left by *Salerno*, and the requirements of the Sixth

[65] United States v. Salerno, 481 U.S. 739 (1987).

Amendment – all converge to make our current pretrial detention hearings in need of reform.

The False Promise of Preventative Detention

In the federal system, preventative incarceration, or detaining the accused based on the potential of future crime, did not become popular until Congress's 1984 Bail Reform Act.[66] In the past thirty years or so, many states have followed suit, allowing their criminal justice systems to detain indicted individuals based on their future dangerousness. Both judges and academics have challenged the bases for this type of determination, however, questioning the entire underlying theory of preventative detention.

Over thirty years ago, in *Barefoot v. Estelle*,[67] the Supreme Court first tackled the suitability of nonjury actors determining and punishing future dangerousness.[68] Although the Court ultimately permitted pretrial incarceration based on determinations of potential danger, the majority of the *Barefoot* Court underlined the importance of the community's role in deciding whether a fellow member of the public is so dangerous as to deserve incarceration on that basis.[69]

More critical for our purpose here, however, is Justice Thurgood Marshall's *Barefoot* dissent, which noted that psychiatrists and other experts might actually be "less accurate predictors of future violence than laymen."[70] This is partially because the lay public lacks a personal bias leaning toward predicting violence, an inclination that can arise from

[66] 18 U.S.C. § 3142.

[67] *See* Barefoot v. Estelle, 463 U.S. 880, 903 (1983) (finding that "[e]xpert testimony, whether in the form of an opinion based on hypothetical questions or otherwise, is commonly admitted as evidence where it might help the factfinder do its assigned job").

[68] In *Barefoot v. Estelle*, the Supreme Court agreed with the lower trial court that the use of psychiatric experts to discuss the potential dangerousness of the defendant *at trial* was permissible because this type of determination was for the jury to decide: "Such disputes are within the province of the jury to resolve. Indeed, it is a fundamental premise of our entire system of criminal jurisprudence that the purpose of the jury is to sort out the true testimony from the false, the important matters from the unimportant matters . . . ." *See Barefoot*, 463 U.S. at 903.

[69] Granted, this holding applied to the propriety of determining dangerousness during an actual trial, not during a pretrial detention hearing, but the larger meaning of the holding would apply to pretrial detention determinations as well.

[70] *Id.* at 922 n.4 (Marshall, J., dissenting).

the responsibility for the erroneous release of a violent individual.[71] If this is true of psychiatric experts, it is equally true for magistrates and trial judges, especially those state court judges who must submit to the pressures of periodic reelection. It is no wonder that the courts almost invariably decide, on the basis of community safety, that pretrial detainees should be incarcerated.

Marshall's dissent also highlighted a key critique that applies widely to all determinations of potential future dangerousness: the general unreliability of these predictions.[72] Citing several studies, the dissent pointed out that long-term prediction of future violence by psychiatrists continues to be extremely inaccurate.[73] This is due in part to the difficulty of identifying any subclass of offenders that has a greater than fifty-fifty chance of reengaging in assaultive conduct,[74] the conduct with which future dangerousness is most concerned. Indeed, a 90 percent error rate for predicting future dangerousness is common.[75]

All these concerns are focused, of course, on expert psychiatric testimony heard by the jury during an actual trial. How much more unreliable might those hasty predictions be when they are issued by an untrained magistrate or trial judge attempting to determine the future dangerousness of a person who has not yet been convicted? At the minimum, to comport with the spirit of the Sixth Amendment, incarcerating an arrestee on the basis of his potential to commit future crimes should be based on stronger science than gut feelings or past conduct. Moreover, it should certainly allow some degree of community participation.

Many of the judicial determinations that lead to pretrial detention are overly harsh or punitive.[76] This is especially true when it comes to predicting future dangerousness. Neither experts nor courts have had

71 *Id.* at 922 n.4.

72 *See id.* at 919 (discussing how "the unreliability of ... predictions of long-term future dangerousness is by now an established fact within the profession," and noting that two out of three predictions of long-term future violence made by psychiatrists are wrong" (citing Brief for American Psychiatric Association as Amicus Curiae Supporting Petitioner at 12, 463 U.S. 880 (1983) (No. 82–6080)).

73 *Id.* at 920.

74 *Id.* (citing Wenk, Robinson & Smith, *Can Violence Be Predicted?* 18 CRIME & DELINQ. 393, 394 (1972)).

75 *Id.* at 921 n. 2.

76 *See id.* at 327 (criticizing the binary model for its inability to take into account "partial degrees of truth").

much success in accurately determining if and when an offender might commit more crimes.[77] Unsurprisingly, then, many harmless defendants are unfairly detained as dangerous.[78] Our current bail system fails to account for the varying degrees of detainability, dangerousness, and culpability that indicted offenders present,[79] painting them all with the same overly broad strokes.

Predicting Violence in the Twenty-First Century

The problems with determining future dangerousness, however, do not end there. Even if it can be accurately predicted, should that necessarily mean that a prediction of potential dangerousness should always equal detention and punishment for arrestees?

The quality of dangerousness is a "peculiarly seductive" one, partly because it can be ascribed as a personal characteristic of the offender, not a judicial imposition.[80] And when dangerousness is seen as a personal trait, it leads to confusion between the determination of dangerousness and the determination of desert, when both usually animate the reasons underlying punishment.[81] As criminal theorists have long noted, "as a matter of justice we should never take power over the convicted criminal on the basis of unreliable predictions of his dangerousness."[82] If this is true for convicted criminals, how much more important is this tenet for those merely indicted? Indeed, the strongest moral argument against predictive detention is, simply, that it is not

[77] See Barefoot v. Estelle, 463 U.S. 880, 919–22 (Marshall, J., dissenting) (emphasizing this problem with the current system). *See also* Joseph J. Cocozza & Henry J. Steadman, *The Failure of Psychiatric Predictions of Dangerousness: Clear and Convincing Evidence*, 29 RUTGERS L. REV. 1084, 1097 (1976) (finding "dangerous" patients no more than nondangerous patients); John Monahan, *The Prediction of Violent Behavior: Toward a Second Generation of Theory and Policy*, 141 AM. J. PSYCHIATRY 10 (1984) (arguing that dangerousness predictions are wrong approximately 95% of the time).

[78] *See, e.g.*, MICHAEL R. GOTTFREDSON & DON M. GOTTFREDSON, DECISIONMAKING IN CRIMINAL JUSTICE: TOWARDS THE RATIONAL EXERCISE OF DISCRETION 122–27 (1980) (articulating reasons that predictions of dangerousness for indicted offenders are often unreliable).

[79] *Id.* at 327–28.

[80] See Franklin E. Zimring & Gordon Hawkins, *Dangerousness and Criminal Justice*, 85 MICH. L. REV. 481, 492 (1986).

[81] *Id.*

[82] NORVAL MORRIS, THE FUTURE OF IMPRISONMENT 73 (1974).

deserved – an objection that remains even if there is an accurate prediction of future dangerousness.[83]

This uncertainly and ambiguity of standards in pretrial detention matters because determining dangerousness is a central preoccupation of the criminal justice system.[84] Indeed, the reliability of preventative detention is a hotly debated topic. The reliability of predictive dangerousness can be challenged in two ways: (1) persons should not be denied liberty on dangerousness grounds unless there is a high degree of certainty that the person will offend in the near future; and (2) actual proof of dangerousness is nearly impossible to obtain.[85]

We frequently rely upon predictive dangerousness to imprison and even execute convicted offenders. For example, the *Barefoot* Court held that the inconsistencies inherent in predicting future dangerousness, even in regard to the death penalty, are largely eradicated by the adversarial process, which usually exposes erroneous views.[86] If we can rely on the shaky credibility of predictive dangerousness to justify an execution, how could it not justify regular pretrial detention, where no life is lost?

The answer here, of course, is specific to pretrial detention. First, there is no adversarial contest in the typical pretrial detention hearing, as there is no right to appointed counsel during bail determination. As the vast majority of those detained without bail are those who cannot afford counsel on their own, it is rare to see defense counsel appear at bail hearings.[87] Thus, there is little to no adversarial process in bail determinations.

[83] *See* ANDREW VON HIRSCH, DOING JUSTICE: THE CHOICE OF PUNISHMENT 125 (1976). Granted, von Hirsch admits that a small fraction of offenders should be confined in preventative detention, including those who have extensive violent records and who were convicted of serious assault crimes. *Id.* at 125–26.

[84] *See* Christopher Slobogin, *A Jurisprudence of Dangerousness*, 98 NW. U. L. REV. 1, 2 (2003) (stating that dangerousness assessments play a role in "death penalty determinations, non-capital sentencing, sexual predator commitment, civil commitment, pretrial detention, and investigative stops by the police").

[85] *Id.* at 3.

[86] *See* Barefoot v. Estelle, 463 U.S. 880, 901 (1983).

[87] Although in *DeWolfe v. Richmond*, ___ Md. ___ (No. 34, S.T. 2011 (January 3, 2012)), the Maryland Court of Appeals recently attempted to require counsel for all pretrial detainees, in April 2012 the Maryland Legislature amended the public defender statute to remove the right to counsel at commissioner hearings but mandated counsel at the initial judicial bail

Second, there is an important difference between assessing future dangerousness for a convicted offender, who is usually subject to punishment of some kind, and assessing the same for someone who has not even been subject to conviction. Taking away the liberty of a person convicted beyond a reasonable doubt (or who has admitted his or her guilt) is a far different matter than imprisoning someone whose actual guilt is still unproven.

Empirical Evidence and National Trends

The actual work of determining dangerousness is a chancy business, filled with pitfalls and indeterminacy. To predict the potential threat of an indicted offender, courts tend to analyze the nature of the charged crime and combine this information with their knowledge of the defendant's past conduct.[88] The court then adds to this assessment its own determination of the accused's circumstances and character.[89] In many states, a more subjective judicial assessment permits courts to consider the totality of the defendant's circumstances and character.[90] Determining dangerousness, then, can be greatly influenced by the court's personal feelings and quirks. Despite claims of scientific accuracy, the determination of dangerousness is based far more on subjective than objective factors.

On the whole, predicting further pretrial crime while an indicted offender is out on bail is an extremely dubious science.[91] In fact, our assumptions about who might be mostly likely to reoffend before trial

review. *See* Maryland Public Defender Act, ss16–101 through 16–403 of the Criminal Procedure Article. Ultimately, in a 4–3 decision, the Maryland Court of Appeals held in DeWolfe v. Richmond, No. 34, September Term, 2011 (decided September 25, 2013), that Article 24 of the Maryland Declaration of Rights guarantees an indigent defendant the right to state-furnished counsel at an initial appearance before a district court commissioner. *See* Kara Fischer, *Maryland Recognizes Constitutional Right to Counsel at Initial Appearance Hearings, available at* http://www.jgllaw.com/blog/maryland-recognizes-constitutional-right-counsel-initial-appearance-hearings.

88 See Baradaran & McIntyre, *supra* note 58, at 508–10. As Baradaran and McIntyre show, there are five states that allow for an even deeper look into a defendants background by allowing judges to factor the defendant's past conduct into their determination. *Id.* at 511.

89 *See id.* (noting that this factor is much broader, to allow for judicial discretion).

90 *See id.* at 510. As the authors note, some state statutes include a list of factors with an "including but not limited to" clause or permit judicial officers to consider "any other factor" relevant to making a determination of dangerousness. *Id.* at 511.

91 *Id.* at 523.

are often not borne out. For example, as demonstrated by one of the few large empirical studies done on defendants released before their trials, those charged with violent crimes are *not* necessarily more likely to be rearrested pretrial.[92] Nationally, 16 percent of defendants released on bail are rearrested for any reason, and 11 percent are rearrested for a felony.[93] Most important, only 1.9 percent of all defendants released on bail before trial are rearrested for a violent felony.[94] Thus one prong of the furor over "dangerous" arrestees loses its force; if only a tiny percent of all defendants released on bail go on to reoffend with violent crimes, then perhaps our fear over the danger posed to the community by the pretrial defendant is overblown.

Interestingly, the greatest predictor for future pretrial crime, dangerous or not, is the existence of past arrests.[95] It is important to note, however, that analysis of prior convictions shows that even defendants with multiple prior convictions are unlikely to be rearrested for a new violent crime while on release.[96]

Moreover, those charged with violent crimes are *not* necessarily more likely to be rearrested pretrial.[97] Critically, although recent research demonstrates that defendants charged with violent crimes have the highest likelihood of being rearrested on bail, there is still a huge variation in how dangerous these violent defendants can be, depending on the specific crime charged.[98] Ultimately, despite the

92 *See id.* at 528. As the authors point out:

> The highest rearrest rates pretrial are for defendants charged with drug sales or robbery (21%), followed by motor vehicle theft (20%), and burglary (19%). Those released who are charged with the "more dangerous crimes," such as murder, rape, and felony assault, have much overall lower rates of pretrial rearrest at 12%, 9%, and 12%, respectively. *Id.*

93 *See id.* at 527.

94 *See id.*

95 *See id.* at 536 ("A person's number of previous arrests is a large predictor of future rearrest; however, whether or not that prior arrest turned into a conviction is largely irrelevant as an additional predictor.").

96 *See id.* (finding that only 5% of all defendants have more than a 5% change of being rearrested on a violent felony charge when released on bail).

97 *See id.* Granted, those charged with violent crimes are more likely to be rearrested for violent crimes on release. *See id.*

98 *See id.* at 528. For example, those defendants charged with murder have a 6.4% violent crime rearrest rate, one of the highest. Similarly, those defendants charged with robbery have a 5.8% chance of rearrest for violent crime, those defendants charged with rape a 3.2% chance of rearrest for violent crime, and those defendants charged with assault reoffend at a rate of 2.9%. *See id.* at 528–29.

large variety of assessments of pretrial "dangerousness," the defendants granted bail before trial are often far less threatening to public safety than most people would anticipate.[99]

There must be a better way of predicting "dangerousness" than our current fumbling in the dark. The charged crime, by itself, is a poor predictor of a threat to the community, except for the most violent ones (such as murder, which by statute usually prevents the defendant from obtaining bail release in any case). The existence of multiple past convictions for similar crimes seems to have the most predictive effect, although even those pretrial recidivism rates are low.

Accordingly, relying on our current system of judicial and prosecutorial decision-making regarding pretrial release – which relies primarily on the charged crime – is not only unfair, but largely ineffective. And considering that roughly 62 percent of the overall jail population consists of pretrial detainees,[100] these decisions make a huge difference.

If, as I contend, the imposition of pretrial detention in today's jails is a form of punishment, then the community must have some say in the matter. One stumbling block to achieving this goal, however, is the Supreme Court's 1984 decision in *United States v. Salerno*,[101] which dismissed a facial challenge to the 1984 Bail Reform Act, thus permitting the detention of arrestees on grounds other than flight risk.[102] The *Salerno* Court specifically noted, however, that it was simply foreclosing a *facial* challenge to the 1984 Bail Reform Act,[103] not foreclosing all challenges for the future.[104] This was particularly significant because, in addressing a facial challenge, *Salerno* only focused on theoretical

[99] *See id.* at 529.

[100] *See id.* at 37 (finding that in 2007, 62% of the overall jail population consisted of pretrial detainees).

[101] United States v. Salerno, 481 U.S. 739 (1987).

[102] In *Salerno*, the Supreme Court held that the 1984 Bail Reform Act, which permitted courts to impose pretrial detention on defendants based on potential dangerousness, had a legitimate regulatory goal (preventing danger to the community) and that the incidence of pretrial detention was not excessive in relation to that regulatory goal. *See Salerno*, 481 U.S. at 747.

[103] As the *Salerno* Court held, "We are unwilling to say that this congressional determination ... on its face violates either the Due Process Clause of the Fifth Amendment or the Excessive Bail Clause of the Eighth Amendment." *Salerno*, 481 U.S. at 755.

[104] *Salerno*, 481 U.S.at 741.

pretrial detention, not actual pretrial detention as experienced by indicted defendants.

Despite its approval of predictive detention practices, the *Salerno* Court did carve out an important exception to its defense of preventative detention: when pretrial detention becomes punishment. Of course, simply because a defendant is detained does not mean that he is being punished.[105] Traditionally, we look to legislative intent to determine whether a restriction on liberty, like pretrial detention, is more like punishment than like regulation.[106] Unless Congress intended on imposing punishment, the classification of a liberty restriction as either punitive or regulatory depends on whether there is an alternative purpose related to the restriction, and whether this restriction seems excessive in relation to the original goal.[107]

The *Salerno* Court itself reserved the right to decide on the constitutionality of a situation in which "detention in a particular case might become excessively prolonged, and therefore punitive, in relation to Congress's regulatory goal."

As I have detailed above, much of pretrial detention, whether based on fears for community safety or flight risk, has an effect virtually indistinguishable from punishment. Thus, despite *Salerno*'s decision generally endorsing preventative detention, there is nothing precluding a state or federal court from finding pretrial detention unconstitutional. This is particularly true for state courts, which process the vast majority of pretrial detention cases, because *Salerno* focuses on a congressional act.

Moreover, *Salerno* did not address the Sixth Amendment implications for the 1984 act, as the defendants did not raise the issue on appeal. Of course, a Sixth Amendment claim at the time of the *Salerno* decision would have been fruitless. Now, however, after the *Apprendi-Blakely* line of cases, an application of the current understanding of the Sixth Amendment jury trial right – requiring that the

[105] See Bell v. Wolfish, 441 U.S. 520, 537 (1979) ("Not every disability imposed during pretrial detention amounts to 'punishment' in the constitutional sense.").

[106] See Schall v. Martin, 467 U.S. 253, 269 (1984) ("Absent a showing of an express intent to punish on the part of the State, that determination generally will turn on 'whether an alternative purpose to which [the restriction] may rationally be connected is assignable for it, and whether it appears excessive in relation to the alternative purpose assigned.'" (citing *Kennedy v. Mendoza-Martinez*, 372 U.S. 144, 168–69 (1963))).

[107] Kennedy v. Mendoza-Martinez, 372 U.S. 144, 168–69 (1963).

community be the only arbiter of punishment for an offender – makes a great deal of sense.

In the end, the Supreme Court left room in its doctrine to determine in both state and federal courts whether and how pretrial detention can be punishment. This issue is best explored through the dimensions of the Sixth Amendment community jury trial right.

Punishment, Community Rights, and Pretrial Detention

Recall that in *Blakely*,[108] the Supreme Court held that the jury is the only body that can find facts that increase the maximum punishment for an offender. Put another way, *Blakely* contended that a criminal offender must have a jury, or the local community, determine all aspects of punishment.[109] This newfound understanding of the Sixth Amendment jury trial right applies to all aspects of our criminal justice system, including bail and jail. In fact, all of our constitutional guarantees should apply with more force to the pretrial stage, since at this point the offender still maintains the presumption of innocence. But the spirit of the Sixth Amendment jury trial right has yet to be applied to the determination of pretrial detention.

When we apply the community jury trial right to the pretrial detention hearing, various problems with the bail hearing are illuminated. One problem is the lack of adversarial context when determining the future dangerousness of an indicted offender. Since the adversarial process is crucial for the proper community understanding and imposition of punishment, the lack of it raises equity and possibly even constitutional concerns.

Although Congress does permit the right to legal assistance, the right to cross-examine prosecution witnesses, and the right to testify and present witnesses in a federal bail hearing,[110] the accused does not

[108] *See* Blakely v. Washington, 542 U.S. 296, 296 (2004) ("Because the facts supporting petitioner's exceptional sentence were neither admitted by petitioner nor found by a jury, the sentence violated his Sixth Amendment right to trial by jury.").

[109] *See, e.g.*, United States v. Booker, 543 U.S. 220, 226 (2005) (applying *Blakely* to Federal Sentencing Guidelines, making guidelines advisory); *Blakely*, 542 U.S. at 296.

[110] 18 U.S.C. § 3142(f).

have a right to compulsory process,[111] which is a key factor in any properly adversarial contest. Indeed, evidence submitted by the prosecutor may be submitted by proffer.[112] In the states, moreover, there are no guarantees of any of the foregoing rights. Furthermore, the amount of disclosure required by the states varies widely; some districts comport with *Brady* requirements for bail hearings, and some do not.

The failure to require full disclosure of evidence by the prosecutor at the pretrial detention stage means that indicted defendants often cannot challenge the evidence presented by the government to establish the accused's future dangerousness. Although the Supreme Court has held that the pretrial detention hearing does not generally require "the full panoply of adversarial safeguards," the establishment of potential dangerousness by the government is so questionable that the adversarial process should apply. Especially since the standard of evidence required from the prosecutor at this stage is relatively low – only probable cause[113] – it seems only fair that the accused get a greater disclosure of evidence when she is subject to potential detention based on dangerousness.

At minimum, more and better disclosure of prosecutorial evidence is needed to help the offender challenge the request for pretrial detention.[114] When the defendant lacks knowledge of the evidence against him, he cannot properly challenge the detention request, meaningfully participate in the hearing, or refute any secret evidence, because the proceeding is one-sided.[115]

Even more troubling in the view of adversarial process is the lack of the right to *appointed* counsel at the pretrial detention stage. Simply put, this means that the vast majority of defendants, both state and federal, do not have any legal representation at the bail hearing at all,[116] since

[111] Rinat Kitai-Sangero, *Due Process at the Pretrial Detention Stage – What Will Become of the Innocent? – A Call for Pretrial Discovery Rules*, 46 CRIM. L. BULL. 452, 452 (2010).

[112] *Id.*

[113] *See id.* at 464 (stating that "the prosecutor is only required to show probable cause that the accused has committed the offense attributed to him in addition to proving the ground of detention: obstruction of justice or dangerousness").

[114] *See id.* at 465 ("Disclosure could be of paramount importance to the accused in contesting the evidence against him.").

[115] *Id.* at 466.

[116] But see Maryland, *supra* note 86.

the average criminal defendant cannot afford legal representation on his own.

This lack of adversarial context and the one-sided nature of the detention hearing also implicates the community jury trial right. If, as the *Apprendi-Blakely* line of cases instructs us, the community is supposed to decide all potential punishments for an offender after observing an adjudicatory process, then there should be some sort of adversarial process during the detention hearing.

Although a full adversarial procedure would not be feasible, a detention hearing should provide a few more procedural safeguards. At the very least this should include the requirement of a minimum proffer of prosecutorial evidence at the hearing, proved by a standard of probable cause, in any case in which the indicted defendant might potentially be detained due to community safety concerns. Better still would be provision of some minimum of appointed counsel for all criminal defendants who want one. These two changes would provide a modicum of adversarial process for the detention hearing.

The animating principle behind *Apprendi-Blakely* – that the community should determine all punishment to be meted out to the defendant – has import for not just the jury trial, but for other areas of criminal procedure too. *Apprendi-Blakely* applied first and foremost to sentencing, but there is no reason why it should not be applied to the pretrial detention hearing as well.

Quite simply, recent conditions in pretrial detention centers have rendered any sort of time in them a form of punishment. This is in addition to all the negative externalities that flow from a pretrial loss of liberty. Not only is this punishment imposed before a determination of guilt, but it is also imposed by a judge, not a jury – a violation of the Sixth Amendment jury trial right to determine all punishment for a criminal offender.

The question becomes, then, under what circumstances does the judicial determination of pretrial detention turn into an imposition of punishment? When denial of bail equals an imposition of punishment, this might mean that the community should play a role, particularly in determinations of its own safety.

The Community Deciding Danger to Itself

Considering that pretrial detention often confines offenders before trial due to their supposed threat to community safety, it is ironic that this determination currently lacks any community imprimatur. Surely members of the community would be better able to assess who might pose a danger to their own neighborhoods than would a line prosecutor, who often has other concerns on his or her mind when determining whether an indicted offender may post bail before trial. This is equally true for a judge, who is not always part of the community she governs and may be more interested in uniformity (or in some cases, reelection) than individual justice.

It is true that the prosecutor is both technically and legally the public's representative.[117] The prosecutor's function as the people's representative, however, can be subsumed by a gradual inclination to align with the government and a desire to achieve a positive win-loss record. Too often, prosecutors have "their own agendas, both personal and administrative."[118] For prosecutors, the concepts of *public interest* or *justice* can be terms too diffuse and elastic to constrain. A prosecutor's simultaneous representation of both the state and the people can get submerged in the everyday details of doing his job, particularly when the indicted offender is a high-profile defendant and there is considerable media scrutiny and pressure in the case.

Allowing some slice of the community to help determine whether the accused is truly a threat to community safety makes both logical and ethical sense. First, the community often knows the offender far better than either the prosecutor or the judge, especially in a state or local forum. Despite the persistent fear of crimes perpetuated by strangers, people commit most crimes within their communities. Thus, who better than a representative of the community to help determine whether the accused might pose a danger if granted bail?

In addition, granting the community power to determine whether pretrial detention should be imposed would likely foster a feeling of

[117] As the Supreme Court has noted, the prosecution's interest "is not that it shall win a case, but that justice shall be done." Berger v. United States, 295 U.S. 78, 88 (1935).

[118] Abraham S. Goldstein, *Converging Criminal Justice Systems: Guilty Pleas and the Public Interest*, 49 S.M.U. L. Rev. 567, 569 (1996).

participation and investment in the criminal justice system, something that many members of the public lack. Being given the opportunity to make real decisions on community safety would hopefully make these citizens, and by association their families and friends, feel far more connected to how the criminal justice system works. Put another way, instead of envisioning the criminal justice system as a faceless, remote entity, the local public, through their participation in the pretrial detention hearing, would realize that they are part of the justice system as well. This would generally promote the legitimacy of and public confidence in the justice system, something that has been lacking of late.[119]

Finally, having the community become involved with pretrial detention determinations will result in the public's increased understanding of the criminal justice system. Particularly with high-profile cases, the current lack of transparency in pretrial detention procedures can create both disappointment and a sense of helplessness in the local community. For example, when disgraced financier Bernard Madoff was granted bail after his confession to the police, the local and international public was angered and dismayed.[120] The public's integration into the pretrial detention hearing through participation in the procedure can eliminate some of the concerns inherent in imposing pretrial detention or granting bail by exposing the public to the actual debate over individual bail determinations.

Having an informed segment of the community take part in pretrial detention determinations will also assist with the accuracy of the "future dangerousness" predictions. Currently, judges tend to use their own intuition to determine how dangerous an indicted offender might be, or they rely on a prosecutor's statement of disrupted community safety. This can result in overprediction of future dangerousness. Naturally, a

[119] *See generally* STEPHANOS BIBAS, THE MACHINERY OF CRIMINAL JUSTICE (2012).

[120] See *Madoff Debate: Should He Be Free on Bail?* MSNBC.COM, Jan. 7, 2009, *available at* http://www.msnbc.msn.com/id/28540171/ns/business-us_business/t/mad off-debate-should-he-be-free-bail/ (last visited July 30, 2012) (discussing how investors, editorial writers, and the general public expressed outrage regarding the granting of Madoff's bail, while prosecutors argued that Madoff should be thrown behind bars because he could flee or hide his assets); *see also* Larry Neumeister, *Bernie Madoff Escapes Jail, Judge Declines To Revoke Bail*, HUFFINGTON POST, Jan. 12, 2009, *available at* http://www.huffingtonpost.com/2009/01/12/bernie-madoff-jail-hearin_n_157049.html (discussing how "[t]here is a thirst for blood that transcends just those who have been victimized").

prosecutor would have an interest in the defendant remaining in custody as long as possible, both to ensure cooperation and that no further crimes happen that might reflect negatively on the prosecutor's office.

Judges also have a tendency to be biased in favor of predicting violence, in part because they will be responsible if they erroneously release a violent individual.[121] Moreover, judges, like all experts who routinely make these types of dangerousness determinations, may also have a tendency to generalize from experiences with past offenders on bases that have few, if any, relationships to future violence.[122]

Members of the community, on the other hand, do not have some of these pressures and biases. First, even if they participate in some sort of pretrial detention hearing, they would not bear any ultimate responsibility if the indicted offender were to commit another crime before trial. Equally important, the small cross-section of the public that would be involved in determining whether the accused obtained bail would not have the aforementioned tendency to generalize from prior experiences, permitting them to make the determination of pretrial detention from a fresh perspective.

Proposal: Reform and Revision

Some of the ills of our criminal justice systems can be traced to the dissociation between our local communities and their ability to effect change on the system. Insufficient local control is a serious issue, pervading all aspects of criminal justice. As William Stuntz passionately argued,

> To the suburban voters, state legislators, and state and federal appellate judges whose decisions shape policing and punishment on city streets, criminal justice policies are mostly political

[121] See J. MONAHAN, THE CLINICAL PREDICTION OF VIOLENT BEHAVIOR 13, 22–25 (1981) (noting that psychiatrists might be less accurate predictors of future violent than laymen because of personal bias arising from fear of responsibility for erroneous release of a violent person).

[122] See Saleem A. Shah, *Dangerousness: A Paradigm for Exploring Some Issues in Law and Psychology*, 33 AM. PSYCHOLOGIST 224, 229–30 (1978) (arguing that when prior probabilities of the outcome, or base rates, are very low, the predictions are of poor reliability).

> symbols or legal abstractions, not questions the answers to which define neighborhood life. Decisionmakers who neither reap the benefit of good decisions nor bear the cost of bad ones tend to make bad ones. Those sad propositions explain much of the inequality in American criminal justice.[123]

This is particularly true in pretrial detention hearings, where the question of whether an indicted defendant is released or not before his trial often rests on decisions made by remote legislators or senior district attorneys. The local community has little or no say in the matter.

But this result is neither preordained nor necessary. One way to get the community more involved in the criminal justice process – thus making them feeling more invested in the system – is to invite their participation in the pretrial detention hearing, allowing them to give their opinion on whether the suspect is a true threat to community safety.

If the community is actively involved in determining what would best serve community safety, this not only meets the demands of the community jury trial right, but it might also provide more leniency toward the pretrial release of indicted, low-level offenders. The social consequences of mass incarceration are myriad. By incarcerating too many nonviolent criminals, either before or after conviction, poor and minority communities are increasingly harmed by the massive scale of incarceration, and many of these nonviolent offenders do become dangerous after being exposed to violent criminals in jail or prison.[124] Thus, the short-term decision to incarcerate pretrial offenders for purposes of "community safety" ends up backfiring on a number of levels in the long run.

In theory, of course, imprisonment in local jails removes the accused from their existing social communities with the intent of creating safer, better neighborhoods, ones better able to enforce their own social codes.[125] In reality, however, the removal that pretrial detention

[123] William J. Stuntz, *Unequal Justice*, 121 Harv. L. Rev. 1969, 1974 (2008).

[124] *See, e.g.*, Jeffrey Fagan & Tracey L. Meares, *Punishment, Deterrence and Social Control: The Paradox of Punishment in Minority Communities*, 6 Ohio St. J. Crim. L. 173, 201–05 (2008) (discussing the social consequences of mass incarceration); James Forman, Jr., Book Review, 108 Mich. L. Rev. 993, 999 (2010) (reviewing Paul Butler, Let's Get Free: A Hip-Hop Theory of Justice (2009)).

[125] *See* Marcia Johnson & Luckett A. Johnson, *Bail: Reforming Policies to Address Overcrowded Jails, the Impact of Race on Detention, and Community Revival in Harris County, Texas*, 7 Nw. J. of L. & Soc. Pol'y 42, 72 (2012).

imposes has a significant negative impact on arrestees' families and children.[126] The loss of income and employment alone has obvious negative effects on both a pretrial detainee's family and the community as a whole.[127] No matter what amount of time the defendant is jailed, the deleterious consequences of detention remain.

Adding to the problem, communities that experience higher rates of incarceration often begin to reject the stigma of incarceration. This can lead to greater numbers of community members being locked up. Specifically, the mass imprisonment of African American young males "poses a distinctive harm to African-American communities, damaging social networks, distorting social norms, and destroying social citizenship."[128]

Incorporating the community into the bail hearing, however, might help offset some of these problems. Not only is it more likely that many more low-level offenders would be granted more freedom, but it is also possible that the public would gain an increased understanding of the criminal justice system, the restored benefit of criminal adjudication's educative function, and a sense of investment and trust in the system.

So how would this integration of the community happen? And why would it be a positive force? First, and most basically, the current bail hearing process – like so much else in the criminal justice system – functions out of sight of the average citizen. The local citizenry has a meaningful interest in uncovering the procedures involved in denying or granting bail, especially since so many taxpayer dollars are being used to incarcerate those who have not yet been determined guilty. For this reason alone, the integration of the local community is justified.

Second, enhancing local, popular participation within an existing criminal justice institution,[129] such as the bail hearing, creates the positives of community involvement without requiring new courts,

[126] *See id.* at 72.

[127] As the Justice Institute Policy Report has amply documented, "jail disrupts the employment and economic outcomes of a person who has been admitted." PRETRIAL JUSTICE INSTITUTE REPORT, *supra* note 29, at 17.

[128] *See* Johnson & Johnson, *Reforming Policies to Address Overcrowded Jails*, *supra* note 125, at 74.

[129] See Adriaan Lanni, *The Future of Community Justice*, 40 HARVARD C.R.-C.L. L. REV. 359, 363 (2005) ("The best way to introduce the community justice goal of greater citizen input into the administration of justice is not to scale up current community justice programs, but to provide for enhanced local, popular participation within existing criminal justice institutions.").

vast infusions of money, or immense change in the existing system. Through citizen involvement, the "cynicism and contempt" created by our more secretive criminal justice system will be minimized.[130] This is especially important for communities that have felt distanced and isolated by the criminal justice system; by allowing these communities to determine whether one of their own is "safe" enough to release pretrial, the local public may feel some investment or purchase in the workings of the system.

As Judith Resnik powerfully argued, "[t]hird-party scrutiny illuminates the treatment of suspects, detainees, prisoners, and immigrants, all reliant on government for their well-being."[131] Permitting the community to observe and participate in the routine preventative detention hearing of a domestic defendant, then, would vindicate a number of rights, including, of course, the community jury trial right. As Resnik contends, "law ought to oblige open decision making when confinement is at stake."[132]

In addition, allowing a cross-section of the community to decide a detainee's "dangerousness" would offer a less jaded sensibility to the pretrial detention determination. Although normally we defer to courts to make such decisions, having fresh eyes look at each individual situation, from a body that is not beholden to reelection or reappointment processes, would inject both transparency and fairness into the proceedings. A bail jury, in other words, could make decisions informed by their own knowledge of the community and unburdened by judicial pressures and biases.

This kind of open decision making – and open participation by the local public – is most likely to take place in the state court system, which processes a vast percentage of pretrial detainees in the country. As

[130] Kenneth Kipnis, *Plea Bargaining, A Critic's Rejoinder*, 13 LAW & SOC'Y REV. 555, 557 (1979).

[131] See Judith Resnik, *Detention, the War on Terror, and the Federal Courts: An Essay in Honor of Henry Monaghan*,110 COLUM. L. REV. 579, 670 (2010). Although Resnik is primarily envisioning courts as this public oversight, she admits to a possible role for other third parties. As she notes, speaking of the general public's right of audience during these impositions of detention, "[e]mpowered, participatory audiences can therefore see and then debate what legal parameters ought to govern." *Id.*

[132] *Id.* This is particularly true when, as now, the Court has "repeatedly insulated the federal judiciary from addressing the merits to decide when an individual is wrongfully convicted or detained in intolerable conditions." *Id.* at 681.

Resnik notes, "[t]he last few decades have brought attention to state courts as a font of constitutional jurisprudence that can be more rights-protective than federal precepts."[133] Because of this, it would be easy enough to draw from the county jury rolls to create a body of local fact-finders for bail hearings, the members of which would be selected in a manner similar to those citizens selected for the grand jury.

These "bail juries" could sit for a week or two at a time, focusing their decisions on the community safety issue: in other words, whether the indicted defendants brought before the court would be eligible for bail. If the "bail jury" deemed defendants safe for release out into the community – perhaps using a preponderance-of-the-evidence standard, then barring any true evidence of danger to the public – they would be released either on their own recognizance or electronically monitored until trial or guilty plea date.

Potential Problems

Admittedly, a cluster of concerns center around the implementation of a bail jury, its potential costs, complexity, and time. One serious critique of the bail jury is its impracticality, both in terms of cost and delay. In these fiscally stretched times, any procedure that would add to the cost structure of the criminal justice process is viewed with great suspicion. And incorporating a bail jury into the pretrial detention hearing would potentially increase costs; although the bail jury could be drawn from the same rolls as the grand jury, the more citizens drawn, the more money needed to fund per diems, reimburse transportation costs, and pay court staff to organize such juries.

As noted above, however, the potential amount of savings that a properly working bail jury would provide could be vast. Even a 30 percent reduction in those incarcerated before trial could save the state thousands of dollars. And although there are no guarantees that a bail jury would be more lenient on matters of pretrial release than the traditional judicial arbiter, it is likely that a more informed body of decision makers – that is, a cross-section of the community – might

[133] *Id.* at 682.

not believe that all criminal defendants, whether low level or violent, are a threat to public safety.

As for delays, it is possible that the incorporation of the bail jury would slow down the pretrial detention somewhat. But that is not necessarily a bad thing. Part of the problem with our current bail hearings is the speed at which these critical determinations take place. Since there is no right to appointed counsel at a bail hearing, often they are very fast, as the prosecutor presents evidence regarding the defendant's incarceration and the court makes a decision. Although the bail jury does not tidily solve all of the problems of our framework of bail and jail, it provides a partial solution to some of the glaring inequities of pretrial detention.

Reducing the haste of the process might also ensure that both the court and the prosecutor take the process more seriously; since the bail jury will not be criminal justice insiders, they will likely focus on each individual case more intensely, requiring the prosecutor to more fully explain her reasoning for denying bail. The court, too, may spend more time on the decision, since it will need to incorporate the bail jury's decision into its own. Thus, the delay in imposing pretrial detention or granting bail might be a positive one, opening up the procedure to some much-needed sunshine and scrutiny.

The use of a bail jury, combined with increasing monitored pretrial release,[134] would begin to solve both constitutional and procedural problems. First, the bail jury would help ameliorate the Sixth Amendment issue, allowing the community a chance to help decide any pretrial punishment imposed on indicted offenders. Second, giving local citizens a say in who is released back into their community has a practical aspect to it; instead of having the prosecutor and the judge, both representatives of the government, be the only ones to determine community safety, it makes sense to have some input from the very community that the government is trying to protect. Third, the addition of increased electronic monitoring of those offenders released before trial would be a relatively easy, cost-effective way to permit those accused who either cannot afford to make bail or about whom the

[134] *See generally* Wiseman, *The Right to Be Monitored*, *supra* note 7.

community or judge still have some reservations to avoid detention in jail.

As both a practical measure and a fundamental matter of constitutional fidelity, the people should be involved in the machinations of criminal punishment. This includes the procedures that happen before trial. Our current system of pretrial detention lies in shambles, incarcerating those not yet convicted in punitive conditions often far worse than those existing in prisons. Allowing the community a say in the matter and broadening the ambit of those who can be released pretrial is one way to shine light into the darkness.

7 INFUSING COMMUNITY THROUGH CRIMINAL PROCEDURE: THE PLEA JURY

The preceding chapters arguing for a collective jury right have all raised one overarching question: In a world of guilty pleas, how important can this community right to the jury trial right be? In response, this chapter explores how the Court's new jury-centered philosophy of punishment affects the procedures of the guilty plea – by far the most common way of adjudicating criminal indictments. Although the Court focused its analysis on community participation in juries, I conclude that there is nothing in *Apprendi-Blakely* or its progeny to suggest that this type of participation should be limited only to the criminal trial. Thus, a logical next step in following the dictates of the jury trial right is the incorporation of the community into the guilty plea procedure, through the use of a plea jury.

The Court's recent concentration on the jury and the rights of the community applies to all aspects of criminal process, as the Court has continually taken pains to point out. It goes without saying that the function of the petit jury – to represent the community – is deeply entwined with our general understanding of legitimacy, democracy, and punishment. And the Court's reliance on the historical origins of the criminal's jury trial signifies a return to a more robust community right. But this community right has been almost completely excised from modern criminal process, the guilty plea procedure being the most dramatic example.

Our current configuration of the criminal guilty plea leaves no room for the community's voice. Guilty pleas, although critical to the smooth processing of criminal justice, have become hasty and rote, allowing little to no expression of the community's voice. Moreover, the chronic imbalance of prosecutorial power over the past thirty years has shrunk to much smaller roles those of the defendant, the defense attorney, and the trial court.

Looking at plea bargains through the lens of the community jury trial right highlights their constitutionally subversive nature, since the very process neatly excises the community's role in criminal adjudication. Thus, changing the guilty plea procedure to make it more trial-like in form – by including the jury – would be a way of restoring full constitutional rights to the most frequently used form of criminal adjudication.

This question of how to integrate the community criminal jury trial right also pays homage to the expressive, restorative retribution implicit in the Sixth Amendment's collective jury trial guarantee. The issue is particularly salient because, in today's world, there are so few criminal trials and so many criminal guilty pleas. The next step, then, is how to expand the Sixth Amendment community jury function into the guilty plea procedure.

The best and simplest way to incorporate the community into the plea bargain process is through use of a plea jury. Integrating a special community-based jury into the plea process serves a number of functions. First, the use of a plea jury would allow the community, as jury, to finally inject its voice back into the criminal procedure (the guilty plea) that disposes of the majority of criminal indictments. Second, utilizing a plea jury would return the community to its longstanding, constitutional role as decider of guilt and imposer of punishment, while retaining the essential structure of the guilty plea. Third, the introduction of a fresh, less jaded element into the business of plea bargains, through the incorporation of the lay public, would provide renewed attention to the often-overlooked procedural rights of the defendant.

Equally important, with the use of a plea jury, the factual basis of the plea – that is, the actual crime to which the defendant pleads guilty – would receive greater scrutiny, helping link punishment more tightly with what crime was actually committed. Finally, inserting a plea jury in the standard guilty plea process would apply the Court's recent reaffirmation of the jury's constitutional rights and powers to all aspects of criminal adjudication. Considering that the primary tool of modern criminal justice has been the guilty plea, not the trial, focusing the

Court's new jury-centered jurisprudence on criminal trials only addresses a small area of criminal process.

With its enshrinement of the jury trial, the Sixth Amendment community jury trial right delineates one of the most important rights in our criminal justice system – a right that has for too long been neglected. As a fundamental matter of democratic political theory, it is the people who should run the government, not the legal elite. This extends to the criminal justice arena as well as the legislature and the executive. The inclusion of a plea jury returns the community to the center of the criminal decision-making process, where it belongs.

Restoring the community jury right to the vast bulk of criminal adjudication can be achieved by envisioning the community's integration into the guilty plea, theoretically as well as procedurally. In doing so, this chapter will illustrate not only how a standard plea jury would be incorporated, but also why the critical norms embedded into jury participation could help improve existing guilty plea procedure. In this way, I hope to build a bridge between our standard punishment theory (based primarily on criminal trials) and everyday criminal practice, providing in the process a principled, theoretical account of plea process.

Incorporating the community jury right and its underlying jurisprudence into the practice of guilty pleas will both reestablish the lost voice of the people and instigate much-needed change in our current criminal justice system. Restoring the community voice to its full volume, in the form of a plea jury, will not only permit us to follow the constitutional requirements of the Court, the Sixth Amendment, and Article III,[1] but also provide balance and new energy into the business of adjudicating criminal cases.

A THEORY OF GUILTY PLEAS

From the beginning of the American colonial experiment, as discussed in Chapter 2, the community right to a public trial was heavily

[1] *See* U.S. CONST. Art. III, § 2, para. 3 ("The Trial of all Crimes, except in Cases of Impeachment, shall be by Jury.").

intertwined with a combined retributive and restorative understanding of punishment. This was a philosophy closely tied to the sovereign will of the people, the community's traditional role in determining moral blameworthiness, the importance of popular authority, the public right to trial, and the community's willingness to forgive wrongdoers and eventually restore their rights. The use of expressive, restorative retribution was inexorably tied to the community's right to determine punishment for wrongdoers.

But how do we translate that community jury trial right, and its underlying philosophy of expressive, restorative retribution, into our current criminal justice system? Unquestionably, we now live in a world of guilty pleas; it is unregulated, devoid of much due process, and lacking a credible theory of punishment. Although various theories of guilty pleas have been offered – a contractual view, a motive theory, a crime control theory, a social cohesion theory – none has truly worked on both a practical and a philosophical level. As Ron Wright has persuasively argued, "We need an alternate theory of guilty pleas, one that transcends the hidden intentions and grudgingly spoken words of defendants and the contradictory incentives at work on prosecutors in particular cases."[2]

The consistent use of a plea jury, supported by an underlying framework of expressive, restorative retribution, would meet this need for an alternate theory of guilty pleas. Thus, my vision of the plea jury process operates on two levels: one theoretical and one practical.

The incorporation of the community into the primary vehicle of criminal adjudication and sentencing would permit all three aspects of expressive, restorative retribution to function. First, although the full expressive aspects of a trial do not occur with the plea jury, there is still the offender's expiation of his crimes to a segment of the public. With use of the plea jury, the guilty plea is no longer enacted only before a limited audience of the judge, the prosecutor, and the defendant, thus helping restore the public aspect of community adjudication.

[2] Ronald F. Wright, *Trial Distortion and the End of Innocence in Federal Criminal Justice*, 154 U. Pa. L. Rev. 79, 96 (2005). Wright argues for a midlevel theory of plea bargaining that evaluates plea bargaining as an artifact of a particular criminal justice system, with different features depending on different practices. *Id.* at 99–100.

Second, requiring a plea jury to decide whether the offender's allocution is truthful and whether the sentence is appropriate satisfies the basic requirements of retributive justice, as it permits the injured community to impose punishment on its offenders. This is something lacking in today's criminal process, leading to all sorts of problems, as I discussed in previous chapters.

Finally, restorative justice also plays its part in the plea jury process, since the participation of the lay public not only allows the community to impose punishment but also allows the demonstration of mercy and forgiveness as well. If the community sees that the offender is truly remorseful for his actions, then they are hopefully more likely to accept a shorter sentence, as well as be more supportive of the offender's reintegration into the community after release from incarceration.

If truly integrated into the procedure of the guilty plea, the jury's position as the community representative functions in a number of roles, both theoretical and practical.

THE PROBLEM WITH GUILTY PLEAS

Guilty pleas have thoroughly colonized the criminal justice system. With 90 percent to 95 percent of all convictions resolved by a guilty plea,[3] what was once an infrequent disposition has now become the norm.[4] This change in adjudication from criminal trial to criminal plea, however, has not been accompanied by an equal shift in either constitutional protections[5] or punishment theory.[6] As William Stuntz

[3] *See id.* at 90–91.

[4] *See* Ronald Wright & Marc Miller, *The Screening/Bargaining Tradeoff*, 55 STAN. L. REV. 29, 30 (2002).

[5] As John Langbein trenchantly noted, our shift from criminal trials to guilty pleas means that there is an "astonishing discrepancy between what the constitutional texts promise and what the criminal justice system delivers," making "our guarantee of routine criminal jury trial . . . a fraud." John H. Langbein, *On the Myth of Written Constitutions: The Disappearance of Criminal Jury Trial*, 15 HARV. J.L. & PUB. POL'Y 119, 120 (1992).

[6] *See* Stephanos Bibas, *Plea Bargaining Outside the Shadow of Trial*, 117 HARV. L. REV. 2464, 2468 (2004) (describing how plea bargains and guilty pleas rely on sentencing factors such as wealth, sex, age, education, and intelligence rather than any traditional theories of criminal punishment).

astutely observed, "criminal settlements do not efficiently internalize the law."[7]

In short, guilty pleas are largely unregulated and have been implemented with a focus on efficiency and disparity rather than any particular theory of criminal punishment. Among other problems, this has given short shrift to the Sixth Amendment community jury trial right. In John Langbein's terminology, we have come to rely on a system of "condemnation without adjudication."[8] The practical landscape of the current criminal justice system, enmeshed as it is in pleas, leaves no room for the recently reinvigorated theoretical importance of the jury trial right. Currently, the Court's *Apprendi-Blakely* jurisprudence has found only a limited toehold in the practical workings of the justice system, confined as it has been to jury trials and some sentencing procedures. This plea jury proposal, however, expands that hold.

Legal response to the current realm of guilty pleas has been varied. On the whole, prosecutors, defense attorneys, and courts have easily accepted this dramatic procedural shift.[9] Plea bargaining is supported by the belief that "any harm to the public or to third parties from the enforcement of plea bargains is outweighed by the benefits of enforcement."[10]

Once we accept the middle ground on guilty pleas – that although imperfect, they are here to stay – we also need to develop a better, more nuanced framework of plea bargains, one that is "capable of endorsing some plea deals while disapproving of others."[11] This kind of normative framework must acknowledge what has been lost by the move from the

[7] William J. Stuntz, *Plea Bargaining and Criminal Law's Disappearing Shadow*, 117 HARV. L. REV. 2548, 2548 (2004) (emphasis omitted).

[8] John Langbein, *Land Without Plea Bargaining: How the Germans Do It*, 78 MICH. L. REV. 204, 204 (1978).

[9] *See* GEORGE FISCHER, PLEA BARGAINING'S TRIUMPH 16 (2003). Fischer particularly notes that for the prosecutor and judge, not only did the plea bargain alleviate crushing workloads, but it also spared them both the risk of loss and the potential humiliation of defeat. *See id.*

[10] Nancy J. King, *Priceless Process: Nonnegotiable Features of Criminal Litigation*, 47 UCLA L. REV. 113, 116 (1999).

[11] Michael M. O'Hear, *What's Good About Trials?* 156 U. PA. L. REV. PENNUMBRA 209, 209 (2007), *available at* http://www.pennlawreview.com/online/156-U-Pa-L-Rev-PENNumbra-209.pdf. O'Hear explains that this sort of normative framework must discuss not only the innocent but also the guilty defendants, including their sentencing reductions, the role of victims, and which procedural rights they are allowed to surrender. *Id.* at 211.

trial to the guilty plea, despite the gains in efficiency and cost.[12] Although there have been a few "middle course" proposals that recognize this truth, many do not. My plea jury proposal meets such a challenge head-on.

None of the middle-course guilty plea modification proposals have proposed the incorporation of the jury into the plea process. The reason seems obvious: How can there be a jury if the defendant has waived that right? But looking at the inclusion of the jury as solely the right of the defendant is a mistake. As we discussed previously, the jury has long been the primary way through which the community plays its part in criminal decision-making, a rule clearly marked out for the people in both Article III and the Sixth Amendment. Recall that since the sanctions applied in the criminal justice system can be severe, the Framers expected the community, in the role of the jury, to prevent abuses of state power.[13]

So this raises an interesting question: If the collective right of the community to determine punishment rises to a constitutional level – or even if it doesn't – does the defendant's waiver of "his" jury trial right in favor of a guilty plea eliminate the role of the jury? Logically, the answer seems to be no. If, as the Supreme Court seems to imply, the community has a right to determine an offender's punishment, then it follows that the community's right cannot be waived by the defendant. In other words, the defendant does not have the ability to waive the collective right, only his own.[14] Accordingly, if the collective jury right is distinguished from the defendant's, then we must address how to integrate the community jury right into all forms of criminal adjudication.

Partitioning the right to a criminal jury trial between the community and the accused would serve a variety of purposes. First, restoring some measure of the jury trial right to the local community would comport with the original understanding of the procedure, both as practiced in the eighteenth century and as formalized in the Bill of Rights. If the

[12] *See* O'Hear, *Trials*, *supra* note 11, at 210.

[13] *See* Langbein, *Myth of Written Constitutions*, *supra* note 5, at 123–24.

[14] As Nancy King points out, the procedural rights remaining in the guilty plea process "may serve a variety of social or public goals that will not always coincide with the preferences of defense and prosecution." King, *supra* note 10, at 132.

Supreme Court is now basing some of its criminal jurisprudence on the historical practices of the jury trial, focusing on the rights of the community, then the original meaning of the jury trial right has renewed import.

Although modern courts, until quite recently, have assigned the jury trial right almost exclusively to defendants,[15] there is no reason why the rights of the people could not have more of a role in modern criminal procedure. In fact, in another facet of the right to a jury trial we do that very thing. I am referring, of course, to *Batson v. Kentucky*[16] and its progeny, which hold that a juror has a right not to be excluded from a petit jury based on race, ethnicity, or gender.

The best example for how to share a right to a jury trial comes from another aspect of criminal procedure: the peremptory challenge. The body of case law surrounding peremptory challenges initially addressed the prosecution's illegal dismissal of jurors due to race or ethnicity, but it gradually grew to include the illegal dismissal of jurors by either the defense or the prosecution, based on the right of the juror herself to serve. It is this kind of division of jury rights – based on the rights of the community itself – that I propose to apply to the guilty plea.

One reason the Court found a community right to a fair and balanced jury in the *Batson* line of cases is because it determined that discrimination in jury selection impacts not only the litigants and the individual jurors who have been subject to peremptory challenges, but their community as well.[17] As the lower courts have understood it, "[j]ury service – a privilege and duty of citizenship – is . . . a fundamental means of participating in government."[18]

For one aspect of criminal adjudication, then, the Court has held that the public has a jury right independent of the defendant. As the

[15] *See* United States v. Patton, 281 U.S. 276 (1930) (assigning jury trial right to defendant).

[16] 476 U.S. 79 (1986). Over time, as the Court developed its case law on peremptory challenges, its original holding expanded significantly. The *Batson* peremptory challenge, originally based only on race-based discrimination, has been variously extended to include challenges of jurors of a different race than the defendant, civil actions, third-party standing to raise improper exclusion for prosecutors, and gender discrimination.

[17] *See* Johnson v. California, 545 U.S. 162, 171–72 (2005); Batson v. Kentucky, 476 U.S. 79, 87 (1986).

[18] New York v. Allen, 653 N.E.2d 1173, 1177 (N.Y. 1995) (citations omitted).

Court noted in *Powers*: "Although '[a]n individual juror does not have a right to sit on any particular petit jury . . . he or she does possess the right not to be excluded from one on account of race.'"[19] By ensuring that no juror is struck for constitutionally impermissible reasons, the *Batson* procedure allows the community's interests to manifest in criminal jury selection. As the Court concluded, when a juror is illegally stricken under *Batson*, harm is done not only to the defendant, but also to the individual juror and the community at large, as the "harm from discriminatory jury selection extends beyond that inflicted on the defendant and the excluded juror *to touch the entire community*."[20] The competing offender and community aspects of the jury right undergird the entire body of law regarding peremptory challenges.[21]

The community's right to serve on a jury must be weighed against the defendant's right to an impartial jury. The *Batson* procedure manages to simultaneously balance both rights. Similarly, the guilty plea process can emulate this balancing act by utilizing a plea jury. Like the *Batson* procedure, my envisioned procedure of the plea jury strikes a middle ground between two competing interests: the efficiency of the guilty plea versus the need for community involvement in criminal adjudication.

There are a few important ways in which the local community, through the use of the plea jury, could be directly involved in the guilty plea. These procedures are supported both practically and through the use of expressive, restorative retribution, which, as we have seen, supports the Sixth Amendment jury trial right. Expressive, restorative retribution, as filtered through twenty-first-century mores, not only permits the community a true opportunity to exercise its jury trial right, but it also pushes offenders to take more responsibility for their wrongdoings, since the community is able to get involved in imposing punishment and restoring the balance disturbed by the offender's bad acts. This type of community involvement reestablishes a much-needed step, one that has long been missing from our criminal adjudication.

[19] *Powers v. Ohio*, 499 U.S. 400, 409 (1991).

[20] *Johnson*, 545 U.S. at 171–72 (emphasis mine); *See also Batson*, 476 U.S. at 87.

[21] *See* Nancy S. Marder, *Beyond Gender: Peremptory Challenges and the Roles of the Jury*, 73 TEX. L. REV. 1041, 1046 (1995).

THE PLEA JURY: PROCESS AND POLICY

Applying a collective jury right to the procedure of a guilty plea can seem rather counterintuitive. After all, the whole rationale for a guilty plea is to *eliminate* the jury aspect of the trial. But upon further inspection, incorporating the jury into the mechanics of the guilty plea is a positive both for the community and for reifying the substantive values underlying our criminal justice system. Before we explore the *why* of the plea jury, however, we should first look at the *how* – that is, how the plea jury would actually work.

First, it is helpful to briefly outline the rudiments of the modern guilty plea, which consists of several stages. First is the charging decision, a decision that is generally left almost entirely to the prosecutor's control and discretion.[22] In fact, sometimes even before the grand jury returns the indictment, the prosecutor and the defense counsel will have a preliminary meeting to discuss possible plea deals for the charged or potentially charged crimes.[23]

Usually, defense counsel will then meet with her client and advise him of a variety of matters, including his right to accept or reject a proposed plea bargain, the merits or demerits of the facts and the law, any plea offers made by the prosecutor, the consequences of accepting these offers, the range of the sentence if found guilty after trial, the necessary allocutions to be made to the court, and what, if any, fundamental rights will need to be waived.[24] Upon discussion with the client, defense counsel returns to the prosecutor[25] and either a deal is struck or bargaining continues until an agreement has been negotiated.[26]

Plea bargains, however, are not merely simple negotiations of guilt, acceptance, and sentence length. Today's guilty pleas often involve

[22] G. Nicholas Herman, Plea Bargaining 26 (2nd ed. 2004). At the screening phase, prosecutors tend to "err on the side of charging." Josh Bowers, *Punishing the Innocent*, 156 U. Pa. L. Rev. 1117, 1120, 1126 (2008).

[23] Herman, Plea Bargaining, *supra* note 22 at 62, 78.

[24] Herman, *id.* at 62–63. Granted, some plea deals are struck without defense counsel ever truly consulting the client, but I am charting how guilty pleas should be made, without reference to the shortcuts sometimes made in the heat of the moment.

[25] The defendant is rarely present for the plea negotiations between the prosecutor and the defense counsel. *See id.* at 79.

[26] *See id.* at 77–96.

haggling over such provisions as dismissing or reducing a charge against a third person, limiting the factual proffer or stipulation of facts, a defendant's cooperation or testimony against another party, a defendant's agreement to leave the jurisdiction, stipulating to testimony in another case, waiver of civil liability, and charge bargaining.[27] All of this complex bargaining, along with the resolution of matters normally decided within a more public and formal legal sphere, is now determined in private meetings between the prosecutor and the defense counsel, far from the public eye. Thus, the plea jury's participation is all the more important in the next step.

Once the plea bargain has been struck, it must be brought before the court to be finalized and approved.[28] In most plea agreements, the court has the ultimate power to accept or reject the plea agreement, which includes the imposition of sentence.[29] Thus, for a guilty plea to be accepted by the court, all three players must come before the court so the defendant can "take" his plea in front of the judge. Before the defendant can plead guilty, the court must advise him of all of his rights,[30] and it must also explore the factual basis for the plea during the defendant's allocution. This is where the plea jury would come into play.

In the standard guilty plea, a defendant makes an allocution to the particulars of his crime(s) before the court.[31] Formally, this is the time when the court determines whether the defendant's conduct was intentional and actually constituted the charged offense as well as whether the plea is knowing and voluntary.[32] This is where I envision the entrance of the plea jury.

[27] *See id.* at 93–94.

[28] *See* Div. for Pub. Educ., Am. Bar Ass'n, Steps in a Trial: Plea Bargaining, *available at* http://www.abanet.org/publiced/courts/pleabargaining.html.

[29] Herman, *supra* note 22, at 96. "Under . . . the Federal Rules of Criminal Procedure and rules of some state jurisdictions, a judge is expressly prohibited from participating in plea discussions." *Id.* However, some states, like Vermont, allow participation after counsel have reached an agreement. *Id.* at 96 n.31.

[30] *Id.* at 11–12. These rights include the right to a jury trial, to assistance of counsel at trial, to confront and cross-examine witnesses, and the right against self-incrimination. *Id.*

[31] *See, e.g.*, U.S. Attorneys' Manual, Title 9: Criminal Resource Manual § 623, *available at* http://www.justice.gov/usao/eousa/foia_reading_room/usam/title9/crm00623.htm.

[32] *See id.*

My plea jury proposal is relatively straightforward. The defendant would direct his plea to a special guilty plea jury, under the supervision of the trial court. The guilty plea jury would then make a three-part determination: (1) whether the facts stated fit the alleged crimes; (2) whether the plea was knowing and voluntary; (3) and whether the proposed sentence was appropriate.

To incorporate this plea jury more smoothly into the vast, bureaucratic machinery of guilty pleas, the jury would function as a cross between a grand jury and a petit jury.[33] Like a grand jury, it would serve more than once, for at least two weeks at a time. Like a petit jury, it would probably consist of twelve or fewer people. Like a grand jury, it would be comprised of people randomly selected from the community, with no peremptory or for-cause challenges to shape its ranks. Like the petit jury, it would focus primarily on the facts of the charged offenses, although in this case, the plea jury would also help determine whether the suggested punishment – both charge and sentence – was acceptable.

There would, however, be two important procedural differences between the plea jury and the petit jury and grand jury functions. First, with the plea jury, the watchful eye of the court would always be a buffer between any irrational or patently unfair jury decisions rejecting a proffered plea, on either charging or sentencing grounds. In other words, the trial court could, with proper discretion, reject or overturn a plea jury's decision on a plea deal if the court determined the decision was unreasonable.

Although I envision this discretionary oversight being used infrequently, the existence of a safety valve in the process would protect against common concerns about the jury, such as bias or ignorance, and it would be similar to the court's discretion over a criminal jury's "irrational" guilty verdict.

Second, with the plea jury, unlike with most criminal petit juries, there would be no requirement for unanimity. Instead, a majority vote would suffice.[34]

[33] For a detailed look on how the grand jury functions as a populist, community body and for a defense of its discretion, see Roger A. Fairfax, Jr., *Grand Jury Discretion and Constitutional Design*, 93 CORNELL L. REV. 703 (2008).

[34] Both Oregon and Louisiana permit nonunanimous jury decisions in criminal trials: Apodaca v. Oregon, 406 U.S. 404 (1972); Johnson v. Louisiana, 406 U.S. 356 (1972).

A crucial aspect of the plea jury's role is its part in listening to the defendant's allocution. Instead of pleading guilty and explaining his offenses solely to the judge, the defendant would now direct his plea and allocution to the plea jury. The plea jury would then determine whether the facts admitted by the defendant matched the original facts of the crime; whether the plea was knowing, willing, and voluntary; and whether the proffered sentence was appropriate. Although the court would still first need to advise the defendant about the nature of his offense, the range of statutory penalties, and the like, the defendant's actual allocution would be addressed primarily to the plea jury.

If the plea jury were to reject one or more aspects of the defendant's proposed plea, whether for reasons of involuntariness, lack of knowledge, disbelief in the factual proffer (i.e., that the specific defendant actually did the crime she admits in her allocution), or disagreement over the proposed punishment, then the defendant would have several options. First, the defendant could back out of the plea deal entirely and take her chances with a trial. Alternatively, the judge could grant a continuance, and during that time the prosecutor and the defense counsel could fashion a different plea deal, responding to the concerns of the plea jury. Finally, if the problem was a matter of sentencing, the plea jury could recommend an appropriate sentence for the crime committed, the final sentence to be ultimately refined and imposed by the court.[35]

In cases where the prosecution and defense counsel object that the plea jury's rejection of the proposed plea or sentence was unfair or biased, the presiding judge or magistrate could make a ruling determining the propriety of the plea jury's decision. If the decision violated any legal or ethical standard, the plea jury's conclusion could be overruled. Because the jury's conclusion would not be a formal verdict, the court's override would not violate any constitutional roles. Normally, however, under this scheme, the plea jury's decision would stand, whether favorable or unfavorable to the fate of the proposed plea agreement.

[35] In the federal system, the defendant's guilty plea and the court's imposition of sentence are usually two separate procedures. Therefore, it would be important to have the same plea jury convened for both the guilty plea and the sentencing hearing. This might mean that federal plea juries are called for a longer period – possibly two or three months, similar to the service of grand juries.

Although the inclusion of a lay jury into a traditionally bureaucratic, administrative-like proceeding such as a guilty plea may seem, at first glance, surprising or quixotic, incorporating a panel of community members into this important criminal adjudication has many benefits. There are substantive legal and theoretical values that are strengthened and improved by this integration of the public into the private workings of the criminal justice system.

It is no secret that our system of guilty pleas shortcuts many classic substantive and procedural values, ones taken for granted in criminal justice. The principles that justify our imposition of punishment in public jury trials rapidly disintegrate in the informal, private realm of plea agreements. This difference between "promise and performance, between text and reality,"[36] is particularly acute with guilty pleas because of the vast distance between the rights elaborated in the Sixth Amendment and the workings of the guilty plea process.

Meaningful lay participation, in the form of a plea jury, would shrink the current distance between the criminal law's "legitimizing promise and [the] systemic reality"[37] of guilty pleas. Moreover, the plea jury would inject some genuine adjudication into our system of plea bargains, something that is badly needed.[38]

One important way in which the plea jury would bridge this gap is in helping determine the voluntariness of the defendant's guilty plea. Although courts technically supervise the voluntariness of guilty pleas,[39] the reality is quite different. First, a prosecutor's immense power as both charging instrument and adjudicator of the guilty plea can compromise the defendant's ability to make a knowing and voluntary decision to relinquish constitutional rights.[40] The prosecutor's vast charging discretion includes her ability to manipulate the offenses on

[36] Markus Dirk Dubber, *American Plea Bargains, German Lay Judges, and the Crisis of Criminal Procedure*, 49 STAN. L. REV. 547, 548 (1997).

[37] *Id.* at 551 (arguing that our modern system of punishment has failed to live up to its legitimizing promise because of the hypocrisy pervading state punishment).

[38] *See* Langbein, *supra* note 5, at 126.

[39] *See* Abraham S. Goldstein, *Converging Criminal Justice Systems: The Guilty Plea and the Public Interest*, 49 S.M.U. L. REV. 567, 569 (1996) ("Judges have an affirmative obligation to police the guilty plea and with it the bargaining process.").

[40] *See* Tracy L. Meares, *Rewards for Good Behavior: Influencing Prosecutorial Discretion and Conduct with Financial Incentives*, 64 FORDHAM L. REV. 851, 852 (1995).

which the accused is charged,[41] both by charging offenses that may not be provable beyond a reasonable doubt at trial and by charging offenses higher than necessary to induce a plea on a lower charge.[42] These potential abuses of discretion affect the ability of the accused to plead guilty in a knowing and voluntary fashion, because they affect the offender's ability to accurately assess the risks and benefits of going to trial.[43]

This potential for abuse in plea bargaining is not necessarily balanced out by the role of defense counsel. Often, defense counsel feel that it is in the client's best interests – and their own – to follow in the path of a plea arranged almost entirely by the prosecutor.[44] Although under *Brady v. United States*[45] such induced pleas might technically meet the minimum legal definition of voluntariness, they do not fit our normative sense of what "voluntary" really means.

When the prosecutor unilaterally decides innocence or guilt along with the charged offense and sentence, plea proffers tend to become coercive.[46] Because the criminal defendant often does not have the same access to information as the prosecutor – discovery rules do not require the prosecution to give a defendant free access to information[47] – the prosecutor often acts as the sole judge and jury of the case.[48]

To compound this problem, the quick colloquy that the judge has with the defendant regarding the voluntariness of her plea is often rote and perfunctory for all participants. If the defendant parrots the correct phrases, the judge is unlikely to scrutinize the plea any further. This lack of scrutiny hinders the defendant's ability to avail herself of her

[41] *See id.* at 863.

[42] *Id.* at 864.

[43] *See id.* at 867.

[44] *Id.* at 869. This is often due to defense counsel's heavy caseload and the hope of continuing the relationship with the prosecutor in the future. *Id.*

[45] 397 U.S. 742, 745 (1970) (holding that a guilty plea encouraged by the fear of a possible death sentence was legal because it was both voluntary and intelligent). However, the meaning of "voluntary" differs in different criminal contexts. Meares, *supra* note 40, at 872. For example, the voluntariness standard for confessions is much more stringent than the voluntariness standard for guilty pleas. *Id.* at 872.

[46] *See* Máximo Langer, *Rethinking Plea Bargaining: The Practice and Reform of Prosecutorial Adjudication in American Criminal Procedure*, 33 AM. J. CRIM. L. 223, 224 (2006).

[47] *See* Richard A. Rosen, *Disciplinary Sanctions Against Prosecutors for* Brady *Violations: A Paper Tiger*, 65 N.C. L. REV. 693, 695 (1987).

[48] *See* Langer, *supra* note 46, at 224.

full due process rights.[49] The trial court's inquiry into voluntariness should be made with full appreciation that the plea takes place in a questionable context and framework,[50] but it rarely is.

Although judges could certainly take a more active role in reviewing plea bargains, due to their institutional role they are in a weak position to actually do so. In part because of separation-of-powers concerns, courts are poorly situated to oversee prosecutorial charging decisions or factual bases for these charges.[51] Indeed, judges rarely interfere with "discretionary decisions over charges or plea bargains."[52] Considering the "crowded dockets and little personal or institutional investment in the resolution of particular cases,"[53] judges lack incentives to scrutinize plea deals.

In addition, judges are major beneficiaries of the guilty plea's efficiency, resulting in even less motivation to carefully question a defendant's allocution. Finally, claiming involuntariness on appeal to later overturn the plea is not often successful, leaving the voluntariness of defendants' pleas virtually without scrutiny.

In sum, there is rarely, if ever, any deep investigation by the court into government practices that may have helped induce the plea. As Markus Dubber has dryly noted, "American courts have fallen into the comfortable habit of regarding defendants who complain about involuntary pleas as smooth operators who copped a deal with the assistance of a savvy defense lawyer."[54]

Allowing a plea jury to determine voluntariness, however, helps break this troubling pattern. Inserting a representative section of the lay public into the guilty plea process injects a fresher, less jaded audience to listen to and determine whether the plea is actually voluntary. Insiders, like trial courts, which hear hundreds of guilty pleas a

[49] *See, e.g.*, Dubber, *supra* note 36, at 598 (contending that "[s]ince courts do not seriously scrutinize the voluntariness of guilty pleas, the Due Process clause effectively does not apply to the vast majority of criminal proceedings in the United States").

[50] *See id.*

[51] *See* Albert W. Alschuler, *The Trial Judge's Role in Plea Bargaining*, 76 COLUM. L. REV. 1059, 1075 n.59 (1976).

[52] *See* Stephanos Bibas, *Prosecutorial Regulation Versus Prosecutorial Accountability*, 157 U. PA. L. REV. 959 (2009).

[53] Russell Covey, *Fixed Justice: Reforming Plea Bargaining with Plea-Based Ceilings*, 82 TUL. L. REV. 1237, 1267 (2008).

[54] *See* Dubber, *supra* note 36, at 598.

year, generally do not pay much attention to a plea's voluntariness unless the level of involuntariness or coercion is extreme.[55] In contrast, an outsider body[56] like the plea jury would likely scrutinize each defendant's level of voluntariness with much more care, by virtue of its lack of cynicism and more open views about the process. Moreover, this reinvigorated scrutiny by the plea jury may well include an inquiry into the defendant's knowledge of the alleged facts.

A guilty plea cannot be considered voluntary unless the defendant is aware of the relevant circumstances and likely consequences of the guilty plea.[57] But the court's cursory assessment of the defendant's voluntariness might differ from an assessment by a plea jury, because the judge is often habituated to the rote articulations of the defendant's colloquy. Of course, judges definitely have a stake in plea bargains; they are invested in the procedure, at minimum, for the streamlining of their docket, and try to facilitate guilty pleas as much as possible.[58] This investment in smooth process can inure courts to the sometimes questionable voluntariness of the pleading defendant. Indeed, judges have seemingly abandoned the voluntariness part of the guilty plea inquiry, usually satisfying themselves with a pro forma statement from the defendant that her guilty plea was not coerced.[59]

A plea jury, on the other hand, can be more sensitive to whether the defendant is pleading guilty under any undue coercion or influence, by virtue of its multiple eyes. First, the amount of explanation required by a plea jury to understand the workings of an individual plea would

[55] *Id.* at 599 (contending that "plea hearings today are too perfunctory to ensure that even minimum voluntariness requirements for pleas have been met"); *see also* WILLIAM F. MCDONALD, U.S. DEP'T OF JUSTICE, PLEA BARGAINING: CRITICAL ISSUES AND COMMON PRACTICES 135 (1985) (explaining that courts deny a mere 2% of guilty pleas).

[56] For the concept of inside and outside players in the plea bargaining process, I am indebted to Stephanos Bibas. *See* STEPHANOS BIBAS, THE MACHINERY OF CRIMINAL JUSTICE (2012); Bibas, *Transparency and Participation in Criminal Procedure*, 81 N.Y.U. L. REV. 911 (2006).

[57] Brady v. United States, 397 U.S. 742, 748 (1970) (holding that standard as to voluntariness of guilty plea is that "a plea of guilty must be entered into by a person fully aware of the direct consequences" of plea).

[58] GEORGE FISCHER, PLEA BARGAINING'S TRIUMPH, *supra* note 9, at 175–80.

[59] Wright, *supra* note 2, at 93. Wright goes on to explain how the very environment of the guilty plea can be coercive, making voluntariness questionable, as the "size of the differential between the post-trial sentence and the post-plea sentence can become enormous." *Id.*

necessarily uncover much more of the prosecutor's charging decisions. A plea jury would likely require some minimal presentation of the evidence as well as all indictments made by the prosecutor's office. Such a presentation would not only clarify matters for the plea jury, but also allow the defendant to potentially reconsider her plea based on the evidence offered, permitting her to make a more meaningful decision on whether to plead guilty.

In addition, due to its outsider status, the plea jury can better understand and empathize with the defendant, who is thrown into the complex rules of the criminal justice system. A court's decision that a defendant understands the "direct consequences"[60] of a guilty plea may contain a very different calculus than that of laypeople. Even the most sophisticated defendant usually does not possess the understanding and general wherewithal commanded by the prosecution, defense counsel, and trial court.

In cases involving chemical impairment, a plea jury might be equally, if not better, suited to determine the voluntariness of the guilty plea. Legally, when a defendant informs the court of recent use of alcohol or drugs, "a court must inquire further into the defendant's mental state."[61] This brief colloquy usually satisfies the requirement of a "meaningful engagement" to further examine the defendant's state of mind.[62] Courts, however, are not any more qualified than laypeople to make a determination as to whether the defendant's plea, at the time of his allocution, is voluntary or knowing despite the potential use of any mind-altering substances.

Instead, having the lay public listen to the colloquy, and potentially ask its own queries in addition to the court's questions, could only improve the quality of the voluntariness inquiry. Cass Sunstein, among others, has argued that heterogeneous decision-making, in a group, is often superior to other types of decision-making.[63] There is an

[60] *Brady*, 397 U.S. at 748.

[61] *See Case Law Developments*, 31 MENTAL & PHYSICAL DISABILITY L. REP. 145, 204 (2007).

[62] *See id.*

[63] *See* Cass R. Sunstein, *Deliberative Trouble? Why Groups Go to Extremes*, 110 YALE L.J. 71, 109 (2000) (explaining that eliminating homogeneity in groups improves the deliberative process, because heterogeneous groups build identification "through focus on a common task rather than through other social ties, [and] tend to produce the best outcomes").

undeniable advantage to having a group, instead of a single actor, determine an important question such as voluntariness, since the breadth of a group's experience is necessarily much wider than that of a single individual, regardless of expertise.

The potential for greater diversity is another related benefit of having the plea jury, not the trial court, determine voluntariness. Although strides certainly have been taken in diversifying the bar and the bench, the fact remains that judges are primarily white[64] and defendants are often minorities.[65] The lack of diversity on the bench is true not only for race and national origin, but for gender, sexuality, and class as well.[66] Although there is no guarantee that any individual plea jury would contain an exact cross-section of the community statistically, it is far more likely that ten to twelve lay jurors would embody more racial, ethnic, gender, and class diversity than any one judge.

In sum, the combined experience, diversity, observation powers, and outsider status of a plea jury would provide a better voluntariness review in a defendant's guilty plea. As the Supreme Court has noted, "[A] plea of guilty is more than an admission of conduct; it is a conviction. Ignorance, incomprehension, coercion, terror, inducements, subtle or blatant threats might be a perfect cover-up of unconstitutionality."[67] If courts are too busy or too enmeshed within the system to properly examine the voluntary nature of a defendant's guilty plea, then the plea jury is nicely designed to fill in the gaps.

The plea jury also helps solve a number of more theoretical problems with the current guilty plea process. One of the defining characteristics of plea bargaining is that it "so often fails to internalize the laws that purport to govern it."[68] In other words, although scholars and courts have spent much time and effort defining the criminal law's rules and theoretical boundaries, it is all blithely cast aside when it comes to our most common criminal adjudicatory process.

[64] *See* Am. Judicature Soc'y, *Judicial Selection in the States – Diversity of the Bench, available at* http://www.judicialselection.us/judicial_selection/bench_diversity/index.cfm?state=.

[65] *See* Bureau of Justice Statistics, U.S. Dep't of Justice, Sourcebook of Criminal Justice Statistics tbl.6.28.2007 (2007).

[66] *See* Am. Judicature Soc'y, *supra* note 64, at *id.*

[67] Boykin v. Alabama, 395 U.S. 238, 242–43 (1969).

[68] Stuntz, *Criminal Law's Disappearing Shadow, supra* note 7, at 2568.

This is particularly true when it comes to Article III and the Sixth Amendment, both of which dictate lay participation as a critical element of punishment. As I discussed previously in Chapter 4, the Supreme Court's latest sentencing decisions seem to articulate a philosophy of expressive restorative retribution. Yet this entire philosophy – as well as Sixth Amendment jurisprudence generally – hinges on the inclusion of a jury as a representative of the community, something the current guilty plea procedure simply neglects. The gap between trial-based theory and the criminal justice reality of our criminal justice system exposes the absence of principled accounts of punishment imposition for guilty pleas.[69]

The use of a plea jury helps bridge this gap. Most obviously, it reintroduces the community back into most forms of criminal adjudication, thereby satisfying the constitutional and theoretical dictates of both Article III and the Sixth Amendment. More subtly, however, the use of the plea jury also provides a way to extend the Court's recent punishment philosophy to plea agreements. Only with the incorporation of the community can we extend the theoretical underpinnings of our system of punishment to the guilty plea.

These restorative, retributive underpinnings of our criminal justice system would be more fully realized with the use of an independent local body such as the plea jury, to ensure that the factual basis of the plea matches the offenses allegedly committed. There is too often a discrepancy that occurs between the observed and stated facts of the offense and the defendant's ultimate recital of facts.[70] This disconnect can make the guilty plea an unreliable measure of fair and accurate punishment. The gap is due to a number of factors, including prosecutorial overcharging and the resultant charge bargaining, deal making between the prosecution and defense counsel, and judicial disinterest.

Despite all these problems, it is extremely rare to have a plea agreement rejected because of discrepancies between the crime charged and the crime committed. This remains true even when the gulf between the

69 *See* Dubber, *supra* note 36, at 602 ("[A]ll too little thought has been expended on the question of how to choose among the multitude of possible systems of punishment imposition that would satisfy the vague and modest requirements of the Constitution.").

70 *See* David Yellen, *Probation Officers Look at Plea Bargaining, and Do Not Like What They See*, 8 FED. SENT'G REP. 339, 339 (1996).

two is so dramatic that even nonjudicial court officials have found cause for concern. In a recent study, 40 percent of federal probation officers believed that the majority of cases were not supported by offense facts that accurately and completely reflected all aspects of the case.[71] The disconnect frequently found between the crime committed and the crime charged has not, however, forced a change in plea procedure.

This issue is not merely a concern for court officials and those people involved in the criminal justice system; it has larger ramifications. When the crime for which the defendant is convicted has little or no relation to the crime that was committed, there is a distorting effect on the criminal justice system.[72] Too much distance between the actual offense and the punished offense collapses the retributive framework of punishment, because the link between the actual crime and the appropriate punishment is severed.

Having an offender recite the facts of her crime to a plea jury helps link the crime back to the proposed punishment. A layperson body such as the plea jury is much less likely to accept a plea of guilty to a vastly different crime than the reported offense and would likely be less tolerant of puzzling disconnects between the two.[73] If the plea jury is briefed prior to the allocution with a short summary of the facts, most likely from the pre-sentence report (which often contains witness statements, police reports, confessions, and the like), then it is more likely to spot any substantial divergence between the actual offense and the charged offense, as well as any contradictions among potential punishments. If the plea jury is comfortable with the lesser proposed punishment, then it may approve the plea agreement. If it is not, it can reject the agreement and direct the parties to find a closer fit between the crime committed and the crime charged.

Furthermore, the role of the plea jury as a listening body for the defendant's factual allocution provides a safety valve for defendants who have been pressured by prosecutors, and sometimes defense counsel, to accept convictions for crimes they did not commit. A defendant's

[71] *See id.*

[72] *See* Goldstein, *supra* note 39, at 574.

[73] This is because a plea jury, as members of the local community, arguably would want to see some sort of retributive justice occur, and thus presumably would desire some correlation between the reported offense and the convicted offense.

obvious discomfort with or patent lack of knowledge about the crime to which she is supposedly pleading guilty is often overlooked or even ignored by the court, as long as the defendant can stumble through the facts. With the use of the plea jury, however, the formal processes of presenting the lay jury with the facts of the offense immediately before the defendant's allocution will make the jury more focused on the actual particulars of the committed crime. This knowledge will help warn the plea jury when a defendant is entirely unfamiliar with the specifics.

Allowing the plea jury to hear and weigh the factual basis of the plea agreement thus helps reestablish the theoretical link between the imposed punishment and the committed offense. The importance of retaining such a link – particularly in a world where more and more acts are criminalized – helps tether the apparatus of the guilty plea to both punishment theory and retributive practice itself, two bases of our criminal justice system.

Now that we've dealt with the how, it is time to address the why. Restoring this community voice to the imposition of punishment within the plea process serves both theoretical and practical interests. As I expand upon below, these positive aspects include the public's increased understanding of the criminal justice system, a restoration of criminal adjudication's educative function, a better fit between imposed punishment and the constitutional theory of the Sixth Amendment, and greater moral consensus among the community.

First, and most basically, the current guilty plea process functions out of sight of the average citizen, because modern plea procedure prevents the public from learning about the defendant's crime.[74] The guilty plea hides the criminal justice process from the community in two ways: (1) citizens do not get to decide the proper punishment for community wrongdoers; and (2) the community does not get to publically be informed of misconduct by offenders, except in notorious cases. This can create not only transparency concerns but also ethical problems, because either the prosecutor or the defense might negotiate a plea agreement to cover up other matters, including police misconduct, wide-scale fraud, or undiscovered crimes.

[74] Wright, *supra* note 2, at 81.

The public has a very real interest in uncovering these issues. Requiring plea agreements to pass before the eyes of a plea jury would at least partially illuminate back-door dealings, because any major discrepancies between the original charges and offense descriptions and the details of the agreement would be scrutinized by community members. In addition, enhancing local, popular participation within an existing criminal justice institution, such as the plea bargain, combines the positive attributes of community involvement with no need for new courts or upheaval of the existing system.

True, the prosecutor is both technically and legally the public's representative. As the Supreme Court noted over seventy years ago, the prosecution's interest "is not that it shall win a case, but that justice shall be done."[75] This role as the people's representative, however, frequently gets subsumed by a gradual inclination to sympathize with the prosecuting ethos and desire to achieve a positive win-loss record. Often, concepts of "public interest" or "justice" are too diffuse and elastic to constrain prosecutors.[76] A prosecutor's simultaneous representation of both the state and the people can get lost in the everyday details of doing her job.

Many prosecutors, in an effort to strengthen their plea bargaining position, regularly charge offenses that either do not fit the crime or that they have no plan to take to trial. As a result, the office of the prosecutor often turns a blind eye to practices such as pressuring defendants to take unfavorable pleas or offering pleas that do not properly consider societal interests. Thus, the goals of the individual prosecutor are often incongruent with those of the public.[77]

Defendants, in contrast, are (understandably) primarily focused on their own immediate problems[78] and are rarely concerned with broader

[75] Berger v. United States, 295 U.S. 78, 88 (1935).

[76] *See* Bibas, *Transparency and Participation in Criminal Procedure*, *supra* note 56, at 961.

[77] *See* Stephen J. Schulhofer, *Plea Bargaining as Disaster*, 101 YALE. L.J. 1979, 1987 (1992). Schulhofer goes on to explain how a district attorney's goals (such as a high conviction rate, a good relationship with influential private attorneys, an absence of high-profile losses) can differ from the goals of a frontline prosecutor (such as career advancement, job satisfaction, manageability of cases), further complicating the matter. *Id.* at 1987–88.

[78] Although, as a recent report from the Vera Institute illustrates, a plea bargain is not always the best result for a defendant either. In the county of New York, black and Latino defendants were much more likely to obtain a custodial sentence after a plea bargain than whites or Asians, with blacks being 13% more likely and Latinos 5% more likely to receive

principles of legality or public interest. And as I discussed above, courts are concerned with proportionality and neutrality, not with validating the people's rights. The three major players in the guilty plea process, then, fail to represent the public interest in any meaningful way. As a result, the public "lose[s] faith in a system where the primary goal is processing and the secondary goal is justice."[79]

Far too frequently, reviewing guilty pleas outside of the standard plea bargain process is necessary because none of the actors involved can be relied upon to protect the public interest.[80] Although opinions differ as how to best achieve this goal, one way to inject public scrutiny and accountability is through the use of the plea jury. Like a trial, a plea proceeding is normally open to the public, which permits any member of the community to attend and observe. Unlike trials, however, the average plea proceeding is rarely publicized or scheduled openly, making it highly unlikely that even interested community members would attend. The plea jury, in contrast, indelibly inserts the public into the process.

Ultimately, through the vehicle of the plea jury, the community will come to understand that criminal justice is an open, accessible proceeding by participating in the process. Through repeated involvement in guilty pleas, the community will come to better understand how the system adjudicates and punishes crime, which itself will help educate the public about how criminal justice actually works. Through citizen involvement, the "cynicism and contempt"[81] for the criminal justice system that is invariably created by secretive proceedings will be minimized.

Equally important, the current complex, behind-the-scenes machinations of guilty pleas can greatly frustrate the public. Where the initial charges and the ultimate charge and punishment are incongruent

prison time than other defendants. *See* Besiki Kutateladze, Whitney Tymas & Mary Crowley, *Race and Prosecution in Manhattan* viii (Vera Institute, July 8, 2014), located at http://www.vera.org/sites/default/files/resources/downloads/race-and-prosecution-manhattan-technical.pdf.

79 Wright & Miller, *supra* note 4, at 33.

80 *See* Wright, *supra* note 2, at 96. Wright is not the only scholar to hold this view. *See* Schulhofer, *Plea Bargaining as Disaster*, *supra* note 77, at 1985–90 (contending that prosecutors and defense counsel both ignore issues of the public interest in plea agreements).

81 Kenneth Kipnis, *Plea Bargaining, A Critic's Rejoinder*, 13 LAW U[.] SOC'Y REV. 555, 557 (1979).

and this discrepancy is never publicly explained, there can be disappointed expectations and, often, community demoralization. Relatedly, the prosecutor sometimes authorizes pleas to nonexistent, inapplicable, or time-barred crimes, or sentences that the public has not legally authorized through statute. These prosecutorial actions further frustrate the public. Finally, some plea agreements include the closure of court proceedings and sealing of court records, eliminating the opportunity for public scrutiny.[82] Allowing the lay public into the courtroom to weigh these choices will, at minimum, shed light onto the process for the community. The public may also have concerns that innocent defendants are pleading guilty or that the criminal justice system allows defendants to barter away constitutional rights for a lesser punishment. Thus, a lay citizen's integration into the guilty plea process, through participation in the plea jury, can either stop some of these practices (pleas to nonexistent crimes or nonstatutory sentences), solve some other concerns (inclusion of the community, through the plea jury, in closed or sealed proceedings), or eliminate concern over much of the rest of the problems inherent in guilty plea practice (by personally scrutinizing the defendant's allocution for innocence or coercion).

In addition, the local jury's ability to integrate community values into criminal justice decision making helps the jury fulfill one of its primary duties under the Constitution, resisting the governmental abuse of power against the public, as well as counteracting any judicial bias or corruption. The fact that the jury has been entirely eliminated from the current plea process means that the experiences of average members of society have also been eliminated from the criminal justice system.

Finally, criminal law plays a critical part in helping sustain the moral agreement needed to maintain social norms in our diverse society. The jury, as representative of the community, needs to participate in all forms of criminal punishment, because this community determination of social norms is invariably the only decision that can override cultural and ethnic differences.[83] By eliminating the role of the jury, our current guilty plea procedure robs us of an important norm-creating

[82] *See* Joseph A. Colquitt, *Ad Hoc Plea Bargaining*, 75 TUL. L. REV. 695, 740 (2001).

[83] *See* Paul H. Robinson, *Competing Conceptions of Modern Desert: Vengeful, Deontological, and Empirical*, 67 CAMBRIDGE L.J. 145, 154 (2008).

opportunity in the realm of criminal justice. Restoring jury participation to this most common of criminal procedures likewise restores the community's role in creating meaningful social norms.

THE POWER OF ALLOCUTION

The plea jury's role in hearing the defendant's allocution gives it much of its power. This feature of the guilty plea process is central to the plea jury's ability to change aspects of the procedure for the better – in practical, theoretical, and normative ways.

One key aspect of the plea jury is its role as an outsider. A vast gulf divides insiders and outsiders in the criminal justice system. Insiders, such as prosecutors, defense counsel, and judges, possess power and knowledge, while outsiders, such as crime victims, bystanders, and the general public, frequently feel excluded and confused.[84] This divide creates a tension between the two groups, which hinders the public's faith in law's legitimacy and blocks the criminal law's moral, instrumental, and expressive goals. With the guilty plea rate as high as it is, outsiders undergo considerable frustration when they are excluded from the workings of the criminal justice system.

The plea jury fits in nicely as a kind of innovation to help fix this insider/outsider problem. Regarding transparency, the plea jury opens a window into the workings of the criminal justice system, highlighting hidden processes such as the work of the probation officer, the pre-sentence report, and the function of post-release supervision, as well as better illuminating the sentencing statutes and guidelines, state or federal, that constrain and shape punishment. Because part of the role of the plea jury is to study the pre-sentence report and the descriptions of the crime before hearing the plea, the public gains a much wider understanding about the complex mechanisms of substantive criminal law and criminal procedure.

Since most hearings, including plea hearings, are not well publicized, having a formal mechanism to incorporate the lay public into important criminal process will unquestionably shed light into the

[84] *See* Bibas, *Transparency and Participation in Criminal Procedure*, *supra* note 56, at 912–13.

black hole. This transparency has important trickle-down benefits. The public will have a more realistic understanding of criminal penalties and the proportionality of sentences, with better access to and comprehension of how guilty pleas work. As a result, hopefully the community will rely somewhat less on stereotypes, news stories, and media hysteria to round out its understanding of criminal justice.[85]

The participatory benefits of the plea jury similarly accrue. There are few roles for the public in the modern criminal justice system. Grand juries are controlled by prosecutors, jury trials are few and far between, the local public has virtually no role at sentencing hearings, and both incarceration and post-release supervision often occur far away from the community. At most, the public can affect the practice of criminal law by electing district attorneys and judges or through referendums, and even this is relatively hands-off and controlled by imperfect information. Thus, the plea jury supplies a way for many different citizens to partake in the practice and imposition of criminal justice, one that is frequent, inclusive, thoughtful, and meaningful – an exercise that has become increasingly rare in the modern era.

The plea jury also helps mend the substantive gulf between criminal procedure and criminal values. By better fostering the lay public's understanding of criminal process and by clarifying the link between crimes and specific penalties, the plea jury both educates the community as a whole and reinforces retributive justice, which requires that offenders must know the punishment for crimes before they are committed.

The plea jury's scrutiny of the defendant's allocution and proposed plea agreement requires deliberation of whether the actual crime matches up with the pled crime, as well as whether the crime is properly punished by the proposed penalty. This kind of a review of the defendant's enumerated crimes and potential punishments will not only help impose proper punishments, but will also hopefully assist in bringing home the lessons of retributive justice in a concrete way. Indeed, "the

[85] *See id.* at 927. Importantly, Bibas explains how constant "misperceptions about average sentences fuel spiraling sentences and discontent with criminal justice. Because voters are badly misinformed, they clamor for tougher sentences, three-strikes laws, and mandatory minima across the board." *Id.* at 929.

criminal law's most important real-world effect may be its ability to assist in the building, shaping, and maintaining of these norms and moral principles."[86]

Local citizens are also more likely to think that the criminal justice system is fair if they have had a direct part to play in its workings. This is especially true if the community helps impose punishment on offenders who have, more likely than not, committed crimes in the local neighborhood. If impenetrability reduces the public's belief in the law's legitimacy, then the plea jury, by participating in the sentencing of the community's wrongdoers, permits the public to see how guilty pleas work both procedurally and substantively. This, in turn, allows some lost trust in the system to be rebuilt. There is an unmistakable value in reassuring the outside public that guilty pleas are not exercises in self-serving or random lenience for the insiders, but rather a principled and fairly conducted practice.[87]

The plea jury also assists in inculcating public preference directly into the criminal law. There are few, if any, majoritarian ways in which the citizenry may straightforwardly affect change in any administrative-type body, let alone one as important as the criminal justice system. Having the community partake in an active process like the plea jury cannot replace the power and consequence of the jury trial, but it is a decent compromise: the lay public still gets to decide whether a defendant's punishment is acceptable, but there is no tremendous sacrifice in efficiency or procedural change. Combined, potentially, with proposed restraints on charge bargaining and sentence bargaining, the plea jury procedure could bridge the worst aspects of the insider/outsider gulf while improving the system's fairness, transparency, and legitimacy.

Finally, there is undeniably an important civic interest in having some inquiry and adjudication occur in front of the community, particularly for a serious crime. Allowing the public to learn, through the use of the plea jury, the circumstances of the crime and the proposed punishment provides a positive externality. Although there is not the public expiation of a trial, the plea jury provides at least some measure of how our institutions have responded to current events.

86 Robinson, *supra* note 83, at 148.
87 *See* O'Hear, *supra* note 11, at 216.

The plea jury strikes a balanced medium between the need for fairness and probity and efficiency requirements. The reality of the modern criminal justice system prevents any significant increase in full jury trials due to time, money, and processing costs. But the guilty plea system has become increasingly problematic. We have moved primarily to a de facto administrative regime "where prosecutors interpret the law and adjudicate cases without written standards or hearings"[88] and the usual constitutional rights surrounding criminal procedure are largely irrelevant or ignored. The adversarial system inherent in the jury trial has been replaced with a balancing of faulty bargains on one end against faulty bargains on the other, attempting to approximate justice.

The plea jury spans the gap between full-blown jury trials and unregulated plea agreements. The guilty plea process as a whole is relatively untouched; the prosecutor and the defense counsel may still bargain as they will to dispose of cases, retaining the efficiency gained when the formal adversarial process is bypassed. And integrating the selection of the plea jury into the already-existing apparatus for calling and selecting both petit and grand jurors is as simple as accessing the data rolls and choosing a body of jurors randomly selected from the community. Thus, the plea jury can efficiently be called and chosen from the extant jury rolls and sent to whichever courtroom and judge has need of them for the day.

Because the plea jury would serve for a minimum of two weeks, their required training would not need to be excessive. As a benchmark, we routinely expect petit juries to absorb an immense amount of complex legal information in a short period of time during jury instructions. Therefore, it does not seem unrealistic to expect a panel of citizens to be able to understand its role in examining the voluntariness, knowingness, and factual basis of the defendant's plea, along with the appropriate level of punishment within a sentence structure.

The most important task of the plea jury – to weigh the voluntariness and truthfulness of the defendant's allocution – provides the lynchpin between the current state of the jury trial and the guilty plea. Through the plea jury, the lay public gets to participate in the guilty plea process,

[88] Susan R. Klein, *Enhancing the Judicial Role in Criminal Plea and Sentencing Bargaining*, 84 TEX. L. REV. 2023, 2027 (2006).

but only in a traditional, jury-like capacity: determining the truthfulness of the defendant, the voluntary nature of the testimony, and the crimes for which the defendant should be held liable. The plea jury's responsibility in helping assess the appropriateness of the agreed-upon punishment is paralleled in the work of sentencing juries, an aspect of jury trial now common in many states.[89]

Equally important, however, the function of the plea jury – listening to and weighing the defendant's allocution and proposed punishment – is limited in nature. It does not interfere with the prosecutor's or the defense counsel's normal roles in shaping the initial agreement. It does not require the lay public to have any extra knowledge of criminal law or sentencing. And it does not usurp the traditional role of the judge in managing and supervising all legal functions that come before her court.

There is a strong need for predictability in our current plea-heavy criminal justice system. Having a plea jury would continue that predictability, as the procedure would inject a familiar element into the plea process while roughly maintaining the plea's current structure. The participation of both the plea jury and the court in the guilty plea allows these two bodies to function as proper ballasts to the power of prosecutors, injecting more procedural and substantive fairness into the process. By balancing the enormous discretion of prosecutors with the scrutinizing power of the plea jury and the oversight of the court, we could reach a middle ground – admittedly imperfect, but definitely an improvement.

Another important benefit of integrating a plea jury within the guilty plea process is the power of expressing social norms. One of the most powerful aspects of the plea jury's part in evaluating the defendant's allocution is its expressive role. Traditional jury trials have a strong expressive element to them, because any crimes for which the offender is accused are publicly aired out and determined in a community arena.

This expressive element, however, is completely absent in the current guilty plea process, where the defendant's rote allocution to the court is simply an empty rehearsal of the deal made in private by the prosecutor and the defense counsel. Although technically held in a

[89] For more on noncapital sentencing juries, see Nancy J. King & Roosevelt L. Noble, *Jury Sentencing in Non-Capital Cases: Comparing Severity and Variance with Judicial Sentences in Two States*, 2 J. EMPIRICAL LEGAL STUD. 331 (2005).

public courtroom, guilty pleas are poorly publicized, if at all. Even victims of the crimes frequently do not receive notice of or attend guilty pleas. Because public display is still an important part of our modern criminal justice system, we should increase the legitimacy of the guilty plea itself by making these private machinations both public and meaningful.

The offender's allocution to the plea jury works its expressive power in a variety of ways. First, the involvement of a more impartial body such as the plea jury helps give the impression of fairness to the general public. The public understandably feels that justice is best left in the hands of more neutral decision-makers, such as the plea jury and the judge. This is particularly true because the procedures surrounding the guilty plea are relatively untouched by constitutional regulation. The combination of the judge and the plea jury in the allocution process means that the community is better able to trust the conviction and sentence resulting from a guilty plea. This trust forms a direct link between public participation and public confidence in the administration of justice. By having a plea jury participate in the open allocution, the public gains a far better understanding of how the criminal justice system approaches, judges, and punishes crime.[90]

If part of the court's role in American society is helping express our social values,[91] then the public's ability to see the community impose these values, through the work of the plea jury, is particularly useful. By requiring the criminal justice system to incorporate the lay public into the guilty plea process, the plea jury helps signal to everyone that fairness and procedural due process is an intrinsic part of the criminal justice system, one that cannot be eliminated by the defendant's waiver of his jury trial right.

The plea jury allocution also has value for the defendant. By openly admitting her guilt and articulating her offenses to the plea jury, the defendant is able to publicly accept her blameworthiness and show remorse to the community. In so doing, she is able to fulfill a key aspect of jury trials – the outward expression of guilt. Because the defendant is willingly admitting her wrongdoing and asking for a reduced sentence, she not only shows the community an acceptance of her responsibility,

[90] *See* Wright & Miller, *supra* note 4, at 34.

[91] *See* Robert Cooter, *Expressive Law and Economics*, 27 J. LEGAL STUD. 585, 586 (1998).

but also publicly reinforces the link between offense and societal punishment.

Furthermore, the acknowledgment of wrongdoing to a plea jury may well have a positive effect on the defendant. By allocuting only to the trial court, the defendant is likely to attribute her punishment to the state and shrug off the appropriate feelings of responsibility or awareness of her wrongdoing. In contrast, when there is a subsection of the community listening to her admission of guilt, the wrongdoer has more difficulty avoiding the burden of criminal responsibility, because her fellow citizens, her community, and her peers have both literally and figuratively become part of the expiation process. The plea jury's seal of approval on the proposed sentence impresses upon the defendant that the public has had at least some say in the punishment, even if the actual bargaining was done between the prosecutor and the defense counsel.

If the public has lost faith in a criminal justice system where the first step is processing and the secondary step is justice,[92] then a visible, plein air guilty plea process and public allocution facilitates renewed belief in the workings of criminal procedure. The plea jury's role provides a public resolution of the offense without requiring a full jury trial, and the requirement that the defendant allocute directly to the panel fosters more responsibility and acceptance of wrongdoing.

The defendant's allocution to the plea jury is also a significant feature in the context of restorative justice. By admitting her crimes to a subsection of the community, the offender literally *pleads* to the community itself, and not only for the reduced sentence or punishment that she hopes will be approved. In accepting culpability for her bad acts, the defendant acknowledges her communal breach and asks for mercy and reconciliation. This is even more powerful if the victim is also in the courtroom listening to the allocution and plea.

As we discussed previously, restorative justice removes the offender, victim, and community from their usual passive roles, encouraging all three to become actively involved in resolving the conflict. The plea jury's removal of the guilty plea from the back rooms of the criminal justice system, while also creating a role for the community, plays an integral role in facilitating restorative justice.

[92] *See id.* at 33.

The community as a whole is also more likely to allow the offender to be eventually restored to its good graces if it has heard her acknowledgement of wrongdoing. When it is time for the offender to be released from whatever punishment has been imposed, the community, having literally seen and heard the offender's plea of guilt through its work as the plea jury, will potentially be more willing to forgive the offense and move on. Having been given a measure of empowerment by hearing the defendant's allocution, the local public will hopefully be more willing to allow the offender back into the neighborhood and local polity, whether by restoring felon voting rights, allowing halfway houses in the community, assisting with job training, or supporting other important reintegrative procedures.

The transformative potential inherent in the plea jury's restorative-justice aspect is one that has been little explored since the decline of rehabilitation forty-odd years ago. The plea jury allocution helps bridge the gap between the accused, the victim, and the community, reuniting compassion and punishment, re-envisioning justice as a community mandate.[93]

Finally, having a plea jury helps inculcate an important aspect of deliberative democracy into the criminal justice process. This is partially because the jury is generally acknowledged as a critical part of democratic government. The creation of jury-like systems in new democracies illustrates how important the incorporation of citizens into legal decision-making can be to polities seeking democratic legitimacy.[94] Indeed, citizen participation in lawmaking promotes democracy, because the express participation of community members enhances the legal system's legitimacy, widening its receptivity to local values. Such popular participation in legal deliberation, via the plea jury, provides a way for citizens to resolve moral disagreements in a quasi-public sphere, using collective, reasoned discussion.[95]

[93] *See* Anthony V. Alfieri, *Community Prosecutors*, 90 CAL. L. REV. 1465, 1479 (2002). Alfieri makes a similar point about drug courts.

[94] *See* Valerie P. Hans, *Introduction: Citizens as Legal Decision Makers: An International Perspective*, 40 CORNELL INT'L L.J. 303, 306 (2007).

[95] *See* Jeffrey Abramson, *Two Ideals of Jury Deliberation*, 1998 U. CHI. LEGAL F. 125, 125 (1998).

The very diversity of the plea jurors also encourages the group to entertain arguments that ultimately move them toward mutually acceptable outcomes. The more reflective the jury is of diversity in society, the better it will democratically embody the beliefs of the community it represents. Only a representative jury, one drawn randomly from a representative cross-section of the population, can truly make legitimate decisions for its community. A representative jury not only provides democratic decision-making, but it also exposes each juror to the diversity within his or her actual community.

The democratically deliberating jury is also a local jury. Only the local citizen can truly bring the values of the community into the courtroom, whether for a trial or a plea bargain. Although "strangers" can equally hand down the law, they would not bring the peculiar standards and morals that only those living in the actual community would truly know.

Jury service is the primary way in which this country incorporates its citizens into the legal process, whether in grand juries or petit juries. Although surface complaints about the inconvenience of jury service are common, post-trial surveys of jurors who have actually served have shown that jury service seems to produce public support for both the courts and the legal system.[96] As the Jury and Democracy Project has shown through its research, jury service has strongly positive effects on civic participation and engagement.[97] In general, the jury may more powerfully promote democracy and citizenship than any other type of organization.[98]

Jury service through the petit jury has been drastically reduced over the past thirty years, and this elimination of civic participation may come with hidden costs for both democratic principles and political participation. To begin with, eliminating or sharply reducing jury service directly affects the ability of citizens to interact, not only with each other but also with the polity. Jury service permits political participation that can be, among other things, inspiring, empowering, educational,

[96] *See* Hans, *supra* note 94, at 306.

[97] *See* John Gastil, Perry Dress, Phil Weiser & Cindy Simmons, The Jury and Democracy: How Jury Deliberation Promotes Civic Engagement and Political Participation (2010).

[98] *See id.*

and habit forming,[99] mediating the divide between the state, political society, and civil society (which includes the individual and the community).

In addition, recent studies have suggested that those who participate in jury duty are more likely to vote. More specifically, the enhancement in voting occurs only with participation in criminal, not civil, trials, and it happens with any jury body that deliberates. This means that participation in a plea jury would also likely provide such a benefit. Another benefit that results from criminal jury participation is, interestingly, increased activity in charitable groups by those jurors who decided on a guilty verdict, perhaps inspired by a desire, conscious or not, to further improve their community. Reviving jury service through the use of a plea jury, then, would provide all of these positive externalities, in addition to restoring classic criminal procedure values such as voluntariness, expressive retribution, and articulation of the public interest.[100]

Restoring interest, power, and accountability to the local community is a critical step in fixing some of the current problems with our criminal justice system. There is a tremendous need to restore a populist aspect to the punishing and sentencing of criminal offenders. When the public feels too distant from the workings of crime and punishment, and only sees the media representation of crimes and the occasional (in)famous trial, they often react by calling for ever harsher and lengthy sentences. In contrast, allowing the community to participate in a much larger slice of criminal procedure gives the lay public a more realistic – and more personalized – view of the criminal justice system, hopefully fostering a less punitive streak.

As both a practical measure and a fundamental matter of political theory, the people should be involved in the machinations of criminal punishment. Our current system of plea bargains and guilty pleas cuts the lay public entirely out of the picture. Although there is no one perfect solution to the complicated reality of the guilty plea world, involving the community via the plea jury is one way to start, a way that reflects our constitutional history, our democratic structure of government, and our desire to ensure that criminal justice is both fair and proportional.

[99] *See id.*
[100] *See id.*

8 ERADICATING THE BENCH TRIAL

One simple yet meaningful way we can exercise the community jury trial right is by eliminating bench trials. Bench trials occupy an uneasy middle ground in the realm of the jury trial right. Neither a full waiver of the jury trial, such as a guilty plea, nor a carefully regulated criminal procedure such as a full jury trial, the bench trial is a strange beast. As such, it requires a full reevaluation under our new understanding of the community jury right.

Historically, bench trials have been highly disfavored. From the start of the colonial criminal justice system, jury trial waivers were "isolated instances" and "clear departures from the common law."[1] Indeed, until 1827, the English common law provided only a jury trial option to criminal defendants.[2] Following the adoption of the Constitution, bench trials were virtually unknown. Justice Story, while sitting on a Massachusetts case, contended that trial by jury was the only permissible method of trial.[3] State courts, in interpreting their own constitutions, espoused similar views.[4]

The Supreme Court originally expressed the view that the Constitution required the jury trial to be the exclusive method of determining guilt in all federal criminal cases.[5] By the 1930s, however, the Court rather reluctantly held that a criminal defendant "may forego" a

[1] Singer v. United States, 380 U.S. 24, 26 (1965).
[2] *Id.* at 28.
[3] United States v. Gibert, 25 F. Cas. 1287, 1294 (C.C.D. Mass. 1834) (No. 15,204).
[4] *Singer*, 380 U.S. at 32 n.6.
[5] *See* Thompson v. Utah, 170 U.S. 343, 354–55 (1898).

jury trial with the express consent of the government and the court.[6] The Court did note that "trial by jury has been established by the Constitution as the normal and ... preferable mode of disposing of issues of fact in criminal cases."[7] Importantly, though, various courts, including the Supreme Court, have held that there is no constitutional right to a bench trial.[8]

The modern bench trial was completely unimaginable in the eighteenth century,[9] when our criminal justice system was created. In an era when guilty pleas were themselves extremely uncommon, the idea of the accused waiving his right to a jury of his peers in favor of the government as sole fact finder would have been unthinkable. Today, although bench trials are common, they are fraught with problems, both practical and constitutional.

Part of the issue with bench trials is that the harms and losses created by the bench trial procedure are not remediated by the array of rights we currently assign to defendants. Such concerns include the trial court's singular power to grant or deny bench trial requests; the fiction that a court can simultaneously inhabit the role of both judge and jury; the use of bench trials as formalized plea deals when the defendant will not plead guilty but the defense counsel, the prosecution, and the court agree on punishment and sentence; the superior democratic deliberation and decision-making that jury trials provide; and the recently acknowledged acquittal gap between federal bench trials and federal jury trials.[10] All of these concerns about bench trials, combined with the original, historical understanding of the jury trial right, point to the need to eliminate, or at least substantially reduce, reliance upon this procedure.

6 Patton v. United States, 281 U.S. 276, 298 (1930). The Court noted that "the maintenance of the jury as a fact finding body in criminal cases [has] such importance and has such a place in our traditions." *Id.* at 312.

7 *Singer*, 380 U.S. at 35 (citation omitted) (internal quotation marks omitted).

8 *See, e.g., id.* at 36; Gannett Co., Inc. v. DePasquale, 443 U.S. 368, 416 (1979)[.]

9 *See* John Langbein, *Land without Plea Bargaining: How the Germans Do It*, 78 MICH. L. REV. 204, 269 (1978), noting that "In America, where the judiciary's association with the excesses of English colonial administration had led the framers to make jury trial a constitutional right, bench trial was all the harder to envision."

10 *See* Nancy J. King, David A. Soulé, Sara Steen & Robert R. Weidner, *When Process Affects Punishment: Differences in Sentences after Guilty Plea, Bench Trial, and Jury Trial in Five Guidelines States*, 105 COLUM. L. REV. 959, 968–69 (2005).

Of equal concern, using bench trials instead of having the traditional jury trial not only completely curtails the community's voice but also eliminates any public expressive aspect of criminal justice.[11] Although bench trials are not necessarily closed to the public, they are far less likely to attract attention or an audience, and the procedures obviously lack the participation of the community members required by jury trials. The open nature of the criminal jury trial right reflects that, as the Supreme Court has commented, "[w]hat transpires in the court room is public property."[12] This public facet is "an inescapable concomitant of trial by jury, quite unrelated to the rights of the accused."[13]

Likewise, Hale and Blackstone recognized that the public, communal nature of jury trial was essential, and each framed it not in terms of individual liberties but as part of the effectiveness of the common law trial process.[14] Without question, society has an interest in the public trial that is separate from the interests of the criminal defendant.[15]

Bench trials also provide the wrong view of "justice" to the accused, making it seem as if it is entirely the state, and not the community, that is handing down punishment. By contrast, jury trials, where the representatives of the local community literally pronounce a sentence, reflect "the notion, deeply rooted in the common law, that justice must satisfy the appearance of justice."[16] Stated differently, justice is less likely to be perceived as "just" if not deliberated by the defendant's peers and fellow community members. Moreover, the handing down of justice must be done openly, in the public sphere, to maintain the "confidence of the public in judicial remedies."[17]

Taking all of these bench trial irregularities into account, and keeping in mind the concern that a jury-less trial would have originally

[11] *See In re* Oliver, 333 U.S. 257, 270 n.24 (1948) (recognizing that the public aspects of trial provide various benefits to the community) (citation omitted); *see also* Gannett 443 U.S. at, 383 (noting that "great public interest in jury trials as the preferred mode of fact-finding in criminal cases" is one of the reasons why a defendant, standing alone, may not waive a jury trial (citation omitted)).

[12] Craig v. Harney, 331 U.S. 367, 374 (1947).

[13] *Gannett*, 443 U.S. at 419 (Blackmun, J., dissenting).

[14] *Id.* at 421.

[15] *See id.* at 427.

[16] Levine v. United States, 362 U.S. 610, 616 (1960) (citation omitted) (internal quotation marks omitted).

[17] *Gannett*, 443 U.S. at 429 (Blackmun, J., dissenting).

created, it may be time to consider eliminating the bench trial altogether. The rest of this chapter addresses six major problems with bench trials as they currently stand, all of which give additional reasons to eradicate – or severely curtail – the use of the criminal bench trial.

THE POWER SHIFT TO THE TRIAL JUDGE

One baseline problem with the bench trial is that it gives too much power to the trial court to decide whether the offender is permitted to have the bench trial in the first place.[18] The individual judge, and sometimes the prosecution as well, must approve the request.[19] Considering the Founders' deep concern that the government might seize the right to judge offenders, it is ironic that we have now strayed so far from this ideal that in a bench trial, it is *only* the government that decides whether the accused may dispense with the jury.

The need for approval from both the judicial and the prosecutorial arm of the state is one reason why the bench trial, as seen from the vantage of the community jury trial right, is deeply problematic. With a bench trial, the consideration of judgment is twice removed from the imprimatur of the community – first by the agreement of the prosecution, and then by the agreement of the court.

The removal of adjudicative decisions from the jury to the judge contains some philosophical shifts as well. As I previously discussed, the jury's role in adjudicating has some important normative, noninstrumental effects. The process of decision-making is both context-specific and underdetermined by the applicable legal rules.[20] Kyron Huighens has explained how, "in the interstices of the offense definition . . . [there is] some discretion over precisely what the law will require in specific

[18] In New York, the court must approve a defendant's request for a bench trial. N.Y. CRIM. PROC. LAW § 320.10(2) (McKinney 2014).

[19] *See, e.g.* FED. R. CRIM. P. 23(a) (providing that a criminal defendant may elect to be tried by the court rather than a jury, but that the court must "approve" the request and the government must also "consent").

[20] *See* Darryl Brown, *The Perverse Effects of Efficiency in Criminal Process*, 81 VA. L. REV. 183, 213 (2014).

circumstances."[21] How a judge interprets these open spaces is likely to be very different from how a jury does.

A jury's verdicts, then, can markedly differ from those of professional judges, in ways that common law jurisdictions tend to particularly value.[22] The differences between the bench trial and the jury trial are many, including variances in available evidence, legal and moral argument, modes of advocacy or persuasion, and the decision-maker's differing personas.[23]

Moreover, the legal fiction that a judge can simultaneously inhabit the judicial and jury roles without prejudice to the defendant has been repeatedly called into question.[24] The few empirical studies that have measured the trial judge's ability to disregard evidence have shown that judges have just as much difficulty with this as jurors.[25] And although evidentiary rules are meant to shield prejudicial information from fact finders, these rules apply far less rigorously in bench trials.[26] Thus, the proposition that judges can simultaneously be neutral arbiter and fact finder – a cornerstone belief of the bench trial – rests on shaky grounds.

In addition, judges can make as many mistakes as laypeople when acting as adjudicators. Judges often possess three types of blocks to processing information: informational blinders, cognitive blinders, and attitudinal blinders.[27] Regarding information blinders, as mentioned above, judges have difficulty disregarding information they have already internalized, even if it was for another purpose.[28] This means that having the same judge both rule on the motions as well as adjudicate the case is deeply problematic.

[21] Kyron Huighens, *Liberalism, Normative Expectations, and the Mechanics of Fault*, 69 MOD. L. REV. 462, 477 (2006) (book review).

[22] *See* Brown, *supra* note 20, at 213.

[23] *See id.*

[24] *See* Andrew J. Wistrich, Chris Guthrie & Jeffrey J. Rachlinski, *Can Judges Ignore Inadmissible Information? The Difficulty of Deliberately Disregarding*, 153 U. PA. L. REV. 1251 (2005); *see also* Jennifer L. Mnookin, Response, *Bifurcation and the Law of Evidence*, 155 U. PA. L. REV. PENNUMBRA 134, 136 (2006), *available at* http://www.pennumbra.com/responses/12-2006/Mnookin.pdf (questioning a judge's ability to fully set the evidentiary value of an excluded piece of evidence at zero).

[25] *See* Wistrich et al., *supra* note 24, at 1323 ("Judges are indeed human; like jurors, they are often unable to 'close the [v]alves of [their] attention.'" (citation omitted)).

[26] *See* Judith Resnik, *Managerial Judges*, 96 HARV. L. REV. 374, 408 n.137 (1982).

[27] *See* Chris Guthrie, *Misjudging*, 7 NEV. L. REV. 420, 420 (2007).

[28] *See id.* at 422.

Second, judges often struggle with cognitive blinders, including self-serving bias, all of which can cause systematic errors in decision-making.[29] Courts are particularly vulnerable to the self-serving bias, since they tend to be very sure of their adjudicatory skills.[30] Finally, judges also evidence attitudinal blinders, due to the inherently political nature of ascending to and remaining on the bench, whether state or federal.[31]

Although individual jurors are, of course, subject to each of these problems in their processes of decision-making, the group nature of the jury experience helps blunt the negative effects of these blinders on any individual jurors. Assuming that a jury contains members with diverse views, as it usually does, the mix of different ideas and experiences might attenuate the influence of individual attitudinal blinders on the outcome. Judges, in contrast, rule in solitary splendor in a bench trial, with nothing to shelter the defendant from any misjudging on the judiciary's part. Far from providing better decisions than juries, then, sometimes bench trials provide a worse adjudicatory result.

BENCH TRIALS AS SURREPTITIOUS PLEA DEALS

Another problem with bench trials is their occasional use as unofficial, formalized plea deals. Unlike Alford pleas,[32] where the defendant pleads guilty but does not admit to wrongdoing, the bench trial as unofficial guilty plea most often takes place when the accused does not wish to plead guilty but defense counsel, the prosecution, and the trial court agree on the offender's punishment and sentence. In this situation, the accused is seemingly given "his day in court," but the end result is preordained, often without the actual knowledge of the defendant. This

29 *See id.* at 429.
30 *See id.* at 437.
31 *See id.* at 440.
32 *See* North Carolina v. Alford, 400 U.S. 25, 37 (1970) ("An individual accused of crime may voluntarily, knowingly, and understandingly consent to the imposition of a prison sentence even if he is unwilling or unable to admit his participation in the acts constituting the crime."). Alford pleas themselves have recently come under attack. *See* Stephanos Bibas, *Harmonizing Substantive-Criminal-Law Values and Criminal Procedure: The Case of* Alford *and Nolo Contendere Pleas*, 88 CORNELL L. REV. 1361 (2003).

kind of backroom "justice" entirely violates both the defendant's and the community's right to a jury trial, and this is what the right to a jury trial was intended to prevent.

Although this particular issue can be alleviated with a proper colloquy between the court and the accused, ensuring that the defendant truly understands what is going on and what rights she is waiving to obtain a bench trial, stricter regulations need to be enforced by state and local legislatures to ensure that this type of backstairs, insider colluding does not occur, even when it is supposedly in the "best interests" of the defendant.

As we have discussed previously, one recurring problem with the lack of jury trials is that most criminal justice is negotiated – and disposed of – in the backrooms of justice, far from the understanding and the eyes of the average community member.[33] When even the defendant is not fully cognizant of the machinery of criminal justice whirring behind the scenes, it is time to eradicate, at minimum, this kind of winking bench trial/unofficial plea deal.

THE BENCH TRIAL ACQUITTAL GAP

Despite fears about nullifying juries, it is judges who are more likely to acquit defendants than their community counterparts. Recent empirical evidence has shown an acquittal gap between federal judges and federal juries, with courts more likely to acquit than juries.[34] Although defense lawyers may applaud this development, it is troubling that the federal judiciary acquits offenders at a statistically significant rate, considering that adjudicating wrongdoers was originally marked out as a role exclusively for the local community.

Given the history of the jury trial right as a tool to express the collective imprimatur, the continued use of the federal bench trial is problematic in light of new studies. Although a case for bench trials can potentially be made in extremely complicated white-collar criminal

[33] *See generally* STEPHANOS BIBAS, THE MACHINERY OF CRIMINAL JUSTICE (2012).
[34] *See* Andrew D. Leipold, *Why Are Federal Judges So Acquittal Prone?* 83 WASH. U. L.Q. 151 (2005).

cases, there are serious antidemocratic ramifications of having the federal judiciary make determinations of guilt or innocence.

State bench trials raise different concerns. There is some evidence that local state court judges are sometimes easier on DUIs than a proper jury would be. In Massachusetts, for example, a recent report showed that state Supreme Court judges were far more lenient in their conviction rates of those driving under the influence, with an acquittal rate of over 80 percent.[35] This is roughly 30 percentage points higher than the acquittal rate for juries for the same crime.[36] This type of discrepancy is deeply troubling, particularly if the trial judges in question are being overly lenient, as has been alleged.[37]

Furthermore, there is a considerable variation in how frequently state bench trials supplant jury trials. These variations are sometimes the product of deliberate attempts by state legislators and judiciaries to limit the jury trial right,[38] thus providing dramatically different criminal justice procedures to similarly situated defendants.

In particular, different state constitutional laws seem to explain some of the disparity between jury and bench trials in each state.[39] This is due in part to the variation in the Sixth Amendment jury trial right's "petty offense exception," which is generally deemed to be any offense that results in less than six months' imprisonment.[40] Since there is no jury trial right attached to petty offenses, how a state defines a certain offense – as a felony or a misdemeanor – can very much affect a defendant's ability to have a jury trial. Many state constitutions contain analogues to the Sixth Amendment that go above and beyond the standard federal jury trial right, but some do not. This creates unfairness and lack of uniformity among similarly situated defendants, varying wildly from state to state. Accordingly, states should be encouraged

[35] *See* Thomas Farrager, *For Drunk Drivers, a Habit of Judicial Leniency*, BOSTON GLOBE, Oct. 30, 2011, *available at* http://www.boston.com/news/local/massachusetts/articles/2011/10/30/for_drunk_drivers_a_habit_of_judicial_leniency/?page=full.

[36] *See id.*

[37] *See id.*

[38] *See* T. Ward Frampton, Comment, *The Uneven Bulwark: How (and Why) Criminal Jury Trial Rates Vary By State*, 100 CAL. L. REV. 183, 186 (2012).

[39] *See id.* at 198.

[40] *See, e.g.*, United States v. Nachtigal, 507 U.S. 1, 5 (1993).

to be generous with the jury trial right, especially since so few defendants will end up utilizing it when available.

MANIPULATING AWAY THE JURY TRIAL RIGHT

Beyond the difference in state constitutional jury trial rights, another, more disturbing factor in bench trial rates is a state's manipulation of charges and sentences to avoid the jury trial right trigger.[41] Often this manipulation is done precisely to avoid the costs of a proper jury trial, with the benefits of a reduced sentence to the defendant being merely a happy coincidence. But this kind of sentence manipulation ends up eliminating a whole class of offenses from even the possibility of community adjudication.

By widening the class of misdemeanors, which traditionally have a sentence of less than one year, a defendant may get to serve less time for certain minor crimes but now cannot be punished, even in theory, by the very community upon which she has perpetrated such offenses. Considering that most misdemeanors are committed not by strangers but by people within the same neighborhood or community, eliminating the jury trial right entirely takes away whatever power the people might have to disallow a jury trial, in every instance.

Equally disturbing is the prosecutorial trend to aggregate multiple petty offenses into one trial, each offense by itself failing to trigger the Sixth Amendment jury trial right but the offenses together easily exceeding the petty offense/misdemeanor minimum. The Supreme Court gave this practice constitutional muster in *Lewis v. United States*,[42] which held that the Sixth Amendment does not apply to prosecutions of multiple misdemeanors even if, altogether, the sentences result in imprisonment for greater than six months. This is a backdoor way of essentially requiring either a bench trial or a guilty plea for what can turn out to be substantive prison terms, and, as such, violates the spirit of the Sixth Amendment jury trial right.

[41] Specifically, New Jersey, Louisiana, Hawai'i, and the District of Columbia did precisely this to cut down on the number of jury trials required. *See* Frampton, *supra* note 37, at 202, 204.

[42] 518 U.S. 322 (1996).

Finally, many states attempt to pressure the accused into waiving their jury trial rights for the cheaper and easier (for the government, anyway) bench trial or guilty plea. For example, various states impose jury fees that require the defendant to pay a specific fee for the constitutional right to have a jury trial, usually following conviction.[43] For the poor, who make up the bulk of most defendants, these small fees can be prohibitive and negatively affect their ability to take full advantage of the criminal justice system.

DEMOCRATIC DELIBERATION AND IMPROVED DECISION-MAKING

There are a variety of arguments that privilege the decision-making abilities of juries over judges. Studies have shown that the decision-making processes of judges and juries can be very similar,[44] but only juries provide the democratic deliberation so critical to the workings of our democracy.

Fifty years ago, Harry Kalven noted how the jury, as a group of twelve, made better decisions than a single judge: "The distinctive strength and safeguard of the jury system is that the jury operates as a group. Whether twelve lay heads are better than one judicial head is still open to argument, but it should be recognized that twelve lay heads are very probably better than one."[45] This is so because rigidity sometimes comes on the heels of familiarity, so that an expert's accumulated experience and habituated thought processes can create an overly routinized way of approaching conclusions.[46]

In addition, the very action of serving on a jury creates a type of democratic deliberation, a process that is useful to both the individual

[43] *See* Frampton, *supra* note 38, at 210–211. West Virginia and Iowa are two such states.

[44] *See* Jennifer K. Robbennolt, *Evaluating Juries by Comparison to Judges: A Benchmark for Judging?* 32 FLA. ST. U. L. REV. 469, 487 (2005).

[45] Harry Kalven, Jr., *The Dignity of the Civil Jury*, 50 VA. L. REV. 1055, 1067 (1964); *see also* Phoebe C. Ellsworth, *Are Twelve Heads Better Than One?* LAW & CONTEMP. PROBS., Autumn 1989, at 205.

[46] *See* Barbara A. Spellman, Response, *On the Supposed Expertise of Judges in Evaluating Evidence*, 156 U. PA. L. REV. PENNUMBRA 1, 8 (2007), *available at* http://www.pennumbra.com/responses/03-2007/Spellman.pdf.

citizen and the country as a whole. By its very inclusivity of all citizens, democratic deliberation grants a particular political purpose to those participating. By involving the community in the work of government, deliberative democracy gives the people credence in their ability to influence the workings of the polity, and thus multiplies their enthusiasm to continue engaging in politics, even following the jury trial.[47] Therefore, not only do juries enhance democratic decision-making and potentially provide a decision superior in quality to that of a judge, they increase the possibility that citizens will become more involved in the workings of the polity even after their jury service. All this potential is lost, of course, when a bench trial occurs.

BENCH TRIALS AND COMPLEX CRIMINAL CASES

The most common argument for bench trials is the supposed need for the trained minds and greater experience of judges in complex litigation.[48] But does this really bear out in criminal cases?

First, although there are some complex criminal cases, the need for bench trials is comparatively less in average criminal cases. The average criminal case that goes to trial is not a patent case, nor one involving the intricacies of high technology, securities law, or prescription drug side effects. Instead, the most complicated cases likely to be tried in criminal court involve either RICO or DNA evidence – areas in which most jurors comprehend and successfully apply the law. In addition, recent empirical studies have shown that even in complex business cases, juries often add value to dispute resolution – contrary to a widespread perception about their alleged inadequacies.[49]

47 *See* Jenia Iontcheva Turner, *Jury Sentencing as Democratic Practice*, 89 VA. L. REV. 311, 342 (2003).

48 *But see* Louis Harris and Assocs., *Judges' Opinions on Procedural Issues: A Survey of State and Federal Trial Judges Who Spend at Least Half Their Time on General Civil Cases*, 69 B.U. L. REV. 731, 747 (1989) (finding that a slight majority of judges did not favor limiting jury participation even in large, complex civil litigation cases).

49 *E.g. See, e.g.*, Theodore Eisenberg & Geoffrey P. Miller, Do Juries Add Value? Evidence from an Empirical Study of Jury Trial Waiver Clauses in Large Corporate Contracts (Nov. 26, 2006) (unpublished research paper, on file with Cornell Law School Legal Studies Research Paper Series), *available at* http://ssrn.com/abstract=946465.

Furthermore, the empirical research measuring judge versus jury comprehension of complex trials do not fall squarely in the judiciary's favor. There have been no studies that actually prove that judges are better than juries in evaluating evidence, despite the general belief that judges are superior.[50] There is no particular reason to assume that in terms of their attributes, training, or proficiency, trial judges have special qualities at weighting evidence or at fact-finding.[51]

Indeed, given the average age of a judge versus a juror, the advantage may increasingly lie with the jury when it comes to ability to understand complex litigation. As millennials, who in general seem to intuitively grasp complicated and involved technologies, start to populate the jury rolls, we may find ourselves with a jury pool that is better able to handle the demands of difficult criminal cases, particularly those focusing on technology.[52]

Moreover, given the uncertainty as to who is better at fact-finding, juries may be preferable to judges for policy reasons.[53] Combine this doubt with the historical and democratic arguments for a jury trial and it is hard to justify the continued use of bench trials.

Taking all these arguments together, what would we lose if, as a measure of a fuller understanding of the jury trial right, we severely limited the use of bench trials? Obviously, the criminal justice system would lose some efficiency – although not much, since the vast majority of criminal indictments end in guilty pleas. True, it would reduce the choices available to the defendant, but because the real pressure comes with the decision between pleading guilty or going to trial, the effect would not be so great.

On the positive side of the ledger, curtailing the use of bench trials would uphold the community's right to decide upon the offender's

[50] *Cf.* Frederick Schauer, *On the Supposed Jury-Dependence of Evidence Law*, 155 U. PA. L. REV. 165, 189 (2006) (expressing the need for more experiments on judge and jury behavior).

[51] Spellman, *supra* note 46, at 6–7. As Spellman further explains, "trial judges can sit through hundreds of cases and never do the focused study or have the fast reliable feedback necessary for developing expertise." *Id.* at 7.

[52] *See* Andrew Wilhelm, Note, *Complex Litigation in the New Era of the Jury*, 41 PEPP. L. REV. 817, 836 (2014).

[53] *See, e.g.*, Paul H. Robinson & Barbara A. Spellman, *Sentencing Decisions: Matching the Decisionmaker to the Decision Nature*, 105 COLUM. L. REV. 1124, 1138–46 (2005).

moral blameworthiness without taking much away from the bundle of rights we currently assign to the accused. In many ways, bench trials are the most violative of the Sixth Amendment jury trial right, even worse than the plea bargain, as they permit the government itself to adjudicate criminal matters, entirely on its own. The denial of this "great and inestimable privilege of being tried by their peers,"[54] even when chosen by the defendant himself, is a troubling aspect of bench trials, and there is a very real loss to the general community whenever they are implemented. Although impossible to entirely eradicate, the bench trial should be severely limited in use.

[54] Res. of Oct. 14, 1774, in 1 JOURNALS OF THE CONTINENTAL CONGRESS, 1774–1789, at 69 (Worthington C. Ford, ed., 1904).

9 RESTORING THE OFFENDER TO SOCIETY

This chapter, along with Chapter 10, discusses how we can use expressive restorative retribution as a framework to address the problems inherent in the punishment imposed both before and after conviction. The insertion of a community voice into these pre- and post-conviction, or "ancillary," sentences provides a concrete way of implementing a form of expressive, restorative retribution that provides a slice of civic engagement and an improved reentry experience for both the offender and her community.

Not only does expressive[,] restorative retribution give the community a voice and help foster egalitarian and democratic ideals, at its best, it also forces offenders to take more responsibility for their wrongdoings, since the community is involved in the imposition of punishment and restoring the balance disturbed by the offender's bad acts. This type of community involvement is the much-needed step that has long been missing from our punishment in general, but particularly from our nonprison and post-punishment schemes.

Using expressive restorative retribution as a punishment philosophy for ancillary sentencing provides a concrete policy of community involvement and participation to a much-ignored and neglected area of the criminal justice system – a sphere that invariably touches every single offender. Taking a page from the past, Chapters 9 and 10 argue that community involvement can help structure nonprison ancillary sentencing, giving guidance not only to the players in the criminal justice system, but hopefully to the legislative and executive branches as well.

RETRIBUTION AS A GUIDEPOST FOR ANCILLARY CRIMINAL PUNISHMENT

With the benefit of hindsight, it is clear that relying upon utilitarian theories of jurisprudence to guide punishment and sentencing was a failure. Rehabilitation, deterrence, and incapacitation, either singly or combined, have all failed in their distinct ways. In the past, the loose procedural standards (if any) of rehabilitation left too much arbitrary discretion at the hands of judges and correction officials and did not produce the hoped-for restoration and reintegration into society. More recently, current policies of either deterrence or incapacitation, practiced jointly or alone, have not done much to help fix the constant problem of recidivism, despite the complicated supervisory periods and other additional punishments now tacked on to most offenders' sentences.

These failures point to the need for community sanctions, public involvement, and local support for the proper functioning of any sort of prison or post-prison punishment. If such punishments were grounded in the community – if released offenders had to serve their parole or post-release supervision in the very community they had harmed – it is possible that releasees would feel more culpability for their transgressions. Moreover, the community itself would feel more restored to its original state, because it would see the concrete measures of the visibly imposed punishment on resident wrongdoers. Finally, community sanctions provide a measure of restorative justice for both the victims and the community. In that way, parole, probation, and post-release supervision are all essential parts of expressive retributive philosophy translated into the real world.

There are a variety of ways that expressive restorative retribution can be incorporated into ancillary sentencing proceedings. For example, in pre-sentence proceedings, such as pre-sentence reports and the use of persistent violent felony offender statutes, the community should be directly involved in deciding which facts are relevant to increasing sentences – that is, which facts so disturb the offender's immediate community that extra punishment should be imposed. Likewise, with post-prison ancillary sentences, such as parole, post-release supervision, and restitution, the community could become directly involved in determining what local aspects of punishment should be imposed, whether community service, time in a local halfway house, drug and alcohol abuse counseling, or the like. This is particularly important when the community is focused on preventing recidivism, since 33 percent of all prison admissions are based on parole violations.[1] There is a variety of programs the community is in a good position to provide, such as homeless shelters, mental health services, substance abuse programs, adequate health care, education and employment assistance, and family support.[2]

For a general example, Jeremy Travis has proposed drawing heavily on the resources of the community, including families, local employers, and churches, to help better integrate the community into ancillary sentencing.[3] Travis suggests creating an entity to oversee all community supervision in each area. The entity's officials would live and work in the community to avoid the common problem of distance and attenuation. This is one way to create a post-prison version of the community policing model, which would involve the community in concrete problem-solving activities to help reintegrate offenders back into society.

Similarly, a specific transition team could be created for each supervised releasee. Team members could very well include representatives of the institution, community corrections, human service agencies, community-based services, housing providers, local law enforcement, and the court system. New York, Missouri, Tennessee, Florida, and Maryland are among the states that currently have a community transition team in place for offenders with post-prison punishments,[4] and these teams provide the continuing oversight so necessary to extend community involvement throughout all stages of offender punishment. This is a framework of community integration that should spread to all states, both to help increase the quality and the utility of nonprison

[1] *See* California Innocence Project, *Recidivism Rates*, *available at* http://californiainnocenceproject.org/issues-we-face/recidivism.

[2] *See id.*

[3] Jeremy Travis, Senior Fellow, The Urban Institute, *Thoughts on the Future of Parole* 12 (May 22, 2002), *available at* http://www.urban.org/UploadedPDF/410521.pdf.

[4] Re-Entry Policy Council, Report of the Re-entry Policy Council 360–64 (2003), *available at* www.reentrypolicy.org/reentry/Report/Download.

punishments as well as allow that crucial community voice into the ancillary sentencing process.

Another general possibility that involves the community in post-prison sentencing proceedings is faith-based programming. For example, the Ohio Department on Rehabilitation and Corrections has investigated the possibility of using pastoral community members to work with offenders on supervised release. Although using faith-based community initiatives must be carefully squared with First Amendment requirements, it also permits societal input into ancillary sentencing and often provides the most effective type of post-release counseling, whether offenders have religious beliefs or not.

Because it is the resident community that interacts with the offender on the most frequent basis, under my theory of expressive[,] restorative retribution, it is important to get the local citizenry's imprimatur on the length and heft of any pre- or post-prison punishments. The community's role in imposing punishment must not end at the courthouse steps. This is particularly important today, when punishments stemming from ancillary sentences can be equal to or even heftier than the original prison or jail sentence.

There is tremendous potential in applying the lessons of expressive restorative retribution to the world of ancillary sentencing. The community can have greater involvement with the punishment of probationary or released offenders in many ways, and ancillary sentencing proceedings offer us a wealth of possibilities. If we accept that our system of incarceration and punishment is deeply flawed when it comes to preventing recidivism, then we should be willing to extend the philosophy of expressive restorative retribution from these pages to the streets.

American sentencing itself encompasses an extremely complicated range of punishments. The "muddy and complicated realities of multi-actor sentencing systems"[5] include incarceration lengths, prison selection, in-prison punishments, post-release supervision, sex offender registration, community service, rehabilitative programming, criminal fines, and restitution. Sometimes these punishments are determined by

[5] *See* Kevin Reitz, *Modeling Discretion in American Sentencing Systems*, 20 LAW & POL'Y 389, 393 (1998).

the court, sometimes the prosecutor, sometimes the state or federal legislatures, sometimes the probation officer, sometimes the parole board or Department of Corrections. In short, there is no general body overseeing all these various and varied penalties, which makes them, at minimum, confusing and unpredictable, and at worst, injust, not uniform, and potentially unconstitutional.

What all of these proceedings have in common is the potential to enhance an offender's sentence and a lack of input from a jury, the only body constitutionally permitted to increase an offender's punishment. Therefore, many of these ancillary sentencing procedures may violate the tenets of *Apprendi-Blakely* as well as the community jury right.

Throughout the rest of this chapter and the next, I explore the effect of the community jury trial right on a range of front- and back-end sentencing procedures, beginning with pre-sentencing proceedings and ending with post-release supervision, restitution, and fines. I include seven types of proceedings: (1) pre-sentence reports; (2) persistent felony offender enhancement schemes; (3) probation; (4) parole; (5) post-release supervision; (6) restitution; and (7) criminal fines.

Generally, none of the facts determined in these ancillary sentencing proceedings are proven to the jury beyond a reasonable doubt. In fact, most of the time these facts are not even determined by courts, but instead by a laundry list of actors, including police officers, prosecutors, trial judges, parole officers, department of corrections officials, and probation departments, all of whom have a clear effect on sentencing.[6]

In addition, many of these proceedings have minimal procedural due process, often making them arbitrary and hard to appeal. In fact, because guilty pleas comprise such a high percentage of all criminal adjudications, often the sentencing proceedings handing down ancillary punishments are the only "trial-like" procedures that an offender experiences. Accordingly, it is important to get these proceedings right, both for purposes of uniformity and constitutional rigor.

Grappling with the role of the community in ancillary sentencing is particularly important now because America's prison, parole, and

[6] *See generally* Steven L. Chanenson, *Guidance From Above and Beyond*, 58 STAN. L. REV. 175 (2005).

probation populations have greatly increased.[7] More than two million Americans live behind bars, and many millions more are on parole, probation, or post-release supervision. Although state parole has been cut back (and federal parole eliminated) and determinate sentencing has become more popular,[8] many states still use early release to reward prisoners for good behavior.[9] Furthermore, mandatory post-release supervision, a required term of supervision imposed on offenders convicted of committing violent felonies, is routinely imposed in most states.

As ancillary sentencing has developed over the past century, it has gone in a variety of directions, often haphazardly, resulting in differing degrees of success in attempting to reform, house, and punish convicted offenders. An unfortunate result of our historically laissez-faire attitude to sentencing is the lack of meaningful constitutional limits in our approach to prisons, jails, and community sanctions.[10]

With a new focus on the community jury trial right, however, our criminal justice system now has a chance to reevaluate these procedures. In the rest of this chapter, and in Chapter 10, I will discuss a variety of sentencing procedures that badly need the imprimatur of the community.

Front-End Sentencing: The Community and Pre-sentencing Procedures

Although one or two of the proceedings discussed here are not so much "front-end" (i.e., before the sentencing hearing) as midway (during the hearing itself), most take place before the official sentencing hearing

[7] *See* Michael Jacobson, Downsizing Prisons: How to Reduce Crime and End Mass Incarceration 8 (NYU Press 1995).

[8] *See* Kevin Reitz, American Law Institute, Model Penal Code: Sentencing Report to the Council 16 (2004), *available at* http://sentencing.typepad.com/sentencing_law_and_policy/files/mpc_report_to_the_council_2004_for_blog.doc.

[9] Indeed, on November 4, 2014, California voters passed Proposition 47, which reduced the classification of most "nonserious and nonviolent property and drug crimes" from a felony to a misdemeanor. *See* California Proposition 47, Reduced Penalties for Some Crimes Initiative (2014). This resulted in many inmates being freed from their incarceration soon afterward. *See* Paige St. John, *Prop. 47 Jolts Landscape of California Justice System*, L.A. Times (November 5, 2014).

[10] *See* Kevin Reitz, *The New Sentencing Conundrum: Policy and Constitutional Law at Cross-Purposes*, 105 Colum. L. Rev. 1082, 1084 (2005).

actually occurs. These proceedings include pre-sentence reports, persistent felony offender statutes, prior convictions, and probation (or suspended sentences). As I argue below, each would greatly benefit from some evaluation by the local community.

Pre-Sentence Reports

Although a common part of virtually every state sentencing scheme, the pre-sentence report (PSR) exemplifies the nonjury decision-making that is so antithetical to the spirit of the community jury trial right. It is instructive, then, to parse out what parts of the PSR may not comport with *Apprendi-Blakely*'s requirement that juries find all facts that increase an offender's punishment. Equally important is determining how the community's involvement might improve the procedure.

A PSR is an official form assembled by a bureaucratic agency, usually the probation division or the state department of corrections, for use by the trial court at the sentencing hearing. The PSR normally contains facts about the offense (both from the police report and those presented at trial), information on recidivism, and victim impact statements, as well as the offender's prior family history, employment, education, physical and mental health, financial condition, future prospects, and prognosis of rehabilitative promise.

These facts, assertions, and judgments, usually determined by the probation or corrections officer, are utilized by the court to aggravate or mitigate the punishment. In addition, the facts set down in the PSR often influence the court's statements at the sentencing hearing, statements that affect the determination of an offender's discretionary release date (when there is one).

The original purpose of the PSR was to give the court information on the defendant's personal history and criminal conduct, to better achieve individualized sentencing.[11] In recent decades, however, the PSR has become much more focused on offense characteristics over offender characteristics, with the exception of the oft-misused "offender prognosis," where the probation officer gives her assessment on the rehabilitative potential of the offender. The offender prognosis can be

[11] *See* Daniel Macallair, *The History of the Presentence Investigation Report*, Center on Juvenile and Criminal Justice, located at www.cjcj.org/pubs/psi/psireport.html.

particularly damaging to a defendant if treated casually or in a biased manner against the offender.

The probation department's creation of PSRs and the trial court's use of them can have a large impact on the ultimate length and severity of a prison term. These factual determinations, which usually include an interview of the defendant, a summary of his future prospects and employability, and a recommendation for leniency or harshness, are often hastily done with little oversight from the defense bar or the courts.

Defendants have few, if any, rights when it comes to their PSR. Although most states permit the defendant to review the report's content, there is little recourse for any inaccuracies. The burden is on the defendant to prove that any error is harmful.[12] Moreover, in *Gregg v. United States*, the Supreme Court held that PSRs need not have any "formal limitations on their contents, and they may rest on hearsay and contain information bearing no relation whatever to the crime with which the defendant is charged."[13] Thus, there is no evidentiary limit to what may go in the pre-sentence report.

Pre-sentence reports can range in content from simply noting the fact of a prior conviction (still constitutional under *Almendarez-Torres*) to much more thorough documentation. California law, for example, has several recidivist factors memorialized in the PSR, all of which can increase an offender's total sentence. A California offender's PSR may include his poor performance on a previous term of parole, something itself determined by a parole officer, a purely bureaucratic functionary.

Likewise, in cases eligible for probation, a California offender, for example, has her fitness evaluated by a probation officer, who investigates "the circumstances surrounding the crime and the prior history and record of the person, which may be considered either in aggravation or mitigation of the punishment."[14] The probation officer normally makes a written report of his findings to the court, including any recommendations as to whether probation is deserved and which conditions should be imposed. If negative, these determinations are particularly damaging, since courts tend to rely heavily on the

[12] *See id.*
[13] *See Gregg v. United States*, 394 U.S. 489, 492 (1969).
[14] *See* CAL. PENAL CODE § 1203(b)(1).

recommendations of the pre-sentence report, rarely challenging its factual findings, even if these findings would increase the offender's punishment. This practice leaves some very influential fact determinations to an unelected functionary of a bureaucratic institution.

Jones v. United States[15] illustrated how recommendations in PSRs can ultimately end up violating an offender's right to have a jury determination of all key facts. In *Jones*, the PSR recommended that the defendant be sentenced to twenty-five years for a carjacking because one of the victims had suffered serious bodily injury; the recommended punishment was duly imposed.[16] The *Jones* Court, however, overturned the underlying conviction, because the crime of inflicting serious bodily injury should rightfully have been classified as an offense element, to be determined by the jury, and not a sentencing enhancement to be determined by the court.[17] In other words, *Jones* teaches us how a factor in a PSR – a seemingly insignificant fact determination – can become an element of a crime when it "not only provide[s] for steeply higher penalties, but condition[s] them on further facts (injury, death) that seem quite as important as the elements either in the original indictment or statute."[18] Parallel to the situation in *Jones*, many facts in the PSR are similarly left to the probation officer's investigation, determination, and invention, without oversight or regulation. Ultimately, the principles underlying the community jury right strongly suggest that certain aspects of the PSR may no longer pass muster.

Granted, a narrower understanding of the community jury trial right might not require juries to find every fact that might increase an offender's sentence, particularly when such facts do not comprise any part of the offense element, as in the PSR. This counterargument works on two levels. First, as a basic historical issue, American courts in the constitutional era dealt with very few felonies, unlike the plethora of crimes and wide array of pre- and post-sentencing procedures that exist today. As this line of thinking goes, the Founders never imagined applying the Sixth Amendment right to facts not constituting part of the offense elements.

15 526 U.S. 227 (1999).
16 Jones v. United States, 526 U.S. 227, 231 (1999).
17 *Jones*, 526 U.S. at 235.
18 *Jones*, 526 U.S. at 233. A sentencing factor in a PSR also becomes an offense element where it has elsewhere been treated as defining an offense element. *Id.* at 235.

Therefore, any sentencing proceeding that did not exist during the Constitutional period need not meet Sixth Amendment's strictures.

This type of historical argument, however, can be defeated by reviewing the constitutional requirements in other criminal law contexts, many of which also did not exist during the Founders' era. We apply constitutional protections to a variety of procedures unheard of in the late eighteenth century, including police infrared searches, car stops, and *Miranda* rights, to name a few. So, the fact that the pre-sentence report is a twenty-first-century sentencing tool cannot assist in avoiding application of Sixth Amendment principles.

A second, more practical argument contends that pre-sentence report facts are *minor* ones that do not truly require determination by the jury. This understanding of the scope of the community jury right argues that the offender's personal and correctional history (including unproven charges), the description of the crime (using facts from both the police report and the trial), and the prognosis of rehabilitative promise are insufficiently critical to truly merit the full panoply of Sixth Amendment jury rights.

What this argument fails to consider, however, is how these offender-based characteristics and offense-based facts can potentially increase an offender's punishment. For example, pre-sentence reports commonly include statements about the crime from the police report, many of which have never been admitted into evidence, some of which are pure hearsay, and none of which have been presented to the jury. Allowing the court to determine the reliability and impact of these facts on an offender's punishment seems a simple end run around the Sixth Amendment community jury right.

The descriptions of the offender's personal and correctional history can be equally unreliable. Although prior convictions are still acceptable terms upon which to increase a sentence, often the pre-sentence report contains information about prior arrests and dismissed indictments, information that can negatively influence the court's determination of punishment. Furthermore, in cases where the jury finds that certain offenses were not proven, the court may still take the facts of those offenses – often listed in the PSR – into account. In other words, an offender can be punished for crimes that were never proven beyond a reasonable doubt, surely a violation of constitutional proportions.

In addition, the statements made about an offender's correctional history and rehabilitative promise – determined by probation officers, prison officials, and other unelected, unrepresentative bureaucrats – can be extremely arbitrary, especially since these determinations are often collected from functionaries with only minor interactions with the offender. Thus, the PSR can contain a variety of unsubstantiated or biased determinations treated as "fact" by the court, far from the eye of the jury.

Stated differently, the PSR depends on nonadjudicated findings of prior fact for which the defendant has never received his right to a jury or had these findings proven beyond a reasonable doubt.[19] Accordingly, allowing a sentencing jury to weigh the evidence presented is one solution, giving the local public some power to determine the facts contained within the PSR. Thus there would be a bifurcated sentencing procedure wherein a jury (for simplicity's sake, likely the same jury from the trial or plea bargain) would formally determine which PSR facts are the most reliable – that is, which facts would be eligible to increase or decrease the offender's punishment. If there were any questions, either the probation officer, the corrections official, or the prosecutor could respond, explain, and clarify. In this way, all the information on recidivism, victim impact statements, and the offender's prior family history, employment, education, physical and mental health, financial condition, future prospects, and prognosis of rehabilitative promise would be reviewed by a type of jury, which would scrutinize the provided facts to weed out the dubious or inflammatory. Allowing some sort of sentencing jury to weigh PSR facts would not only spur probation and corrections officers to make sure the information was correct, but would also give some sort of determinative power to the community, instead of leaving the entire process to a hidden arm of the bureaucratic state.

Persistent Felony Offender Schemes

A number of states permit sentence enhancement based on statutes that mix recidivism, past violence, and statements on PSRs. These schemes, sometimes dubbed "three strikes" laws, have important Sixth Amendment implications, particularly in the wake of *Apprendi-Blakely*.

[19] *See* Robert Weisberg, *Excerpts from "The Future of American Sentencing: A National Roundtable on* Blakely," 2 Ohio St. J. Crim. L. 619, 648 (2005).

Although California can lay claim to one of the most infamous three-strike laws, New York has a persistent felony offender statute that runs counter to the animating principle of the jury trial right. For example, a New York trial court is authorized – but not required – to sentence an offender with two prior felony convictions to a much longer incarceration period than would normally be permitted. The determination of whether the offender is eligible for the "persistent felony offender" status, however, is left to the judge alone, which tramples upon the community jury trial right.

Under New York law, when the prosecutor requests persistent felony offender status for a defendant, the trial court holds a hearing to determine whether the severity and number of the offender's past crimes requires adjudication.[20] An enhanced punishment must be based on judicial weighing of the history and character of the defendant and the nature and circumstances of his criminal conduct. Although some procedural due process is used during the hearing, none of the facts that lead to the imposition of persistent felony offender status is determined by a jury. Instead, the relevant facts are provided by the prosecutor and defense counsel, and the New York trial court, in a special sentencing hearing, determines whether the convicted offender is classified as a persistent felony offender by evaluating her past criminal history.

In New York, like in many other states, an offender's criminal history can include past behavior on parole, prior convictions, statements from probation and parole officers, and acquitted conduct. Because persistent felony offender classification results in a lengthened sentence for the offender – substantially greater than any maximum sentence allowed – and is based on facts not determined by a jury, the persistent felony offender statute runs against the mandate of the community jury right.[21]

The best result here, as pointed out by E.D.N.Y. Judge Gleeson, would be either to subject all persons convicted of a felony who have two

[20] *See* N.Y. Penal Law § 70.10 (McKinney 2014).

[21] Although New York's discretionary persistent felony offender statute has been challenged in both state and federal courts as violating *Apprendi-Blakely*, both the New York Court of Appeals and the Second Circuit have rejected this claim. *See* Portalatin v. Graham, 624 F.3d 69 (2d Cir. 2010)(en banc); People v. Rivera, 5 N.Y.3d 61 (2005).

prior nonviolent felony convictions to the possibility of life imprisonment (thereby eliminating the factual determination aspect) or to submit to a jury the issue of the defendant's history and character and the need for extended incarceration and supervision.[22] To continue to have a trial court determine whether a defendant is eligible for the persistent felony offender classification seems to violate both the principle and the spirit of the Sixth Amendment jury trial right, despite the current understanding of the Second Circuit.

Prior Convictions

One area of ancillary sentencing that has resisted the incursion of the community jury right is in the use of prior convictions.[23] This is an area ripe for change. Specifically, both *Apprendi* and *Blakely* state that their rule requiring that certain facts be either proven to a jury beyond a reasonable doubt or admitted by the defendant only applies to facts "other than the fact of a prior conviction." This exception conflicts with the Sixth Amendment jury trial right's animating principles, since disputed prior convictions, which unquestionably increase the offender's maximum punishment, are invariably determined by the sentencing court.

Although they may sound like a relatively simple sentencing determination, prior convictions are often inaccurate or confusing, as the category encompasses old convictions, out-of-state convictions, and foreign convictions. To make matters even more complicated, sometimes an offense can be a felony in one state and a misdemeanor in another, or the same facts can be punished differently by different jurisdictions. Thus, the realm of prior convictions is extremely complex, with serious punitive results, and is, yet again, a domain adjudicated solely by the court, not the jury.

The theoretical basis of *Almendarez-Torres*'s "prior conviction" exception has been repeatedly questioned, most recently by Justice Thomas. Thomas got straight to the heart of the matter in his denial of certiorari dissent in *Rangel-Reyes v. United States*. Citing

[22] *See* Portalatin v. Graham, 478 F. Supp. 2d 385, 386 (E.D.N.Y. 2007).

[23] As I discussed earlier, one result of *Almendarez-Torres* was the preservation of the "prior conviction" exception for sentencing procedures.

Apprendi numerous times, he argued that if a crime includes all facts used as a basis for imposing or increasing punishment, then the prior conviction exception is grounded not in the Constitution, but only in Supreme Court precedent: "[T]he exception to trial by jury for establishing 'the fact of a prior conviction' finds its basis not in the Constitution, but in a precedent of this Court."[24]

By thus demoting the prior conviction exception from constitutional rule to mere precedent, Thomas set the stage for possibly overruling the exception. And in repeatedly referring to *Apprendi*, Thomas returned to the heart of the Sixth Amendment jury trial guarantee – that only a jury may find facts that increase an offender's punishment. The implication is that the *Almendarez-Torres* exception could be overruled as a court-made rule.

On a more practical note, Justice Thomas also noted that a majority of the current Court rejected the exception, and it was its positive duty to "address the ongoing validity" of the exception – not only because addressing the exception was the Court's sole prerogative, but also because, until the exception is reversed, "countless criminal defendants will be denied the full protection afforded by the Fifth and Sixth Amendments, notwithstanding the agreement of a majority of the Court that this result is unconstitutional."[25] Thomas's return to the bedrock guarantees of the Fifth and Sixth Amendments, and his concern over the shortchanged rights of criminal offenders, helps illustrate the continuing importance of the Court's "rediscovered" right to a jury trial for all facts enhancing punishment, precedent and *stare decisis* notwithstanding. For Thomas, and for a growing number on the Court, the animating principles of the Sixth Amendment trump any judge-made rules.

Thomas's dissent in *Rangel-Reyes* foretold his concurring opinion in *Descamps*. *Descamps* held that courts may not apply the modified categorical approach[26] to determine whether a prior offense was a violent

[24] Rangel-Reyes v. United States, 126 S. Ct. 2873, 2874 (2006) (Thomas, J., dissenting) (citations omitted).

[25] *Rangel-Reyes, id.* at 2875.

[26] The Armed Career Criminal Act increases the sentences of certain federal defendants who have three prior convictions "for a violent felony," including "burglary, arson, or extortion." 18 U.S.C. § 924(e): To determine whether a past conviction is for one of those crimes, courts use what has become known as the "categorical approach." They compare

felony under the Armed Career Criminal Act (ACCA), when the crime for which the defendant was previously convicted has a single, indivisible set of elements.[27] In *Descamps*, the defendant, who had a prior burglary conviction, was improperly sentenced under the ACCA (thereby increasing his punishment) when the court looked at the underlying facts of his prior conviction, instead of just the statutory charge. The *Descamps* trial court decided to upgrade the defendant's offense to an ACCA conviction, based on his supposed acquiescence to a prosecutorial statement during state court plea colloquy that he "broke and entered," although this was irrelevant to the charged crime of burglary under California law.

The Supreme Court in *Descamps*, however, held that the modified approach could not convert Descamps's burglary conviction into an ACCA predicate, because California law defines burglary more broadly than the generic offense. In other words, the Court held that the district court improperly relied on its own finding about a nonelemental fact to increase the defendant's maximum sentence. In doing so, the trial court violated the Sixth Amendment requirement that any fact, except the fact of a prior conviction, used to increase a sentence beyond the prescribed statutory maximum must be submitted to a jury and proven beyond a reasonable doubt.

Thomas's concurrence in *Descamps*, agreeing with the majority's judgment though not its reasoning, focused on the utility of the prior conviction exception. Thomas first argued that generally the ACCA violated the Sixth Amendment jury trial right because it permitted the judge to "mak[e] a finding that raises [a defendant's] sentence beyond the sentence that could have lawfully been imposed by reference to facts found by the jury or admitted by the defendant."[28] Under *Apprendi-Blakely's* reasoning, Thomas contended, a court may not find facts about a prior conviction when such findings increase the statutory maximum. Thus, according to Thomas, the ACCA as a whole is unconstitutional.

the elements of the statute forming the basis of the defendant's conviction with the elements of the "generic" crime – *i.e.*, the offense as commonly understood. The prior conviction qualifies as an ACCA predicate only if the statute's elements are the same as, or narrower than, those of the generic offense.

27 133 S.Ct. 2276.

28 *Descamps*, *id.* at 2294 (Thomas, J., concurring).

In addition, Thomas strongly hinted that the entire prior conviction exception is untenable, noting that the only reason the Court even considered *Descamps*'s ACCA enhancement is because it has "not yet" reconsidered *Almendarez-Torres*.[29] As he argued, *any* judicial fact-finding, no matter what the framework, violates the Sixth Amendment jury trial right. In so arguing, Thomas endorses the purest form of understanding the community's right to determine all punishment, at all stages of criminal adjudication.

PROBATION

In contrast to prior convictions, probation has been little scrutinized by the courts. Probation is most often imposed on convicted defendants in lieu of a sentence, or as part of a suspended sentence.[30] In many states, a term of probation means a suspension of the execution of a sentence and an order of conditional and revocable release under the supervision of a probation officer. One hallmark of this kind of dispositional departure is the trial court's flexibility in shifting from a presumptive, non-incarcerative sentence – such as a nonprison disposition – to a term of incarceration. More troubling, decisions to impose these dispositions are often based entirely on a judicial factual determination, which violates the spirit of the Sixth Amendment jury trial right.

Most supervised probation follows similar patterns. These include a requirement to meet regularly with a counselor or probation officer (often, but not always, from the Department of Corrections), a long list of forbidden activities and associations, and some sort of procedure in which the facts of an alleged violation can be determined and adjudicated – most often under a preponderance of the evidence standard. Although the prosecutor has the burden of persuasion at these revocation hearings, she is not required to prove the violation beyond a

[29] *Descamps*, *id.* at 2295.

[30] *See generally* Scott H. Ikeda, *Probation Revocations as Delayed Dispositional Departures: Why* Blakely v. Washington *Requires Jury Trials at Probation Violation Hearings*, 24 LAW & INEQ. 157 (2006).

reasonable doubt, as she would at trial.[31] An offender's violation of probation terms usually results in incarceration, either for the first time (as in a sentence stay) or as a return to prison.

The Supreme Court has held that the determination of a probation violation is entitled to the minimum requirements of due process, including written notice of the claimed violations.[32] Likewise, most states require some sort of minimal due process hearing in front of a court before probation is revoked and a person is returned to prison. For example, in Massachusetts, a violation of a condition of probation must be found "at least to a reasonable degree of certainty."[33] In Florida, a probationer must receive proper notice of the claimed violation, as well as some minimum due process, before probation can be revoked.[34] In Connecticut, a revocation of probation hearing has been determined to be less formal than a criminal trial, and requires only that the state prove its case by a preponderance of the evidence.[35]

Often, state court judges have the ability to lengthen the sentence at a probation violation proceeding, something *Apprendi-Blakely* may now require to be left in the hands of the jury or at least some representative of the community. For example, in North Dakota, a court may resentence a defendant to a sentence harsher than the one originally imposed, under the reasoning that this technically does not expose him to multiple punishments for the same offense.[36]

To best see the great discretion given to courts and state corrections boards in the area of probation, it is helpful to study a state's statutes in depth. One excellent example is California, which processes a large number of offenders through its prisons on a yearly basis. California

[31] *See* Brian G. Bieluch, *Thirty-First Annual Review of Criminal Procedure: IV. Sentencing: Probation*, 90 GEO. L.J. 1813, 1826 (2002).

[32] *See* Gagnon v. Scarpelli, 411 U.S. 778, 786 (1973) (holding that a probationer under a suspended sentence entitled to minimum requirements of due process before probation could be revoked); Morrissey v. Brewer, 408 U.S. 471, 486–87 (1972) (explaining minimum due process proceedings required at probation revocation hearings).

[33] *See* Commonwealth v. Maggio, 605 N.E.2d 1247, 1250 (Mass. 1993). *See also* Commonwealth v. Durling, 551 N.E.2d 1193, 1195 (Mass. 1990) (defendant at probation revocation proceedings entitled to certain due process protections).

[34] *See* State v. Spratling, 336 So. 2d 361 (Fla. 1976) (where probationer failed to receive proper notice of claimed violation serving basis of probation revocation, not afforded due process).

[35] *See* State v. McDowell, 699 A.2d 987, 989 (Conn. 1997); State v. Davis, 641 A.2d 370, 378 (Conn. 1994).

[36] Davis v. State, 625 N.W.2d 855, 858 (N.D. 2001).

governs its ancillary sentencing procedures through either judicial or bureaucratic actors, with very little jury (or democratic) participation. In that sense, it is about as far from the animating principles of the Sixth Amendment as a state can get.

In adjudicating probation, California's trial courts determine whether a convicted offender may receive a sentence of probation "the suspension of the imposition or execution of a sentence and the order of conditional and revocable release in the community."[37] In cases involving hate crimes, the trial court has the authority to require the convicted offender's participation in a variety of alternative sanctions *in addition* to the sentence of probation, including the completion of a class or program on racial/ethnic sensitivity or civil rights, additional restitution to programs or agencies that provide service, and reimbursing the victim for reasonable costs of counseling. Since the imposition of these punishments is fully discretionary on the part of the court, and increases the offender's punishment, this seems to qualify as a Sixth Amendment jury trial right violation.

Once outside the courtroom, California's probationary fact-finding shifts from judicial to wholly bureaucratic – moving further and further away from Sixth Amendment legitimacy. Supervision of the probationer falls to the county probation officer, who establishes both the kind and type of supervision consistent with the court-ordered conditions of probation. The probation officer is the sole determinant of whether the defendant has violated any of the terms of probation, despite being a wholly bureaucratic appointment. This is disturbing, because violation of probation terms usually results in revocation of the conditional release.

Likewise, California's nonviolent drug offender statute contains a variety of fact-finding procedures by nonjury actors that often increase a convicted offender's punishment. California requires a sentence of probation and drug treatment instead of prison for those nonviolent drug offenders arrested for personal use crimes, with exceptions for offenders who refuse or are unamenable to treatment. Decisions about whether the defendant has used drugs personally, refused drug treatment, or is generally amenable to rehabilitation are made solely by the

[37] Cal. Penal Code § 1203(a) (West 2014).

trial court. As a whole, then, California's ancillary sentencing proceedings, like those of many other states, lean heavily toward the bureaucratic and judicial, as opposed to the democratic – a state of affairs in contradiction of the animating principle of *Apprendi-Blakely* and the Sixth Amendment jury trial right.

In general, once the term of probation has been set, a combination of judicial and bureaucratic decision-makers decide the facts that determine whether probation has been properly followed. Usually, the evidence of a possible probation violation is collected by the probation officer or commission, and any decision to revoke the period of probation is made by the court.[38] The jury, however, typically has no involvement in the setting of any probationary terms, from imposition to revocation, despite probation's potential to increase the defendant's type and length of prison sentence.

In sum, a change in sentence from a nonincarcerative probation period to a term of imprisonment, based on factual determinations made by nonjury actors, obviously increases a defendant's maximum sentence. Revoking probation increases an offender's punishment as well. On the one hand, the Supreme Court has made it clear that not every imposition on offenders and/or prisoners constitutes impermissible punishment.[39] On the other, the decision to revoke a sentence of probation, thereby denying the offender her liberty, unquestionably has a punitive effect. As probation is currently constituted in many states, it does not seem to follow the requirements of *Apprendi-Blakely* or the Sixth Amendment community jury trial right. If length of punishment is measured by length of time in prison – as our system, and even the most minimalist interpretation of *Apprendi-Blakely*, currently does measure it – then changes in dispositional departures come into the Sixth Amendment's ambit. As such, it is high time to rethink the vast discretion given to courts and state agencies before, during, and after the sentencing hearing.

[38] *See, e.g.*, CAL. PENAL CODE § 1203.2 (West 2014); CONN. GEN. STAT. ANN. § 53a–32(a) (West 2014); FLA. STAT. ANN. § 948.06(2)(a) (West 2014).

[39] *See, e.g.*, Sandin v. Conner, 515 U.S. 472, 484–85 (1995) (rejecting due process challenge to in-prison discipline).

10 BACK-END SENTENCING: THE SIXTH AMENDMENT AND POST-PRISON PROCEDURES

A criminal offender's sentence does not end upon the completion of the term of imprisonment, of course. A modern sentence includes all the various aspects of supervision the offender must undergo, including parole, post-release supervision, and restitution. Upon a prisoner's release, the terms of her probation and supervised release, initially determined by the state legislature and imposed by the court, are enforced and regulated by parole officers. The trial court or the parole officer collects the amount of restitution, imposed during sentencing, after the sentencing hearing. This system of back-end sentencing, however, has long been obscured from public view. It is these types of sentencing proceedings, which can increase the length and the burden of an offender's sentence, that must also be considered through the lens of the community jury trial right.

The first question to address when thinking about the world of post-prison procedures is whether post-release supervision should be subject to the community jury trial right. Most criminal sentences include a period of supervised release following the completion of the imposed sentence.[1] Violating this condition can result in revocation of the conditional release and sometimes can even lengthen the duration of the original prison term. The trial or magistrate judge determines whether supervised release has been violated, using some minimum level of procedural due process, with the facts provided by a probation officer or the department of corrections.

[1] For example, in New York, all felonies come with a period of post-release supervision between one and five years, depending on the severity of the offense. *See* N.Y. PENAL LAW § 70.45 (McKinney 2014).

Likewise, when prisoners are released before serving their full sentences, they are invariably placed on supervised release. For example, when federal offenders are released from prison, they are supervised for a period imposed by the judge as part of the sentence.[2] The guidelines require that nearly all felony offenders be sentenced to at least two years of supervised release following incarceration, and because most federal courts continue to follow the guidelines to some extent, this kind of supervised release is still in practice. In addition, parole boards still exist in the majority of states, in the federal system for those prisoners who committed their crimes before 1987, and in the military.

To start, having courts or administrative officials deciding facts regarding parole or post-release supervision violation – facts that can have a very real effect on the length of convicted defendants' sentences – may collide with *Apprendi-Blakely* and the Sixth Amendment community jury trial right. If, per *Apprendi-Blakely*, a jury must decide all facts that increase a defendant's maximum sentence, then a variety of parole and post-release proceedings would be subject to this reinvigorated Sixth Amendment right. Furthermore, if *Apprendi-Blakely* is viewed most broadly, in terms of determining punishment, virtually all proceedings determining parole and post-release supervision would fall into its orbit.

Most parole and post-release supervision proceedings have very few procedures and safeguards, and the corrections bureaucracy is the primary decision-maker. Because no one in such systems is responsible for creating systemic, cohesive sentencing policy, the case-by-case decisions of parole boards and probation officers can be entirely random. Such haphazard federal and state procedures are far from the requirements that are inherent in the Sixth Amendment jury trial right. It is time to reevaluate which decision-makers determine the outcomes of post-prison release proceedings, and best determine how the community jury trial right should apply to this aspect.

For greater clarity, I have divided my analysis into four categories: parole, post-release supervision, fines, and restitution.

[2] Kate Stith & Jose Cabranes, Fear of Judging: Sentencing Guidelines in the Federal Courts 5, n.9 (Chicago, 1998). As noted above, parole has been eradicated in the federal system.

PAROLE

Parole is the back-end sentencing procedure with the highest public profile. An offender's parole date can play a substantive role in increasing or decreasing the actual length of his imprisonment. Parole determinations are made not by a judge, a jury, or the legislature, but instead by a disparate assortment of prison officials and department of corrections personnel. Excepting specific statutory regulation, the parole board determines the actual incarceration length by deciding if or when to grant the inmate discretionary parole release.[3] A parole release date relies primarily on two things: the offender's behavior in prison (often characterized as good-time credits or punishment) and the constituency of the parole board.

Discretionary parole release plays an important part in the criminal justice system, but it garners little attention. Although parole has been eradicated in the federal system,[4] it still retains a relatively large role in the states, particularly in those states with indeterminate sentencing systems. Tellingly, roughly one-third of all admissions to state prisons are individuals being returned for parole violations.[5] Thus, parole still plays an integral role on the back end of criminal sentencing procedures.

Although parole has been associated with a primarily utilitarian philosophy, there is support for placing it within the framework of retributive theory. As other scholars have noted, locating moral meaning in parole is important, especially in the retributively based mass incarceration era of today.[6] One way to do so is by reconceptualizing parole as a communicative forum, one that requires mutual acceptance of responsibility among participants.[7]

[3] *See* Steven L. Chanenson, *Guidance from Above and Beyond*, 58 STAN. L. REV. 175, 187 (2005).

[4] *See* STITH & CABRANES, *supra* note 2, at 5. Under the Sentencing Reform Act, federal offenders sentenced to prison can no longer obtain early release on parole, which has been abolished. *Id.*

[5] *See* Jeremy Travis, Prisoner Reentry and Community Policing: Strategies for Enhancing Public Safety 2 (2004).

[6] *See* Netanel Dagan & Dana Segev, *Retributive Whisper: Communicative Elements in Parole*, LAW & SOC. INQ. (forthcoming 2014), at 2 (SSRN draft, on file with author).

[7] *See id.* at 2.

For retributive theory to work within the structure of parole, the parole board process must convey a communicative message.[8] From a communicative perspective, punishment approximates a secular form of penance.[9] In this way, a retributive-based philosophy is well suited for parole, as parole board decisions take place in a welter of determinations focusing on desert and punishment and their effects upon the prisoner, the institution, and the community.[10]

Moreover, the parole board, if properly integrated into the community, plays a special role both by its chronological and physical positioning.[11] First, the closure provided by this most back end of back-end sentencing procedures is important to various constituencies, including the offender and the offender's family, the victim and the victim's family, the police, the prosecutor, and the injured community as a whole. Second, since the parole hearing takes place in the actual prison, if the community is involved, there is an expressive value in having them *come* to the prisoner and show an interest in restoring her back into the fabric of society.[12] Put another way, the parole board, when integrated with the community, helps express the moral voice of the community by telling parolees what they need to do to reintegrate.[13]

Complicating matters, the Supreme Court has had difficulty defining the post-conviction rights of prisoners, particularly in parole decisions.[14] In *Morrissey v. Brewer*, the Supreme Court noted that "parole is an established variation on imprisonment of convicted criminals. ... The essence of parole is release from prison, before the completion of sentence, on the condition that the prisoner abide by certain rules

8 *See id.* at 7.

9 *See* R. A. Duff, *Penal Communications: Recent Work in the Philosophy of Punishment, in Crime and Justice: A Review of Research* 20 (1996). The aim of communicative sentencing is to encourage offenders to repent their crime, reform, and thus reconcile themselves with those they have wronged – in this way, similar to the aims of expressive restorative retribution. Likewise, communicative sentencing emphasizes the reciprocal and rational engagement of the offender, the judge, and the community.

10 *See* Keith Hawkins, *Assessing Evil: Decision Behavior and Parole Board Justice*, 23 BRITISH J. OF CRIM. 102 (1983).

11 *See* Dagan & Segev, *supra* note 6, at 11.

12 *See id.*

13 *See generally* R. A. Duff, *Punishment, Communication, and Community* (Oxford 2001).

14 *See, e.g.*, Greenholz v. Nebraska, 442 U.S. 1 (1979) (discussing parole release).

during the balance of the sentence."[15] In other words, the Supreme Court has essentially shifted its authority to the prisons, holding that parole is less a post-prison sentencing procedure than an in-prison reward. Nonetheless, parole is still subject to constitutional requirements, despite the large amount of discretion allowed to prison administrators.[16]

On first view, parole appears exempt from the scope of the community jury trial right, as *Blakely* itself specifically excludes parole: "[o]f course indeterminate schemes involve judicial factfinding, in that a judge (like a parole board) may implicitly rule on those facts he deems important to the exercise of his sentencing discretion."[17] This exception for a parole board's sentencing discretion, originally articulated by *Morrissey*, does not seem to leave much room for the role of the community in parole hearings.

Viewed more broadly, however, parole may be subject to the Sixth Amendment's animating principle that the community should decide all imposition of punishment – after all, the Sixth Amendment never draws a line between punishment imposed inside and outside a prison. Stated differently, if the *Apprendi-Blakely* line of cases is expansively interpreted – that only juries may find facts that increase an offender's punishment – then parole may come into the Sixth Amendment's ambit.

Under a more expansive interpretation, there are two areas where *Blakely* and the Sixth Amendment could potentially affect parole: in the initial grant of parole by the corrections department, and in the determination of whether a parolee has violated her parole terms. Both types of parole are subject to the same general critique: that parole release, like many other sorts of back-end ancillary sentencing proceedings, has traditionally been unstructured and overly discretionary, subject to vagaries, unpredictability, and lack of uniformity. Furthermore, it is questionable whether parole boards have the abilities and tools to

[15] 408 U.S. 471, 477 (1972).

[16] The Supreme Court opined on Fourth Amendment right of parolees in *Samson v. California*, 547 U.S. 843 (2006), holding that the Fourth Amendment does not prohibit police officers from conducting these sorts of suspicionless prisoner searches, because parole is a type of a prison term that continues outside of the prison, and prisoners are normally subject to suspicionless searches.

[17] *Blakely v. Washington*, 542 U.S. 296, 309 (2004).

realistically predict offenders' future criminal behavior based on the limited information they possess.[18]

Answering these questions requires exploration of the details of parole supervision, at least as it functions in the states. In indeterminate systems, parole is granted at the discretion of parole boards, while in a determinate sentencing system, the earliest release date is fixed by statute and can be granted after a prisoner has served a certain proportion of his sentence, assuming good behavior. When a prisoner is up for parole, he usually goes in front of the prison's parole board, staffed by department of corrections or parole board officials, which determines whether the offender is eligible for early release. Many inmates released today have not "earned" their parole, but have been automatically released as governed by state statute.

Once released, parolees are supervised by parole field services officers. Released offenders must regularly report to an assigned parole officer, who, with the help of the parole board, determines whether or not the parolee has "violated" parole by failing to comply with all terms and conditions of parole.[19] Determining whether the released offender has abided by these regulations is the principal responsibility of the parole agent. The conditions can include, among many others, restrictions on association with felons/gang members; mandatory meetings with parole officers; forbidden possession of weapons; mandatory abstinence from drugs and alcohol; medical or psychiatric treatment; frequent searches of persons, possessions, and residences; travel requests; mandatory child support; school attendance; and community service.

Parole officers, however, tend to have large caseloads and little money to effectively supervise, help rehabilitate, or even meet with their released prisoners on a regular basis.[20] Such limited contact

[18] *See* Steven L. Chanenson, *The Next Era of Sentencing Reform*, 54 Emory L.J. 377, 450 (2005).

[19] *See, e.g.*, Cal. Penal Code § 3060 ("The parole authority [has] full power to suspend or revoke any parole and to order returned to prison any prisoner on parole."); Conn. Gen. Stat. Ann. § 54–126 (providing that the Board of Pardons and Paroles establishes rules and regulations for parole); Fla. Stat. Ann. § 947.13(1)(c) (same); N.Y. Exec. Law § 259-c (McKiney 2005); Or. Rev. Stat. § 144.040 (2005); Tex. Gov't Code §§ 508.045, 508.0441 (same); Va. Code Ann. § 53.1–136(3) (same); Wash. Rev. Code Ann. § 9.95.110 (same).

[20] *See* Thomas J. Bamonte, *The Viability of Morrisey v. Brewer and the Due Process Rights of Parolees and Other Conditional Releasees*, 18 S. Ill. U. L.J. 121, 134 (1993).

between parole officers and parolees means that the officials who determine parole violations on a regular basis have minimal data about the released offenders or their future when making the decision to revoke parole.

Since the 1970s when parole was in first bloom, parole agents have become harsher in their supervision of released prisoners. Parole officer training generally provides little emphasis on casework and service referrals, instead relying much more on law enforcement techniques.[21] This focus on law enforcement, rather than rehabilitation, helps reify the image of parole officers as police officers instead of social workers. To assist with the enforcement of their powers, parole agents have legal authority to carry and use firearms; to search people, places, and property free of Fourth Amendment concerns; to order arrests without probable cause; and to confine parolees without bail. The combination of these powers makes parole officers much more focused on policing than rehabilitating.

This ability to reincarcerate the paroled offender, with little outside oversight, for violating her parole conditions makes the agent a mobile criminal justice system.[22] It is in revocation hearings where a parole agent wields the greatest power. Roughly one-third to one-half of all parolees undergo a revocation action during their time of parole.[23] The hearings are often abbreviated procedures with a predetermined end, resulting in the imprisonment of almost every parolee charged with a violation, without possibility of bail. After *Morrissey*, parolees are rarely represented by defense counsel at these hearings, and there are few, if any, confrontation or cross-examination rights.[24] Indeed, it is no uncommon for a parole revocation to be based on hearsay testim of third parties contained only in police reports. h

Overall, the minimal due process rights of parolees, co ted te to low evidentiary standards, minimal burden of proo defense mounted by defendants means that it is e RISONER

[21] *See* JOAN PETERSILIA, WHEN PRISONERS COME H RCEBOOK OF REENTRY 11 (2003). Flanagan, eds.,

[22] *See id.* at 82.

[23] *See* BUREAU OF JUSTICE STATISTICS, D CRIMINAL JUSTICE STATISTICS 667 (K 1991).

[24] Bamonte, *supra* note 20, at 136.

reimprison released prisoners based on scant evidence: a police report, a short report by a hearing officer, and some nominal paperwork. This is hardly a community-determined imposition of punishment.

Because the parole officer gets to make almost all of the factual determinations about whether these violations have occurred, and then whether to bring the revocation action at all, this bureaucratic decision-making infringes on the Sixth Amendment community jury trial right. Through the transfer of fact-finding power from the jury to a parole officer, the community loses the ability to make the all-important determinations of fact that increase punishment. This removes the determination of facts from the community, where it historically and rightfully belongs, and locates it in an arm of the vast corrections and sentencing industry.

Since parole boards are administrative bodies, often entirely lacking in legal training, and the parole hearings are usually secret, revocation of parole can lead to extra punishment for a released offender, with very few legal protections provided during the revocation hearing. This violates the convicted offender's Sixth Amendment community jury right and runs counter to *Apprendi-Blakely*. The adjudication of parole violations should be viewed as a type of sentencing, and thus entitled to the same protections.

Parole, in sum, is an area much in need of reform. A strong case emerges for the formal expansion of *Apprendi-Blakely*'s parameters to formally include parole if the underpinnings of the community jury right are taken into account. Parole is especially suited to community involvement, as it takes place outside of the prison walls. Instead of aving parole supervised by overburdened parole officers with no ties to er the offenders or the neighborhood, parole could be supervised by ated officials, either appointed or volunteer, who live in the ity.

Ma community members supervise parole, particularly for low-rs, would ground the punishment in Sixth Amendment par out forcing extra burdens on the criminal jury. coul ng some of the community service often ordered of Usin in the neighborhood where the offense occurred community heal, at least with nonviolent crimes. ional resources would bring parole back into the *Blakely*-Sixth Amendment fold while simultaneously improving an area rife with problems.

The community could also be integrated into the parole process through the appointment of local representatives to the parole board. Although American parole boards tend to be composed of correctional bureaucrats, many other countries involve the community when making parole decisions.[25] In this way, parole decisions could better reflect the views of the community, because community beliefs would be enacted in front of the offender with every parole decision. Involving the community in, at minimum, the decision-making of the parole board would be the simplest way of inculcating a kind of expressive, restorative retribution while simultaneously doing good for the community.

Post-Release Supervision

Post-release supervision is entirely distinct from parole. Most states have a supervised period for offenders following their final release from incarceration; some states call it parole as well, some call it probation, some call it supervised release, and some call it post-release supervision. (For simplicity's sake I will refer to this supervised period as post-release supervision, notwithstanding the various nomenclatures currently in use.) The terms and duration of post-release supervision are usually set by the state legislature, with the duration of the supervision tied to the type and level of felony committed.

Post-release supervision functions in addition to any early or conditional release, since it is usually imposed only after the majority of the original sentence has been served. Usually, the more violent or dangerous the offense (as determined by the state legislature), the longer is the term of supervised release. Many states now authorize periods of post-release supervision lasting five or ten years, and sometimes even longer. Although parole supervision was originally used as a way to shorten terms of imprisonment, post-release supervision is now added to the end of a determinate sentence, lengthening the period of state control.[26]

[25] *See* Dagan & Segev, *supra* note 6, at 9. These outside participants include experts in psychology, social work, and even independent members who come from all walks of life.

[26] *See* Cecilia Klingele, *The Role of Sentencing Commissions in the Imposition and Enforcement of Release Conditions*, 26 Fed. Sent. Rep. 191, 192 (2014)

Thus, post-release supervision, overseen by the same bureaucratic and/or judicial functionaries who supervise probation and parole, is another hidden sentencing proceeding that falls under the purview of *Blakely* and the community jury trial right.

Because an offender's post-release supervision term is determined by the legislature, not the trial court, the potential Sixth Amendment issue only arises later, when the defendant is released from incarceration and must meet with his probation or parole officer on a weekly or biweekly basis. Any violation of post-release supervision – which can range from association with known felons, to consuming alcohol, to owning a gun, to failing to meet regularly with a counselor – can potentially result in the released prisoner being returned to prison, for up to ten years in some cases. This system raises a similar problem to that of probation revocations: the failure to have any community input into determining these violations. These violations are important because any and all offender missteps are subject to a form of adjudication that, when meting out punishment, can result in a return to prison.

In some cases, the increased punishment resulting from an offender's violation of post-release supervision can extend the offender's prison term longer than even the maximum envisioned by the legislature. This seems a clear-cut violation of the Sixth Amendment's requirement that only juries can determine facts that increase an offender's punishment.

These Sixth Amendment problems are frequently compounded by the manner of imposition of post-release supervision. In the federal system, there is often automatic imposition of supervised release, an additional punishment that is levied upon offenders without much deliberation concerning either an offender's rehabilitative needs or the safety of the community.[27] This raises questions about resource stewardship; by some accounts, the federal system alone spends an additional $13,000 on each offender's term of post-release supervision[28] – and this is on top of whatever costs are incurred during an offender's actual prison or jail term.

[27] *See* Christine S. Scott-Hayward, *Shadow Sentencing: The Imposition of Federal Supervised Release*, 18 Berkeley J. of Crim. L. 181, 183 (2013).

[28] *See id.* at 184.

By permitting a term of post-release supervision to be tacked on to certain violent felonies *in addition* to the standard term of imprisonment, and allowing this special term to be supervised by the same bureaucracy that enforces parole and probation, the actors increasing an offender's punishment are very far away from the constitutional ideal. Although post-release supervision was originally envisioned, like probation, to help rehabilitate the offender within the community,[29] it has turned into another bureaucratic maze for offender and probation officer alike. The released prisoner must navigate a confusing thicket of rules, restrictions, and regulations to comply with the terms of his release.

Although the phrase "community supervision" often applies to post-prison terms such as parole and post-release supervision, the offender has, in reality, little involvement with the community during post-release supervision. His supervision comes almost entirely from the probation officer who oversees the case. Not only does this vest more power in the probation officer, who, as we have discussed, is entirely a bureaucratic actor, but the offender's interaction with the community that he has injured with his crime is virtually nil.

Post-release supervision offers an even more complicated scheme in the federal system, where much of it is discretionary,[30] not mandatory.[31] For federal crimes, most post-release supervision is an additional, separate order imposed by the court, in addition to the term of imprisonment.[32] Despite its discretionary nature, however, most federal offenders invariably get a term of post-release supervision added to their prison terms. The imposition of this post-prison term is based on the type of original offense committed[,] and until recently was not even affected by criminal history.[33] An offender's substance history has also been taken into account in determining the need for post-release

[29] *See id.* at 189.

[30] *See* 18 U.S.C. § 3583(a) ("[I]n imposing a sentence to a term of imprisonment for a felony of misdemeanor, [the court] may include as part of the sentence a requirement that the defendant be placed on a term of supervised release after imprisonment.").

[31] *See* U.S. SENTENCING COMM'N, FEDERAL OFFENDERS SENTENCED TO SUPERVISED RELEASE 50 (2010), located at http://www.ussc.gov/Education_and_Training/Annual_National_Training_Seminar/2012/2_Federal_Offenders_Sentenced_to_Supervised_Release.pdf.

[32] *See* U.S. SENTENCING GUIDELINES MANUAL ch. 7, pt. A(2)(b) (2014).

[33] *See* UNITED STATES SENTENCING GUIDELINES § 5D1.1 cmt. n.3(B) (amended November 1, 2011).

supervision.[34] In addition, the Federal Sentencing Guidelines also dictate the length of the post-release supervision term, which depends on the offense committed.[35]

There are a variety of problems with this routine imposition of post-release supervision. First, and most obviously, having Article III judges potentially increasing an offender's sentence by tacking on regulation-heavy post-release supervision violates the community jury trial right. Although the Federal Sentencing Guidelines claim that post-release supervision is not imposed for punitive purposes,[36] this claim is belied by both the complex regulatory schema that a released offender must still continue to navigate once the full prison term is completed[37] as well as the fact that the federal trial court looks at almost precisely the same factors to determine whether post-release supervision should be imposed[38] as it does to determine the length of punishment in the first place.

The federal government may claim that post-release supervision is not punishment. The welter of complex regulation accompanying federal post-release supervision, however, proves this untrue. The Sentencing Commission recommends that a list of fifteen "standard" conditions be imposed, which include reporting requirements, employment requirements, drug treatment, mental health treatment, community service, a curfew, restriction of the offender's personal associations, financial disclosure, warrantless searches, providing DNA samples, restrictions from certain jobs, and disclosure of financial information to probation officers.[39] Considering that most, if not all, of these conditions are imposed upon a released offender, the amount of time and effort needed for the offender to comply is substantial and often onerous. In the broadest sense, an offender's attempts to follow and meet all of these arduous requirements can be punishment itself.

After a revocation hearing, if a federal trial court determines that an offender has violated a term of her post-release supervision, it can

[34] *See id.* at § 5.D1.1, cmt. n.3(B).

[35] *See* U.S. Sentencing Guidelines Manual § 5D1.2(a)(2).

[36] *See* Scott-Hayward, *Shadow Sentencing: The Imposition of Supervised Release*, *supra* note 27, at 193.

[37] *See generally* 18 U.S.C. § 3583(d) (2012); U.S. Sentencing Guidelines Manual § 5D1.3 (2014).

[38] *See* USSG, § 3583(c).

[39] *See* U.S. Sentencing Guidelines Manual § 5D1.3(c).

continue the defendant's release without any changes, extend or modify the term, or revoke release and impose a new prison sentence, ranging from three to sixty-three months.[40] The court's ability to find facts in this situation and impose punishment clearly violates the spirit of the Sixth Amendment jury trial right, which reserves solely to the community the right to find facts and impose punishment.

Equally troubling, revocation of post-release supervision is a major driver of state prison growth, accounting for more than half of daily prison admissions in some jurisdictions.[41] Although state legislatures do have the right to impose extra punishments, like post-release supervision, onto particular crimes, the oversight and decision-making power for post-release supervision and its revocation must be improved to meet both the Sixth Amendment and *Apprendi-Blakely*'s requirements.

One way to address these problems with post-release supervision is to better involve the community in this sort of "community supervision." For example, instead of having a released offender report only to a sole, overloaded probation officer, the government could appoint a rotating board of community members to assist the probation officer with overseeing the released prisoner within the community, requiring the offender to check in with a variety of actors in different roles, including clergy, addiction/rehabilitation program directors, housing coordinators, and other officially appointed local citizens. In this way, not only is some burden lifted from the probation office, but the offender also has more interaction with various community leaders, granting him some ability to reintegrate back into the community after his term of post-release supervision is complete.

Fines

Most recently, the Supreme Court held in *Southern Union*[42] that the Fifth and Sixth Amendments apply to the imposition of criminal

[40] *Id. at* ch. 7, pt. A. 2(b). In the federal courts, a trial judge cannot impose or lengthen a revocation sentence in order to promote rehabilitation in prison. *See* United States v. Deen, 706 F.3d 760, 768 (6th Cir. 2013).

[41] *See* Cecilia Klingele, *The Role of Sentencing Commissions in the Imposition and Enforcement of Release Conditions*, 26 FED. SENT. REP. 191, 191 (2014).

[42] Southern Union Co. v. United States, 132 S. Ct. 2344, 2350 (2012).

fines as well as to other criminal penalties. This represents a dramatic change from what many courts have assumed over the years, now that any imposition of a criminal fine is punitive. Accordingly, only the jury may now impose a criminal fine that increases the offender's punishment beyond the maximum.

When the Supreme Court granted Southern Union's petition for certiorari, it was to resolve the mounting conflict between the First Circuit's conclusion that *Apprendi* does not apply to criminal fines and the contrary conclusions reached by the Second Circuit in *United States v. Pfaff* and by the Seventh Circuit in *United States v. LaGrou Distribution Systems*. The latter two courts employed *Apprendi-Blakely* to vacate criminal fines, not to justify them.

In reversing the First Circuit, the *Southern Union* Court held unequivocally for the first time that *Apprendi* applies to the imposition of criminal fines. The Court explained that it does not – and has never – distinguished one form of penal sanction from another, and thus *Apprendi* must apply to all criminal sanctions: "Apprendi's 'core concern,' is to reserve to the jury 'the determination of facts that warrant punishment for a specific statutory offense' … [and] [t]hat concern applies whether the sentence is a criminal fine or imprisonment or death." Ultimately, the Court in *Southern Union* determined that there is no principled basis for treating fines any differently from other penalties: "our decisions broadly prohibit judicial fact-finding that increases maximum criminal 'sentence[s],' 'penalties,' or 'punishment[s]' – terms that each undeniably embrace fines."[43]

Of course, even after *Southern Union*, there are still unresolved questions regarding monetary payments as part of a sentence. The Court did note that the Sixth Amendment right to jury trial does not apply to petty offenses. Accordingly, courts will still have to determine the line between insignificant and substantial criminal fines, with the community jury trial right only applying to the latter.

Moreover, *Southern Union* left open the question of whether the Sixth Amendment and *Apprendi-Blakely* apply to restitution. Although the Court did point out that *Apprendi-Blakely* does apply to any "penalt[y] inflicted by the sovereign for the commission of

[43] Southern Union, 132 S. Ct. at 2350.

offenses," the topic of restitution, which I address next, is a complicated one and as of now still unresolved.

Restitution

Judges often have wide discretion over the restitution imposed on a criminal defendant. Although the decision of *when* to impose restitution is normally decided by the legislature, the *amount* of restitution imposed is usually made solely by the trial court. I include restitution in this chapter's discussion of back-end procedures because although the trial court decides the amount of restitution during the sentencing hearing, the payment of such invariably happens afterwards.

There are two ways in which a judge's determination of the restitution amount violates *Blakely*'s animating principles. First, unless the court is simply imposing a set amount dictated by the legislature, it must find facts to determine the total sum, including the level of harm to the victim, the offender's intent in committing the crime, and the offender's ability to pay.

Moreover, laws that tie restitution to a victim's loss violate the historical Sixth Amendment jury trial right unless the jury is the one to determine the penalty's amount. The history of criminal restitution in this country gives weight to this claim. Up until the nineteenth century, courts usually imposed restitution only when it was based on the facts alleged in the indictment, following a defendant's conviction.[44] This means that a jury had to specifically find, beyond a reasonable doubt, that goods had been lost and a defendant should be punished for this loss by providing restitution to the victim. This is similar to the requirement that juries must find all facts that impose punishment. Thus, looking at the historical parallels alone, logically the jury trial right should apply to criminal restitution.

Following the Court's decision in *Southern Union*, one retired federal judge has fervently embraced the idea that any restitution not imposed by the jury violates the Sixth Amendment. Judge William M. Acker has

[44] *See* James Barta, Note, *Guarding the Rights of the Accused and Accuser: The Jury's Role in Awarding Criminal Restitution under the Sixth Amendment*, 51 Am Crim. L. Rev. 463, 477 (2014).

argued that the Mandatory Victims Restitution Act (MVRA) both violates *Apprendi-Blakely* and is unconstitutional because the act requires courts, when sentencing federal defendants, to order restitution to all possible victims in the full amount of their losses, no matter the financial situation of the defendant.[45] In addition to fixing the amount of restitution, the court must fix a payment schedule.[46] Although *Southern Union* does not specifically mention "restitution," court-ordered restitution is virtually indistinguishable from a fine, and there is no discernible reason that fines would be subject to the Sixth Amendment jury trial right but that restitution would not.

Like so many other aspects of ancillary sentencing, the imposition of restitution, now mandated as an integral part of a defendant's sentence, is essentially controlled by the probation officer, as the pre-sentence report is the sole "evidentiary" source for the restitution order. In the federal system, and in most states, the judge "may accept any undisputed portion of the presentence report as a finding of fact."[47] Indeed, as Justice Scalia noted in his *Booker* dissent, trial courts often must adopt "bureaucratically prepared, hearsay-riddled pre-sentence reports."[48] After reviewing the probation officer's report, the trial court may impose restitution based on the report alone, request additional documentation, or conduct a separate restitution hearing, although the latter two are rare. In other words, under the MVRA, the court may find facts (proven by the government by a mere preponderance-of-evidence standard) and impose additional punishment without the imprimatur of the jury.

Along with setting the amount of restitution, the court must also create a payment schedule for the defendant, with no requirement for input from any of the parties. This means that it is possible for the court to impose an impossible or extremely punitive payment schedule on the defendant, thereby increasing his or her punishment, without any participation from anyone, including the community.

Finally, as with other suspended sentences, a court may revoke probation or supervised release upon finding that a defendant has

[45] *See* 18 U.S.C. § 3663A(a)(1).
[46] *See* § 3664(f)(2).
[47] FED. R. CRIM. P. 32(I)(3)(A).
[48] United States v. Booker, 543 U.S. 220, 304 (2005) (Scalia, J., dissenting).

defaulted on restitution.[49] In other words, the court can send a defendant to prison (or back to prison) for debt. Moreover, many courts have simply assumed that restitution does not constitute criminal punishment and instead is compensation to the victim. The Supreme Court in *Kelly v. Robinson*, however, held that restitution constitutes a criminal penalty and not compensation.[50] Thus, when fact-finding is required, the imposition of restitution should be determined by a jury.

In the spring of 2014, *Paroline v. United States*[51] addressed criminal restitution, focusing on the required proof for imposing full restitution on a convicted pornography trafficker. In 1994, Congress provided a financial remedy for victims of those convicted of trafficking in child pornography, or of other sexual crimes against children, under the Mandatory Restitution for Sexual Exploitation of Children Act (Mandatory Restitution Act).[52] Any restitution penalty imposed is in addition to the sentence imposed upon conviction. The federal appeals courts, however, had been divided on whether this extra penalty should be virtually automatic or whether a link between the crimes and the harms to victims needed to be proved.[53]

The *Paroline* Court interpreted the language of the Mandatory Restitution Act to mean that a trial court must determine the amount of restitution the defendant must pay, and this could be done only after it determined the specific defendant's proximate cause of the victim's loss. As the *Paroline* Court noted, a requirement of proximate cause is more restrictive than a requirement of factual cause alone.[54]

Notwithstanding this slightly heightened standard, however, the Mandatory Restitution Act still vests the trial court with the fact-finding abilities to determine whether restitution is deserved. Viewed through the lens of *Apprendi-Blakely* and the community jury trial right, this is troubling. As the Supreme Court has itself found, "the purpose of awarding restitution ... is ... to mete out appropriate criminal

[49] 18 U.S.C. § 3614(a).

[50] This was in the context of deciding whether restitution under the VWPA was subject to discharge in bankruptcy. *See* Kelly v. Robinson, 479 U.S. 36, 52–53 (1986).

[51] 572 U.S. ____, 134 S. Ct. 1710 (2014).

[52] 18 U.S.C. s. 2251.

[53] *Paroline*, slip op. at 5.

[54] *Paroline*, slip op. at 8.

punishment."[55] There is no question that determining and imposing the amount of restitution is a punitive act. Accordingly, if the jury is not the one to determine the causation by the defendant, then the Mandatory Restitution Act is subject to the same Sixth Amendment community jury trial right problems as the MVRA.

Put another way, laws that tie restitution to a victim's loss, whether through proximate or actual cause, violate the community jury trial right unless the jury is the one to determine the penalty's amount. Imposition of restitution could be achieved according to the Sixth Amendment in one of two ways. First, if the matter is left entirely up to the jury, then part of the jury's required findings of fact could be how much loss the defendant caused the victim, and how much monetary restitution would be required to compensate the victim for her loss. Alternately, if Congress wishes to set the amounts of restitution to correspond with certain levels of loss, then the Mandatory Restitution Act could dictate the monetary amounts that equal specific acts of causation, and the jury could simply find the level of causation perpetrated by the defendant in its findings of fact. Either way, the important determination of facts (which leads to the imposition of punishment) needs to be done by the jury, not the court.

Of course, the imposition of automatic restitution for sympathetic victims is difficult to oppose. Nonetheless, Congress cannot simply ignore the Sixth Amendment jury trial right, which quite plainly precludes nonjury fact-finding whenever this increases the defendant's punishment. All of the restitution procedures that impose punishment upon a defendant without jury input plainly usurp the jury's rightful role and violate our current understanding of both *Apprendi-Blakely* and the community jury trial right.

The time has come to reform ancillary sentencing proceedings to comply with the Sixth Amendment-*Blakely* requirements. First, the Supreme Court's recently expressed understanding of the Sixth Amendment embraces the hidden front and back ends of sentencing proceedings. Second, as a matter of punishment theory, it is unclear whether most ancillary sentencing procedures actually work in the way they are intended, either rehabilitatively, retributively, or on the basis of

[55] *See* Pasquantino v. United States, 544 U.S. 349, 365 (2005).

deterrence. These two problems combine to create a new way to think about both hidden sentencing procedures and the rights due to offenders after the trial has ended and the punishment has begun.

A robust understanding of the community jury trial right calls a whole variety of ancillary sentencing proceedings into question. Not only must the community have its say in sentencing the offender at the actual sentencing hearing, but it also must have some sort of imprimatur in the hidden aspects of our sentencing proceedings, from beginning to end.

Excluding front- and back-end sentencing proceedings from the reach of the community's values is doing precisely what Blackstone foresaw in his crusade against "secret machinations" eroding the jury right. The public's understanding of sentencing has far too often been satisfied with mere superficiality, with little interest in exploring the jurisprudential undercurrents that have animated all aspects of sentencing, front end and back end. Allowing the community back in through the tool of the jury is one way to fix this problem.

When we fully incorporate the community's role in imposing punishment, we may well suffer some "delays" and "little inconveniences" in sentencing offenders. Although the rush to justice may resist the time it takes to fully provide an offender with all of her Sixth Amendment rights, the unregulated, invisible punishments imposed during the hidden phases of sentencing can have an outsized effect.

11 JURY NULLIFICATION AND VICTIM RIGHTS: GOING PAST PROCEDURE

Although profoundly dissimilar, jury nullification and victim's rights have one important aspect in common: they both go beyond the normal envisioning of the criminal adjudication process, tipping the scales in favor of their unique and sometimes quite-powerful voices. Although jury nullification erases an offender's potential punishment whereas victim's rights tend to increase it, both also are the extreme culmination of the community voice expanded to its greatest influence, having tremendous control over either the actual offense found or the punishment imposed. This chapter explores how the community has triumphed in two very different ways through the tools of victim's rights and jury nullification.

JURY NULLIFICATION

Jury nullification erodes the formal paradigm surrounding law.[1] Most broadly, jury nullification takes place when jurors decide, as a body, to reject the law as it is given to them by the court and acquit the defendant.[2] By going outside the standard role of the jury, which is to find facts that determine an offender's punishment, and taking the rule of law into its own hands, a nullifying jury disrupts and destabilizes the standard parade of criminal procedure by rejecting the law's actual application to

[1] *See* Jenny Carroll, *Nullification as Law*, 102 GEO. L. J. 579, 580 (2014). As Carroll notes, a nullifying jury provides the possibility that the jury would view the law as deficient, either generally or in its application to a particular defendant. *Id.* at 582.

[2] *See* Nancy Marder, *The Myth of the Nullifying Jury*, 93 NW. U. L. REV. 877, 881 (1999).

a particular defendant. In becoming part of a nullifying jury, a juror's role shifts definitively from being a passive receiver of the law to an active shaper of it.[3]

Of course, this jury seizure of the role as law's interpreter harks back to the earliest days of our Republic. As we saw in Chapter 2, the jury was originally arbiter of both facts and the law,[4] before and after the Revolution, a double role that was supported by the lower federal courts until the early nineteenth century.[5] There was no specific prohibition against jury nullification until 1895.[6] Only at the turn of the century did the Supreme Court hold that the jury's role is to adjudicate the facts and the judiciary's role is to adjudicate the law. Although juries continue to have the power to nullify, they no longer have a "right" to do so.[7]

As we have discussed, the original notion of the relationship between the citizen and the government and the jury's role in that relationship was very different in the post-colonial era than what it is today. One major difference was in the jury's determination of the law as well as the facts. Jury nullification fit in with the jury's original role as protector of the common man, as it created a device that safeguarded the people's liberty by providing an escape hatch from any governmental overreach of power or incorrect understanding of the criminal law. Although our criminal justice system has largely eliminated this jury role, it still lingers in the possibility of jury nullification.

Although generally disfavored, jury nullification fits in well with the theory of community decision-making in criminal justice. With the power of nullification, "the jury, with its original power to reject (or nullify) laws it finds discordant with the lived experiences of the citizenry, emerges not as a scourge of the rule of law within the democracy but rather as a bridge between the governed and the law, and as a source of the law itself."[8]

[3] *See* Carroll, *Nullification as Law*, *supra* note 1, at 580.

[4] *See* Georgia v. Brailsford, 3 U.S. 1 (1794); *see generally* Mark DeWolfe Howe, *Juries as Judges of Criminal Law*, 52 HARV. L. REV. 582, 584–85 (1939) (illustrating how early American juries had the right to decide questions of both law and fact).

[5] *See* Carroll, *Nullification as Law*, *supra* note 1, at 596.

[6] *See* Sparf & Hansen v. United States, 156 U.S. 51, 83 (1895).

[7] *See* Sparf, 156 U.S. at 74. *Sparf*'s effect, ultimately, was to eradicate standard jury instructions on jury nullification where not explicitly authorized.

[8] Jenny Carroll, *Nullification as Law*, *supra* note 1, at 586.

Interestingly, with all the Supreme Court's interest in both the Sixth Amendment and jury trial rights recently, there has been minimal discussion of the role of jury nullification, either at the beginning of the American experiment or in our modern day.

So where does this leave us? If we are truly interested in the community's involvement in the criminal justice system and desire a stronger interaction and investment between the citizens and the criminal law, then jury nullification might not be that bad. Considered one way, it is the purest form of community arbitration of crime. Under this view, jury nullification is the natural result of a jury's rejection of criminal punishment for a particular defendant or class of defendants. The reasons for this rejection vary, from perceived unfairness of the law, unsuitability of the charge, or overwhelming belief in defendant's innocence, to general dismay at the rigor of the applicable sentencing scheme.

Of course, a constant stream of jury nullification would erase the rule of law as we know it. If the criminal law is never applicable, then there is no community jury right, because there is no framework in which to enact it.

But an occasional use of jury nullification can and should be seen as an extreme but still valid exercise of community cohesion and power in direct response to unfairness and/or inequity in the law. Instead of being passive acceptors of legalized injustice, nullifying jurors actively try to rewrite the law to better fit the world around them. In our current world of inactive and detached citizens, perhaps too much zeal, even if it briefly leads to the upheaval of the rule of law within the courtroom, is better than apathy. A nullifying jury is, if nothing else, a concerned jury, and symptomatic of the great fissures within our criminal justice system.

When the jury decides to nullify, several things happen. First, there is direct communication between the defendant and the local community. Put another way, with jury nullification, the offender can rely upon his fellow citizens to correct the failings or the overzealousness of the criminal law.[9] In addition, the jury's desire to reinterpret and reinvent the law, in contrast to existing structures, can be seen as less a challenge to the judiciary and more a challenge to the modern barriers separating the local community from direct imposition of punishment.

[9] *See id.* at 590.

Normally, the community is happy to rely on these barriers, as manifested in our tripartite form of government, to process any potential offenders. But occasionally these walls are not load bearing but instead barricades to fairness, uniformity, and local democracy. This is particularly true where local jurors have beliefs that differ from those of their elected representatives. In that case, the jury's nullification power might seem to be the only forum for the community's expression of these values.[10] In such cases, occasional jury nullification seems reasonable.

Jury nullification is not as antagonistic to the standard criminal justice process as it is often portrayed. Indeed, jurors who nullify are exercising the same interpretative tools as those who convict.[11] For example, in a traditional jury setting, jurors are often asked to apply the law to the facts. Naturally, there are always gray areas of the law that allow the jury's application of community norms into their interpretative process.[12] The division of facts versus laws, then, is not as complete as courts would have us believe. Thus, whether the jury is finding facts, applying a vague legal standard, interpreting jury instructions, or determining that the law should not apply to a given offender, the intellectual activity is still the same.

Of course, the use of jury nullification as a safety valve for a frustrated, alienated, or concerned community works only if the process is utilized infrequently. Encouraging habitual use of jury nullification as a routine aspect of the criminal justice system[13] would undermine the general rigor of the criminal law and the sanctity of the system, as well as potentially insert racism and sexism into the process.[14] Moreover, many scholars feel that the "right" to nullification is not really a right at all, being instead merely the end result of recognizing two other

[10] *See* Marder, *supra* note 2, at 934.

[11] *See id.* at 880.

[12] *See id.* at 904. Marder calls this interpretative view of jury decision-making the "process" view, based on "a fundamental faith in the jury, and a belief that the jury does and should play important roles because of its unique institutional features." *Id.* at 906.

[13] *See generally* Paul Butler, *Racially Based Jury Nullification: Black Power in the Criminal Justice System*, 105 YALE L. J. 677 (1995) (arguing that African-American jurors should vote to acquit African-American defendants in nonviolent, victimless cases).

[14] *See* Tania Tetlow, *Discriminatory Acquittal*, 18 WILLIAM & MARY BILL OF RIGHTS Q. 75, 75 (2009) (arguing that jury nullification based on discrimination or bias hurts victims and communities).

important rights: the jury trial right and the Double Jeopardy Clause protecting the finality of acquittals.[15] Therefore, the nullifying power of the jury should be used sparingly, as a last resort and not as routine happenstance.

VICTIM'S RIGHTS

One final added wrinkle affecting community jury rights in the criminal justice system is the ever-burgeoning victim's rights movement. Over the past thirty years, the role of the victim in the criminal justice system has increased significantly. Today's crime victim possesses a panoply of rights, including, in the federal system, the right to restitution, the right to meet with line prosecutors, the right to speak at sentencing, and a right to be notified if the offender is paroled.[16] Most states have similar protections for crime victims.[17] Indeed, all fifty states have passed victims' rights statutes, and at least thirty-two states also have state constitutional provisions protecting victims' rights.[18]

Most troubling for defenders of the community jury right is how the quest for victim's rights has succeeded in refocusing the thrust of the criminal law from the needs and desires of the community or local public to the needs and desires of the criminal victim.[19] Indeed, scholars have noted that the victim is now the paramount community member in

[15] *See* Nancy King, *Silencing Nullification Advocacy Inside the Jury Room and Outside the Courtroom*, 65 U. CHI. L. REV. 433, 446 (1998).

[16] *See* Crime Victims' Rights Act, 18 U.S.C. § 3771 (2004).

[17] For example, in New York, victims have a right to financial compensation from the New York State Office of Victim Services, make statements to the Department of Probation for judicial consideration when determining the defendant's sentence, request restitution as part of a defendant's sentence, make an oral statement to the court at the defendant's sentencing, make a written or oral statement to the Division of Parole for consideration, receive notification of the release of an inmate from a city or state correctional facility, and receive notification of the final disposition of the case. *See* New York County District Attorney's Office, located at http://manhattanda.org/victims-rights-guidelines (last visited 6/10/14). California provides similar rights to its victims. *See* Marsy's Law, California Constitution art. I, § 28, section (b).

[18] *See* Andrew Nash, Note, *Victims by Definition*, 85 WASH. U. L. REV. 1419, 1425 (2008).

[19] *See* Brenner M. Fissell, *Abstract Risk and the Politics of the Criminal Law*, 51 AM. CRIM. L. REV. 657, 679 (2014).

need of representation and action by the criminal justice process.[20] Such a focus on one member of the affected community, instead of the community as a whole, has unquestionably skewed the attention of the criminal justice process, as these myriad rights of the victim can usurp what little role the community has left. This is especially true in guilty pleas, where the victim's allocution at sentencing can increase the defendant's sentence without any community imprimatur.

The bulk of the victim's rights problem lies with victim impact statements, which generally concern the impact of the defendant's crime on the primary victim and usually take place during sentencing. Victim impact statements are presented to the judge or the parole officer, either as a document or in person, and are often read aloud at the offender's plea or sentencing hearing. These statements usually contain information that describes the victim's financial losses; denote the victim's physical injuries, including gravity and permanence; depict any changes to the victim's personal welfare or familial relationships; detail any requests for psychological services initiated by the victim or the victim's surviving family; and provide any other information related to the impact of the crime on the victim or the victim's family.[21] The routine insertion of these victim impact statements into post-conviction proceedings should be seen as triumph of the victim's rights movement.[22]

The slow creep of victim impact evidence into virtually every type of criminal adjudication has worrying implications, however. First, it is extremely difficult for the defendant to rebut testimony concerning the victim's character,[23] which understandably makes the crime committed look even more reprehensible and thus more deserving of harsh punishment. Even if the victim (or her family) paints a picture that is almost completely untrue, there is no realistic way for the defendant to disprove such assertions. The very injury visited upon the victim by the offender

[20] *See, e.g.*, JONATHAN SIMON, GOVERNING THROUGH CRIME: HOW THE WAR ON CRIME TRANSFORMED AMERICAN DEMOCRACY AND CREATED A CULTURE OF FEAR 75–88 (2007).

[21] *See* Bryan Myers & Edith Green, *The Prejudicial Nature of Victim Impact Statements*, 10 PSYCHOL. PUB. POL'Y 492, 492 (2004).

[22] *See* Aya Gruber, *A Distributive Theory of Criminal Law*, 52 WM. & MARY L. REV. 1, 42 (2010).

[23] See Wayne Logan, *Through The Past Darkly: A Survey of the Uses and Abuses of Victim Impact Evidence in Capital Trials*, 41 ARIZONA L. REV. 143, 143 (1999).

simply disqualifies any contrasting evidence provided by the defendant. In this way, any decision to increase punishment against the offender is not only not made by the community, but is also made without properly balanced information.

Second, most states have minimal guidance on what kind of evidence can be admitted in sentencing proceedings.[24] The Supreme Court has held constitutional the inclusion of victim impact evidence into an offender's capital sentencing proceeding,[25] but has given little other guidance as to when or how such impact evidence should be utilized. In both the state and federal systems, victim impact evidence is used routinely in noncapital settings.[26] The use of this type of evidence, moreover, can lead to a type of victim "ranking," where crimes against certain victims are punished much more harshly than others, due to race, gender, age, creed, or national origin.

Third, as a general concept, victim impact statements contradict the idea that a crime is an injury to the community and the state, as opposed to an injury to an individual victim.[27] The American criminal justice system did away with private prosecutors during the eighteenth century, turning all criminal prosecution over to the state.[28] Presumably, one of the reasons was to normalize and regularize the types of prosecution and punishment visited upon offenders. All criminal prosecutions are undertaken in the name of the state and community, not individual victims. Using victim impact statements at sentencing shifts the thrust of the criminal justice process away from the injury done to the community and focuses it solely on the victim.

Furthermore, victims are not the only ones directly hurt by an offender's crimes (although, presumably, the most affected). The victim's family and friends, the offender's family and friends, both the victim and offender's workplaces, and the community at large are all

[24] *See* Meghan Ryan, *Proximate Retribution*, 48 HOUS. L. REV. 1049, 1081 (2012).

[25] *See* Payne v. Tennessee, 501 U.S. 808 (1991).

[26] *See* Myers & Green, *Prejudicial Nature of Victim Impact Statements*, *supra* note 21, at 492.

[27] *See generally* Andrew Ashworth, *Victim Impact Statements and Sentencing*, CRIM. L. REV. 498 (1993).

[28] Connecticut was the first colony to eliminate private prosecutors, passing a statute appointing a county prosecutor to prosecute all crimes. *See* JAMES L. WORRALL, PROSECUTION IN AMERICA: A HISTORICAL AND COMPARATIVE ACCOUNT 7 (2008).

injured by the crimes committed. Yet it is currently only the victim who is permitted to directly testify at the sentencing, probation, and parole hearings. The other, more remote harms that are caused are almost completely ignored.[29] If we are truly opening up the sentencing proceeding to all claims of victim grievances, then in the interest of fairness, we should permit all potential victims throughout the community to expound on their injuries. Of course, if we do that, then we should also permit all offender witnesses, family and friends, and supporters to provide mitigating evidence for the court to weigh.

Finally, opening up the doors to victim statements also opens up the question of "victimhood" in general. In society, if not in law, victimhood is a steadily expanding category.[30] Should we permit victims suffering from more remote harms to present victim impact evidence at trial, sentencing, or parole hearings? How do we determine who is too remote a victim? Is it based on the moral blameworthiness of the offender? The level of injury to the potential victim? His or her status in the community? The Federal Sentencing Guidelines, for one, provides no definition of the term "victim,"[31] and few states have specifically defined the term either. This vagueness is particularly disconcerting because, technically, any victim of any stripe could deprive an offender of either her life or liberty interests. Considering the highly affective nature of victim impact evidence, the possibility of increasing or extending punishment to offenders due to harms done to putative victims is greatly worrying.

This one-sided granting of power and affectivity to the victim, as sympathetic as he or she may be, throws a wrench into the original procedures of criminal justice as they were conceived in this nation almost 250 years ago. Allowing victim impact evidence into the criminal adjudication process takes the focus off community adjudication and punishment and refocuses it on the victim. This, in turn, skews attention from the need to impose proper punishment on offenders, one of the primary purposes of the criminal justice system.

[29] *See* Ryan, *Proximate Retribution*, *supra* note 24, at 1082–83.

[30] *See* Jessie K. Liu, *Victimhood* 71 Mo. L. Rev. 115, 128 (2006). As Liu notes, "the broadening of the victim category represents a rejection of what Stephen Carter calls the 'bilateral individualist construction of victimhood.'" *See id.* at 129.

[31] *See id.* at 145.

Both jury nullification and the victim's rights movement can have an outsize effect on the standard procedures of criminal adjudication, whether it is to upend the normal judgments of fact and law or to heavily impact the determination of a defendant's offense and deserved punishment. Both procedures should be used sparingly, as each undermines the proportionality upon which the criminal law rests.

12 CONCLUSION

What might the future of criminal procedure be if the community jury trial right is fully applied to all aspects of the criminal justice system? How might we better our understanding not only of the criminal process, from beginning to end, but also of the plight and abuses suffered by many defendants and prisoners? What might we gain as a community by interacting more closely with the justice system? The possibilities are abundant: better appreciation of the duties and obligations of citizenship, more balanced views on how to punish crime, a more nuanced comprehension of the end results of sentencing, a better sense of who our neighbors are, and an increased investment in the indelible cohesion of our local society – that much-lamented and nebulous civic group.

With the advent of *Apprendi-Blakely*, our standard understanding of the original meaning of the right to a jury trial has been called into question. The Supreme Court's recent work strengthening the jury trial right, based on the people's historical right to determine all punishment, has greater textual and historical warrant than previously supposed. Obscured by over a century of misunderstanding, it is time for the collective jury trial right to once again come into its own. By expansively interpreting this right as community participation in the criminal justice system, the collective jury trial right can be translated, updated, and implemented in ways appropriate for the twenty-first century, not only the eighteenth.

Although the implementation of community participation within criminal adjudication might be challenging and occasion some time and expense, overall it will have positive consequences for both our understanding of and our comfort level with the processes of criminal justice. To combat the feeling and the reality of hurried, incomplete justice, it may indeed be necessary to slow down the inexorable machinery of criminal process. If a system's credibility is proven by how it treats its poorest, weakest, and most disadvantaged, then our criminal justice system is in dire need of reworking. Inserting the community voice into the process may be one of the easier ways of doing so without bringing the whole machinery to a halt.

This participation includes the procedures that take place before trial. Our current system of pretrial detention lies in shambles, incarcerating those not yet convicted in punitive conditions often far worse than those existing in prisons. Allowing the community a say in the matter and broadening the ambit of those who can be released pretrial is one way to shine light into the darkness.

Although there is no one perfect solution to the myriad problems of pretrial detention, the use of a bail jury, combined with increasing monitored pretrial release, would help solve both constitutional and procedural issues in the practice of pretrial incarceration. First, a bail jury would help ameliorate the Sixth Amendment issue, allowing the community a chance to help decide what is unquestionably punishment. In addition, giving local citizens a say in who is released back into their community has a practical aspect to it; instead of having the prosecutor and the judge, both representatives of the government, be the only ones to determine community safety, it makes sense to have some input from the very community that the government is trying to protect.

Second, the addition of increased electronic monitoring of those offenders released before trial would be a relatively easy, cost-effective way to permit the accused who either cannot afford to make bail or about whom the community or judge still have some reservations to avoid remaining in jail until their trials. We have long offered such special privileges to the wealthy; now it is time to extend the basic rights of pretrial release to our poorest and most disadvantaged.

One of the most powerful needs for the community voice, however – even more so than in pretrial detention – is in the world of guilty pleas. Guilty pleas, and the hurried, hush-hush machinations that lie behind them, are now the primary form of criminal adjudication and are very lightly regulated, if at all. Far from the coruscating eye of the public, the backroom deals and bargaining that occur between the prosecutor and the defense attorney count out the judge, the community, and even the defendant. Although technically constitutional, they violate the spirit not only of the Sixth Amendment jury trial right but also of the entire structure of our criminal justice system: that the people, the local citizenry, have the duty and the right to opine on the punishment of an offender, in the public square. The transformation of the criminal process from a public trial to a hidden bargain has been extremely destructive to our comfort level with our system of crime and punishment, distancing and alienating the average citizen.

Involving the community in the workings of the plea bargain is critical. First, a careful look into the inside operations of guilty pleas illustrates that there are real problems in the most common procedures of criminal justice, particularly the grave imbalance of power between the prosecutor and the rest of the participants. Shining light into the ugly reality of guilty pleas, through the use of a lay jury, can only be a positive good. The plea jury, as supported by my theory of expressive, restorative retribution, strikes a solid middle ground: it allows for the current framework of guilty pleas and negotiated sentences to continue, but inserts the local citizenry into the most critical part of the plea bargain – the allocution and sentence.

The vast array of hidden procedures that structure ancillary sentencing also exhibit a great need for the voice and values of the community. It is well past time to reform these proceedings to comply with the requirements of the community jury trial right. Our understanding of sentencing has far too often been satisfied with mere superficiality, with little interest in exploring the jurisprudential undercurrents that have animated all aspects of sentencing – front end and back end.

First, doctrinally, the Supreme Court's understanding of the Sixth Amendment addresses at long last the hidden front and back ends of sentencing proceedings. In the fifteen years that have followed the issuing of *Apprendi*, the Court has fastened more and more firmly upon the tenets of the jury trial right, expanding it most recently to criminal fines and even mandatory minimums. Logically, then, it only makes sense that the *Apprendi-Blakely* reasoning would apply to those aspects of sentencing that can impose serious punishment upon an offender, even when she has been released from prison or jail.

Moreover, in terms of philosophical or theoretical intent, it is unclear whether most ancillary sentencing procedures actually work in the way they are intended, either through rehabilitation, retribution, or deterrence. Applying my theory of expressive, restorative retribution, however, with a focus on the community's participation, creates a new way to think about both hidden sentencing procedures and the rights due to offenders and local citizens after the trial has ended and the punishment begins. By involving local citizens in the probation, parole, and post-release supervision process, the community gets a say in public safety and neighborhood quality, the released offender has a better experience and a more successful return to society, and some of the crushing burden on overworked probation officers is lifted.

On the whole, restoring interest, power, and accountability to the local community is an important step in fixing some of the current problems within our criminal justice system. We need to restore a populist aspect to the punishing and sentencing of criminal offenders. When the public feels too distant from the workings of crime and punishment, and only sees the media representation of crimes and the occasional (in)famous trial, they often react by calling for ever-harsher and lengthy sentences. In contrast, allowing the community to participate in a much larger slice of criminal procedure gives the lay public a more realistic – and more personalized – view of the criminal justice system, hopefully fostering a less punitive streak as well as a better comprehension of the system's structure. The community voice is not a panacea for all of the ills of the criminal justice system, but it is a good start – one that reunites us with the original justification for the framework of American criminal process and one that reunites the local public with a system that has for too long shut them out.

SELECTED BIBLIOGRAPHY

ABRAMSON, JEFFREY, WE, THE JURY: THE JURY SYSTEM AND THE IDEAL OF DEMOCRACY (2001).

Alfieri, Anthony V., *Community Prosecutors*, 90 CAL. L. REV. 1465 (2002).

Alschuler, Albert W., *The Changing Plea Bargaining Debate*, 69 CAL. L. REV. 652 (1981).

—, *Plea Bargaining and Its History*, 13 LAW & SOC'Y 211 (1979).

—, *The Defense Attorney's Role in Plea Bargaining*, 84 YALE L.J. 1179 (1975).

—, *The Trial Judge's Role in Plea Bargaining*, 76 COLUM. L. REV. 1059 (1976).

—, *The Prosecutor's Role in Plea Bargaining*, 36 U. CHI. L. REV. 50 (1968).

Alschuler, Albert W. & Stephen J. Schulhofer, *Antiquated Procedures or Bedrock Rights? A Response to Professors Meares and Kahan*, 1998 U. CHI. LEGAL F. 215, 216 (1998).

AMAR, AHKIL REED, AMERICA'S UNWRITTEN CONSTITUTION: THE PRECEDENTS AND PRINCIPLES WE LIVE BY (2013).

—, THE BILL OF RIGHTS: CREATION AND RECONSTRUCTION (1998).

—, THE CONSTITUTION AND CRIMINAL PROCEDURE (1998).

—, *The Bill of Rights as a Constitution*, 100 YALE L.J. 1131 (1991).

ANDENAES, JOHANNES, PUNISHMENT AND DETERRENCE (1974).

Ashworth, Andrew, *Victim Impact Statements and Sentencing*, CRIM. L. REV. 498 (1993).

Bamonte, Thomas J., *The Viability of Morrisey v. Brewer and the Due Process Rights of Parolees and Other Conditional Releasees*, 18 S. ILL. U. L.J. 121 (1993).

Bandes, Susan, *Empathy, Narrative and Victim Impact Statements*, 63 U. CHI. L. REV. 361 (1996).

Baradaran, Shima & Frank McIntyre, *Race, Prediction & Pretrial Detention*, 10 J. EMPIRICAL LEGAL STUD. 741 (2014).

—, *Predicting Violence*, 90 TEX. L. REV. 497 (2012).

Barkow, Rachel E., *The Ascent of the Administrative State and the Demise of Mercy*, 121 HARV. L. REV. 1332 (2008).

—, *Federalism and the Politics of Sentencing*, 105 COLUM. L. REV. 1276 (2005).

—, *Recharging the Jury: The Criminal Jury's Constitutional Role in an Era of Mandatory Sentencing*, 152 U. PA. L. REV. 33 (2003).

Barron, David, *The Promise of Cooley's City: Traces of Local Constitutionalism*, 147 U. PA. L. REV. 487 (1999).

Barsumian, Todd, Note, *Bail Bondsmen and Bounty Hunters: Re-Examining the Right to Recapture*, 47 DRAKE L. REV. 877, 887–88 (1999).

BECCARIA, CESARE, AN ESSAY ON CRIMES AND PUNISHMENTS (Philadelphia, R. Bell 1778).

Berman, Greg & Audrey Fox, *From the Margins to the Mainstream: Community Justice at the Crossroads*, 22 JUS. SYS. J. 189 (2001).

BIBAS, STEPHANOS, THE MACHINERY OF CRIMINAL JUSTICE (2012).

—, *Plea Bargaining Outside the Shadow of Trial*, 117 HARV. L. REV. 2464 (2004).

—, *Harmonizing Substantive-Criminal-Law Values and Criminal Procedure: The Case of Alford and Nolo Contendere Pleas*, 88 CORNELL L. REV. 1361 (2003).

—, *The Real World Shift in Criminal Procedure*, 93 NW. U. L. REV. 789 (2003).

Bibas, Stephanos & Richard A. Bierschbach, *Integrating Remorse and Apology into Criminal Procedure*, 114 YALE L.J. 85 (2004).

Billings, Warren M., *Law in Colonial America: The Reassessment of Early American Legal History*, 81 MICH. L. REV. 953 (1983).

BLACKSTONE, WILLIAM, COMMENTARIES ON THE LAWS OF ENGLAND (1765).

Blinka, Daniel D., *Jefferson and Juries: The Problem of Law, Reason, and Politics in the New Republic*, 47 AM. J. OF LEGAL HIST. 35 (2005).

BODENHAMER, DAVID J., FAIR TRIAL: RIGHTS OF THE ACCUSED IN AMERICAN HISTORY 86 (1992).

BOORSTIN, DANIEL J., THE AMERICANS: THE COLONIAL EXPERIENCE 27 (1958).

Bowers, Josh, *Punishing the Innocent*, 156 U. PA. L. REV. 1117 (2008).

Bowers, Josh & Paul H. Robinson, *Perceptions of Fairness and Justice: The Shared Aims and Occasional Conflicts of Legitimacy and Moral Credibility*, 47 WAKE FOREST L. REV. 211 (2012).

Braithwaite, John, *Holism, Justice and Atonement*, 2003 UTAH L. REV. 389.

Brenner, Susan W., *Towards a Criminal Law for Cyberspace: Distributed Security*, 10 BOSTON U. J. OF SCIENCE & TECH. L. 1, 65 (2004).

Brown, Darryl, *The Perverse Effects of Efficiency in Criminal Process*, 81 VA. L. REV. 183 (2014).

Burke, Alafair & Bruce Green, *The Community Prosecutor: Questions of Professional Discretion*, 47 WAKE FOREST L. REV. 285 (2012).

Butler, Paul, *Racially Based Jury Nullification: Black Power in the Criminal Justice System*, 105 YALE L. J. 677 (1995).

Carroll, Jenny, *Nullification as Law*, 102 GEO. L. J. 579 (2014).

Chablani, Sanjay K., *Re-Framing the 'Fair Cross-Section' Requirement*, 13 U. PA. J. CONST. L. 931 (2011).

Chanenson, Steven L., *Guidance from Above and Beyond*, 58 STAN. L. REV. 175 (2005).

—, *The Next Era of Sentencing Reform*, 54 EMORY L. J. 377 (2005).

COKE, SIR EDWARD, INSTITUTES OF THE LAWS OF ENGLAND (19th ed., Garland Publishing 1979) (1644).

Colquitt, Joseph A., *Ad Hoc Plea Bargaining*, 75 TUL. L. REV. 695, 740 (2001).

Connor, Henry G., *The Constitutional Right to a Trial by a Jury of the Vicinage*, 57 U. PA. L. REV. 197 (1909).

Cooter, Robert, *Expressive Law and Economics*, 27 J. LEGAL STUD. 585 (1998).

Dancig-Rosenberg, Hadar & Tali Gal, *Restorative Criminal Justice*, 34 CARDOZO L. REV. 2313 (2013).

Dolinko, David, *The Theory and Jurisprudence of Restorative Justice*, 2003 UTAH L. REV. 319.

Dubber, Markus D., *American Plea Bargains, German Lay Judges, and the Crisis of Criminal Procedure*, 49 STAN. L. REV. 547 (1997).

Duff, R. A., *Penal Communications: Recent Work in the Philosophy of Punishment*, in CRIME AND JUSTICE: A REVIEW OF RESEARCH (1996).

—, PUNISHMENT, COMMUNICATION, AND COMMUNITY (Oxford 2001).

ENGLISH BILL OF RIGHTS (Dec. 16, 1689).

Fagan, Jeffrey & Tracey L. Meares, *Punishment, Deterrence and Social Control: The Paradox of Punishment in Minority Communities*, 6 OHIO ST. J. CRIM. L. 173 (2008).

FAIRFAX, ROGER A., JR., GRAND JURY 2.0: MODERN PERSPECTIVES ON THE GRAND JURY (2010).

—, *Grand Jury Discretion and Constitutional Design*, 93 CORNELL L. REV. 703 (2008).

—, *The Grand Jury's Jurisdictional Heritage*, 91 MINN. L. REV. 398 (2006).

Ferguson, Andrew G., *The Jury as Constitutional Identity*, 47 U.C. DAVIS 1105 (2014).

FISCHER, GEORGE, PLEA BARGAINING'S TRIUMPH (2003).

Fissell, Brenner M., *Abstract Risk and the Politics of the Criminal Law*, 51 AM. CRIM. L. REV. 657 (2014).

Forde-Mazrui, Kim, *Jural Districting: Selecting Impartial Juries Through Community Representation*, 52 VAND. L. REV. 353 (1999).

Freeland, Stephen N., Note, *The Invisible Badge: Why Bounty Hunters Should Be Regarded as State Actors Under the Symbiotic Relationship Test*, 49 WASHBURN L.J. 201 (2010).

FRIEDMAN, LAWRENCE M., CRIME AND PUNISHMENT IN AMERICAN HISTORY (1993).

Frug, Jerry, *The Geography of Community*, 48 STANFORD L. REV. 1047 (1996).

—, *Decentering Decentralization*, 60 U. CHI. L. REV. 253 (1993).

GARRETT, BRANDON L., CONVICTING THE INNOCENT: WHERE CRIMINAL PROSECUTIONS GO WRONG (2011).

Garvey, Stephen P., *Is It Wrong to Commute Death Row? Retribution, Atonement and Mercy*, 82 N. CAROLINA L. REV. 1319 (2004).

—, *Punishment as Atonement*, 46 UCLA L. REV. 1801 (1999).

GASTIL, JOHN, PERRY DRESS, PHIL WEISER & CINDY SIMMONS, THE JURY AND DEMOCRACY: HOW JURY DELIBERATION PROMOTES CIVIC ENGAGEMENT AND POLITICAL PARTICIPATION (2010).

Goebel, Julius, *King's Law and Local Custom in 17th Century New England*, 31 COLUM. L. REV. 416 (1931).

Goldstein, Abraham S., *Converging Criminal Justice Systems: Guilty Pleas and the Public Interest*, 49 S.M.U. L. REV. 567 (1996).

GOTTFREDSON, MICHAEL R. & DON M. GOTTFREDSON, DECISIONMAKING IN CRIMINAL JUSTICE: TOWARDS THE RATIONAL EXERCISE OF DISCRETION (1980).

GOTTSCHALK, MARIE, THE PRISON AND THE GALLOWS: THE POLITICS OF MASS INCARCERATION IN AMERICA (2006).

Greenberg, Douglas, *Crime, Law Enforcement, and Social Control in Colonial America*, 26 AM. J. LEGAL HIST. 293 (1982).

Gruber, Aya, *A Distributive Theory of Criminal Law*, 52 WM. & MARY L. REV. 1 (2010).

Guthrie, Chris, *Misjudging*, 7 NEV. L. REV. 420 (2007).

HALE, MATTHEW, THE HISTORY OF THE COMMON LAW OF ENGLAND (1713).

Haley, John O., *Beyond Retribution: An Integrated Approach to Restorative* Justice, 36 WASH. U. L & POL'Y 1 (2011).

HALL, KERMIT L., PAUL FINKELMAN & JAMES W. ELY, AMERICAN LEGAL HISTORY (2010).

Hampton, Jean, *Correcting Harms versus Righting Wrongs: The Goal of Retribution*, 39 UCLA L. REV. 1659 (1992).

—, *A New Theory of Retribution*, in LIABILITY AND RESPONSIBILITY: ESSAYS IN LAW AND MORALS 377 (R. G. Frey & Christopher W. Morris, eds., 1991).

Hans, Valerie P., *Introduction: Citizens as Legal Decision Makers: An International Perspective*, 40 CORNELL INT'L L.J. 303 (2007).

Hawkins, Keith, *Assessing Evil: Decision Behavior and Parole Board Justice*, 23 BRITISH J. OF CRIM. 102 (1983).

HERMAN, G. NICHOLAS, PLEA BARGAINING 26 (2004).

Howe, Mark DeWolfe, *Juries as Judges of Criminal Law*, 52 HARV. L. REV. 582 (1939).

Huighens, Kyron, *Liberalism, Normative Expectations, and the Mechanics of Fault*, 69 MOD. L. REV. 462, 477 (2006).

JACOBSON, MICHAEL, DOWNSIZING PRISONS: HOW TO REDUCE CRIME AND END MASS INCARCERATION (1995).

Johnson, Marcia & Luckett A. Johnson, *Bail: Reforming Policies to Address Overcrowded Jails, the Impact of Race on Detention, and Community Revival in Harris County, Texas*, 7 NW. J. OF L. & SOC. POL'Y 42 (2012).

Kalven, Harry, Jr., *The Dignity of the Civil Jury*, 50 VA. L. REV. 1055 (1964).

KANT, IMMANUEL, THE PHILOSOPHY OF LAW (1887).

Katyal, Neal K., *Digital Architecture as Crime Control*, 112 YALE L.J. 2261 (2003).

—, *Criminal Law in Cyberspace*, 149 U. PA. L. REV. 1003 (2001).

King, Nancy J., *Priceless Process: Nonnegotiable Features of Criminal Litigation*, 47 UCLA L. REV. 113 (1999).

—, *Silencing Nullification: Advocacy Inside the Jury Room and Outside the Courtroom*, 65 U. CHI. L. REV. 433 (1998).

King, Nancy J., David A. Soulé, Sara Steen & Robert R. Weidner, *When Process Affects Punishment: Differences in Sentences After Guilty Plea, Bench Trial, and Jury Trial in Five Guidelines States*, 105 COLUM. L. REV. 959 (2005).

King, Nancy J. & Roosevelt L. Noble, *Jury Sentencing in Non-Capital Cases: Comparing Severity and Variance with Judicial Sentences in Two States*, 2 J. EMPIRICAL LEG. STUD. 331 (2005).

Kipnis, Kenneth, *Plea Bargaining, A Critic's Rejoinder*, 13 LAW & SOC'Y REV. 555 (1979).

Klein, Susan R., *Enhancing the Judicial Role in Criminal Plea and Sentencing Bargaining*, 84 TEX. L. REV. 2023 (2006).

Klingele, Cecilia, *The Role of Sentencing Commissions in the Imposition and Enforcement of Release Conditions*, 26 FED. SENT. REP. 191 (2014).

Kobil, Daniel T., *The Quality of Mercy Strained: Wresting the Pardoning Power from the King*, 69 TEX. L. REV. 569 (1991).

KOLLOCK, PETER & MARC A. SMITH, COMMUNITIES IN CYBERSPACE (1998).

LACROIX, ALISON, THE IDEOLOGICAL ORIGINS OF AMERICAN FEDERALISM (2010).

LANGBEIN, JOHN H., THE ORIGINS OF ADVERSARY CRIMINAL TRIAL (2003).

—, *On the Myth of Written Constitutions: The Disappearance of Criminal Jury Trial*, 15 HARV. J.L. & PUB. POL'Y 119, 120 (1992).

—, *Shaping the Eighteenth-Century Criminal Trial: A View from the Ryder Sources*, 50 U. CHI. L. REV. 1 (1983).

—, *Understanding the Short History of Plea Bargaining*, 13 LAW & SOC'Y REV. 261 (1979).

—, *Land Without Plea Bargaining: How the Germans Do It*, 78 MICH. L. REV. 204 (1978).

Langer, Máximo, *Rethinking Plea Bargaining: The Practice and Reform of Prosecutorial Adjudication in American Criminal Procedure*, 33 AM. J. CRIM. L. 223 (2006).

Langhofer, Kory A., Comment, *Unaccountable at the Founding: The Originalist Case for Anonymous Juries*, 115 YALE L.J. 1823 (2006).

Lanni, Adriaan, *The Future of Community Justice*, 40 HARV. C.R.-C.L. L. REV. 359 (2005).

Leipold, Andrew, *Why Are Federal Judges So Acquittal Prone?* 83 WASH. U. L.Q. 151 (2005).

LEPORE, JILL, NEW YORK BURNING: LIBERTY, SLAVERY AND CONSPIRACY IN EIGHTEENTH-CENTURY MANHATTAN (KNOPF: 2005).

Liu, Jessie K., *Victimhood*, 71 MO. L. REV. 115 (2006).

Logan, Wayne A., *The Shadow Criminal Law of Municipal Governance*, 62 OHIO ST. L. J. 1409, (2001).

—, *Through the Past Darkly: A Survey of the Uses and Abuses of Victim Impact Evidence in Capital Trials*, 41 ARIZ. L. REV. 143 (1999).

Marder, Nancy S., *The Myth of the Nullifying Jury*, 93 NW. U. L. REV. 877 (1999).

—, *Beyond Gender: Peremptory Challenges and the Roles of the Jury*, 73 TEX. L. REV. 1041 (1995).

MCMANUS, EDGAR J., LAW AND LIBERTY IN EARLY NEW ENGLAND: CRIMINAL JUSTICE AND DUE PROCESS, 1620–1692 (1993).

Meares, Tracy L., *Rewards for Good Behavior: Influencing Prosecutorial Discretion and Conduct with Financial Incentives*, 64 FORDHAM L. REV. 851 (1995).

Meares, Tracey L. & Dan M. Kahan, *Black, White and Gray: A Reply to Alschuler and Schulhofer*, 1998 U. CHI. LEGAL F. 245 (1998).

MEYER, LINDA ROSS, THE JUSTICE OF MERCY (2013).

MINTON, TODD D., U.S. DEP'T OF JUSTICE, JAIL INMATES AT MIDYEAR 2011 – STATISTICAL TABLES 1 (2011).

MOORE, MICHAEL, PLACING BLAME: A GENERAL THEORY OF THE CRIMINAL LAW 91 (1997).

MORRIS, HERBERT, *Persons and Punishment, in* ON GUILT AND INNOCENCE, ESSAYS IN LEGAL PHILOSOPHY AND MORAL PSYCHOLOGY 31–58 (1976).

MORRIS, NORVAL, THE FUTURE OF IMPRISONMENT (1974).

MURPHY, JEFFRIE G. AND JEAN HAMPTON, FORGIVENESS AND MERCY (1988).

Myers, Bryan and Edith Green, *The Prejudicial Nature of Victim Impact Statements*, 10 PSYCHOL. PUB. POL'Y 492 (2004).

NELSON, WILLIAM, THE COMMON LAW IN COLONIAL AMERICA: VOLUME II: THE MIDDLE COLONIES AND THE CAROLINAS, 1660–1730 (2012).

—, AMERICANIZATION OF THE COMMON LAW: THE IMPACT OF LEGAL CHANGE ON MASSACHUSETTS SOCIETY, 1760–1830 (1994).

NELSON, WILLIAM E. & ROBERT C. PALMER, LIBERTY AND COMMUNITY: CONSTITUTION AND RIGHTS IN THE EARLY AMERICAN REPUBLIC (1987).

NEW YORK CHARTER OF LIBERTIES (1663).

O'Hear, Michael, *What's Good About Trials?* 156 U. PA. L. REV. PENNUMBRA 209 (2007).

Oldenquist, Andrew, *An Explanation of Retribution*, 85 J. PHIL. 464 (1988).

Pole, J. R., *Reflections on American Law and the American Revolution*, 50 WM. & MARY Q. 123 (1993).

POPE, JACQUELINE, BOUNTY HUNTERS, MARSHALS, AND SHERIFFS: FORWARD TO THE PAST (1998).

POSNER, ERIC A., ED., SOCIAL NORMS, NONLEGAL SANCTIONS, AND THE LAW (2007).

PRETRIAL JUSTICE INSTITUTE, JANUARY–DECEMBER 2011 ANNUAL REPORT (2011).

Rapaport, Elizabeth, *Retribution and Redemption in the Operation of Executive Clemency*, 74 CHI.-KENT L. REV. 1501 (2000).

Reitz, Kevin, *The New Sentencing Conundrum: Policy and Constitutional Law at Cross-Purposes*, 105 COLUM. L. REV. 1082 (2005).

—, *Modeling Discretion in American Sentencing Systems*, 20 LAW & POL'Y 389, 393 (1998).

Resnik, Judith, *Managerial Judges*, 96 HARV. L. REV. 374 (1982).

Robbennolt, Jennifer K., *Evaluating Juries by Comparison to Judges: A Benchmark for Judging?* 32 FLA. ST. U. L. REV. 469 (2005).

ROBINSON, PAUL, STEPHEN GARVEY & KIMBERLY KESSLER FERZAN, EDS., CRIMINAL LAW CONVERSATIONS (2009).

Robinson, Paul H., *Competing Conceptions of Modern Desert: Vengeful, Deontological, and Empirical*, 67 CAMBRIDGE L.J. 145 (2008).

Robinson, Paul H. & Robert Kurzban, *Concordance and Conflict in Intuitions of Justice*, 91 MINN. L. REV. 1829, 1846–92 (2007).

Robinson, Paul H. & Barbara A. Spellman, *Sentencing Decisions: Matching the Decisionmaker to the Decision Nature*, 105 COLUM. L. REV. 1124 (2005).

Rosen, Richard A., Disciplinary Sanctions Against Prosecutors for *Brady* Violations: A Paper Tiger, 65 N.C. L. REV. 693 (1987).

Ryan, Meghan, *Proximate Retribution*, 48 HOUS. L. REV. 1049 (2012).

Schauer, Frederick, *On the Supposed Jury-Dependence of Evidence Law*, 155 U. PA. L. REV. 165 (2006).

Schragger, Richard C., *The Limits of Localism*, 100 MICH. L. REV. 371, 372–73 (2001).

Schulhofer, Stephen, *Plea Bargaining as Disaster*, 101 YALE L.J. 1979 (1992).

Scott-Hayward, Christine S., *Shadow Sentencing: The Imposition of Federal Supervised Release*, 18 BERKELEY J. OF CRIM. L. 181 (2013).

SIMON, JONATHAN, GOVERNING THROUGH CRIME: HOW THE WAR ON CRIME TRANSFORMED AMERICAN DEMOCRACY AND CREATED A CULTURE OF FEAR (2007).

Slobogin, Christopher, *A Jurisprudence of Dangerousness*, 98 NW. U. L. REV. 1, 2 (2003).

Smith, Stephen, *Localism and Capital Punishment*, 64 VANDERBILT L. REV. EN BANC 105 (2011).

STEPHEN, JAMES FITZJAMES, 2 A HISTORY OF THE CRIMINAL LAW OF ENGLAND (1883).

STIMSON, SHANNON C., THE AMERICAN REVOLUTION IN THE LAW: ANGLO-AMERICAN JURISPRUDENCE BEFORE JOHN MARSHALL 59–61 (1990).

STITH, KATE & JOSE CABRANES, FEAR OF JUDGING: SENTENCING GUIDELINES IN THE FEDERAL COURTS (1998).

STUNTZ, WILLIAM J., THE COLLAPSE OF AMERICAN CRIMINAL JUSTICE (2011).

—, *Unequal Justice*, 121 HARV. L. REV. 1969, 1974 (2008).

—, *Plea Bargaining and Criminal Law's Disappearing Shadow*, 117 HARV. L. REV. 2548 (2004).

SULLIVAN, DENNIS & LARRY TIFFT, EDS., HANDBOOK OF RESTORATIVE JUSTICE: A GLOBAL PERSPECTIVE (2006).

Sunstein, Cass R., *Deliberative Trouble? Why Groups Go to Extremes*, 110 YALE L.J. 71 (2000).

Swire, Peter P., *Elephants and Mice Revisited: Law and Choice of Law on the Internet*, 153 U. PA. L. REV. 1975 (2005).

Tetlow, Tania, *Discriminatory Acquittal*, 18 WM. & MARY BILL OF RIGHTS Q. 75 (2009).

TOCQUEVILLE, ALEXIS, DEMOCRACY IN AMERICA (Francis Bowen, trans., Alfred A. Knopf, 4th prtg. 1948) (1835).

TONRY, MICHAEL, ED., THE FUTURE OF IMPRISONMENT (2004).

—, *Rethinking Unthinkable Punishment Practices in America*, 46 UCLA L. REV. 1451 (1999).

Toobin, Jeffrey, *This Is My Jail*, THE NEW YORKER 26 (April 14, 2014).

Tulchin, Matthew T., *An Analysis of the Development of the Jury's Role in a New York Criminal Trial*, 13 J.L. & POL'Y 425 (2005).

Turner, Jenia, *Jury Sentencing as Democratic Practice*, 89 VA. L. REV. 311 (2003).

U.S. CONT'L CONG., JOURNAL OF THE PROCEEDINGS OF THE CONGRESS, HELD AT PHILADELPHIA, SEPTEMBER 5, 1774 (Philadelphia, William and Thomas Bradford 1774).

VON HIRSCH, ANDREW, DOING JUSTICE: THE CHOICE OF PUNISHMENT (1976).

Washburn, Kevin, *Restoring the Grand Jury*, 76 FORDHAM L. REV. 2333 (2008).

Weisberg, Robert, *Excerpts from "The Future of American Sentencing: A National Roundtable on* Blakely," 2 OHIO ST. J. CRIM. L. 619 (2005).

Wells, Philip A., *Shrinking the Internet*, 5 NYU J. L. & LIBERTY 531 (2010).

Wiseman, Samuel, *Pretrial Detention and the Right to Be Monitored*, 138 YALE L.J. 1118 (2014).

Wistrich, Andrew J., Chris Guthrie & Jeffrey J. Rachlinski, *Can Judges Ignore Inadmissible Information? The Difficulty of Deliberately Disregarding*, 153 U. PA. L. REV. 1251 (2005).

WORRALL, JAMES L., PROSECUTION IN AMERICA: A HISTORICAL AND COMPARATIVE ACCOUNT (2008).

Wright, Ron, *Trial Distortion and the End of Innocence in Federal Criminal Justice*, 154 U. PENN. L. REV. 79 (2005).

Wright, Ron & Marc Miller, *The Screening/Bargaining Tradeoff*, 55 STAN. L. REV. 29, 30 (2002).

Yellen, David, *Probation Officers Look at Plea Bargaining, and Do Not Like What They See*, 8 FED. SENT'G REP. 339 (1996).

Zimring, Franklin E. & Gordon Hawkins, *Dangerousness and Criminal Justice*, 85 MICH. L. REV. 481 (1986).

INDEX

Lightning Source UK Ltd.
Milton Keynes UK
UKHW020023051019
351053UK00015B/186/P

9 781107 043541